RoboHELP® 7 For Dummies®

KU-680-554

Owning the Interface

Menu bar	Find all your commands here, from creating and editing topics to inserting links. It's not the fastest way to work, but it's reliable and complete.
Project Toolbar	Click these buttos to do your most important things — like create a Topic or a TOC book.
Project Manager	Step back and manage. Create, delete, and move files and folders. (Also on the left are tabs to the TOC, Index, and Tools panels.)
WYSIWYG Editor	Whatever else you do, you do your main work here. (Also on the right, tabs for TrueCode [HTML code], Link View, and Topics.)
Topic List	Get organized here. Create and delete topics. Drag and drop to the TOC or Index.
Compilation Pane	When you compile, check for messages down here.

Project Manager Menu bar   Project Toolbar   WYSIWYG Editor

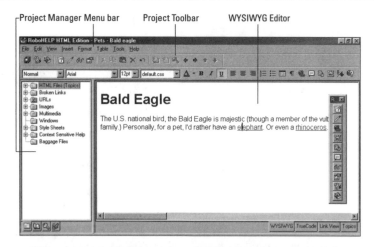

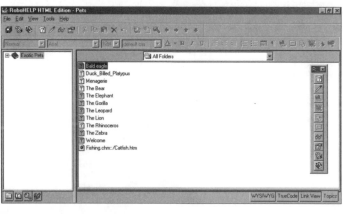

RoboHELP® 7 For Dummies®

Cheat Sheet

Five Really Useful Web Sites

www.bluesky.com	Tours, reviews, success stories, training, tech support.
www.dummies.com	Bone up on all kinds of Help-related computer skills (like graphics, the Internet, Dynamic HTML, and scripting).
msdn.microsoft.com/downloads/	Sample scripts from Microsoft. Free clip art, too.
www.useit.com/alertbox	Great stuff on styles and style sheets by Dr. Jakob Nielsen.
www.dhtmlzone.com	Everything on DHTML — tutorials, articles, examples.

Ten Things To Ask Before You Start

Can I get some training?

How can I keep my programmer(s) happy?

What subject-matter experts should I talk with?

Shall I use the Properties button to manage my time?

What browser or operating system will my audience use?

What does the audience really need?

Will I remember to compile often?

Am I working in modules?

Do I need to create a printed document in the end?

Does anyone understand me?

Five Outstanding Web Techniques

Image Hotspots (clicking a map for details)

Expanding Hotspots

Drop-down Hotspots

Special effects (text that flies onto the page)

Scripts (getting interactive with the reader)

Ultimate RoboHELP Shortcut

Right-click anywhere — a pane, a topic, a TOC item, an Index keyword — to see a menu of your most likely actions.

Most useful right-click? Right-click a topic, and then click Preview Topic to see the topic in a Help format.

Where to Start (Absolute Musts of a Help File)

Topics

Links

Table of Contents

Index

...For Dummies®: Bestselling Book Series for Beginners

ROBOHELP® 7 FOR DUMMIES®

by Jim Meade, Ph.D.

Foreword by Jorgen S. Lien

IDG Books Worldwide, Inc.
An International Data Group Company

Foster City, CA ◆ Chicago, IL ◆ Indianapolis, IN ◆ New York, NY

RoboHELP® 7 For Dummies®

Published by
IDG Books Worldwide, Inc.
An International Data Group Company
919 E. Hillsdale Blvd.
Suite 400
Foster City, CA 94404
www.idgbooks.com (IDG Books Worldwide Web site)
www.dummies.com (Dummies Press Web site)

Library of Congress Catalog Card No.: 99-64848

ISBN: 0-7645-0560-2

Printed in the United States of America

10 9 8 7 6 5 4 3 2 1

1B/RR/QY/ZZ/IN

Distributed in the United States by IDG Books Worldwide, Inc.

Distributed by CDG Books Canada Inc. for Canada; by Transworld Publishers Limited in the United Kingdom; by IDG Norge Books for Norway; by IDG Sweden Books for Sweden; by IDG Books Australia Publishing Corporation Pty. Ltd. for Australia and New Zealand; by TransQuest Publishers Pte Ltd. for Singapore, Malaysia, Thailand, Indonesia, and Hong Kong; by Gotop Information Inc. for Taiwan; by ICG Muse, Inc. for Japan; by Norma Comunicaciones S.A. for Colombia; by Intersoft for South Africa; by Eyrolles for France; by International Thomson Publishing for Germany, Austria and Switzerland; by Distribuidora Cuspide for Argentina; by Livraria Cultura for Brazil; by Ediciones ZETA S.C.R. Ltda. for Peru; by WS Computer Publishing Corporation, Inc., for the Philippines; by Contemporanea de Ediciones for Venezuela; by Express Computer Distributors for the Caribbean and West Indies; by Micronesia Media Distributor, Inc. for Micronesia; by Grupo Editorial Norma S.A. for Guatemala; by Chips Computadoras S.A. de C.V. for Mexico; by Editorial Norma de Panama S.A. for Panama; by American Bookshops for Finland. Authorized Sales Agent: Anthony Rudkin Associates for the Middle East and North Africa.

For general information on IDG Books Worldwide's books in the U.S., please call our Consumer Customer Service department at 800-762-2974. For reseller information, including discounts and premium sales, please call our Reseller Customer Service department at 800-434-3422.

For information on where to purchase IDG Books Worldwide's books outside the U.S., please contact our International Sales department at 317-596-5530 or fax 317-596-5692.

For consumer information on foreign language translations, please contact our Customer Service department at 1-800-434-3422, fax 317-596-5692, or e-mail rights@idgbooks.com.

For information on licensing foreign or domestic rights, please phone 650-655-3109.

For sales inquiries and special prices for bulk quantities, please contact our Sales department at 650-655-3200 or write to the address above.

For information on using IDG Books Worldwide's books in the classroom or for ordering examination copies, please contact our Educational Sales department at 800-434-2086 or fax 317-596-5499.

For press review copies, author interviews, or other publicity information, please contact our Public Relations department at 650-655-3000 or fax 650-655-3299.

For authorization to photocopy items for corporate, personal, or educational use, please contact Copyright Clearance Center, 222 Rosewood Drive, Danvers, MA 01923, or fax 978-750-4470.

 is a registered trademark or trademark under exclusive license to IDG Books Worldwide, Inc. from International Data Group, Inc. in the United States and/or other countries.

About the Author

Jim Meade is author of 20 previous books on computers, including four previous *...For Dummies* books — *SAP R/3 Administration For Dummies*, *LotusScript For Dummies*, *Word Pro For Dummies*, and *Ami Pro For Dummies* (big seller!).

Particularly helpful for this project are programming books — *LotusScript For Dummies* and, even more, *Dynamic HTML Explorer* (an excellent basis for the work in the parts on RoboHELP HTML Edition). The LotusScript book shows experience with compiling, debugging, and using specialized tools for working with code.

The book on Microsoft Dynamic HTML Explorer shows the capability to work with HTML code, Web pages, scripts, style sheets, and ActiveX.

Meade's four books on graphics are also direct preparation for this project, because RoboHELP incorporates graphics and itself works in an additional, presentation dimension (as do graphics). Meade's four books on graphics include the bestseller *Using PowerPoint*.

Books on word processing also are preparation for this book. The tools and interfaces are similar for both, and word processing books provide experience in working with Tables of Contents and Indexes. Meade has five books on word processing.

His three books on Excel are helpful in preparing macros, working with graphics, and in thinking visually.

Also, Meade has prepared documentation for several companies and worked for DEC as a documentation writer (where he gained experience with TOCs and Indexes as well as rules and procedures for preparing documents).

As a software reviewer for *HR Magazine* since 1989, he has examined the Help files on a long stream of products, evaluated their approaches, and offered suggestions.

He admits he may have even peeked into a few Help files himself in preparing those 20 books — many of them in the WinHelp format that's so important in this book.

ABOUT IDG BOOKS WORLDWIDE

Welcome to the world of IDG Books Worldwide.

IDG Books Worldwide, Inc., is a subsidiary of International Data Group, the world's largest publisher of computer-related information and the leading global provider of information services on information technology. IDG was founded more than 30 years ago by Patrick J. McGovern and now employs more than 9,000 people worldwide. IDG publishes more than 290 computer publications in over 75 countries. More than 90 million people read one or more IDG publications each month.

Launched in 1990, IDG Books Worldwide is today the #1 publisher of best-selling computer books in the United States. We are proud to have received eight awards from the Computer Press Association in recognition of editorial excellence and three from Computer Currents' First Annual Readers' Choice Awards. Our best-selling ...*For Dummies*® series has more than 50 million copies in print with translations in 31 languages. IDG Books Worldwide, through a joint venture with IDG's Hi-Tech Beijing, became the first U.S. publisher to publish a computer book in the People's Republic of China. In record time, IDG Books Worldwide has become the first choice for millions of readers around the world who want to learn how to better manage their businesses.

Our mission is simple: Every one of our books is designed to bring extra value and skill-building instructions to the reader. Our books are written by experts who understand and care about our readers. The knowledge base of our editorial staff comes from years of experience in publishing, education, and journalism — experience we use to produce books to carry us into the new millennium. In short, we care about books, so we attract the best people. We devote special attention to details such as audience, interior design, use of icons, and illustrations. And because we use an efficient process of authoring, editing, and desktop publishing our books electronically, we can spend more time ensuring superior content and less time on the technicalities of making books.

You can count on our commitment to deliver high-quality books at competitive prices on topics you want to read about. At IDG Books Worldwide, we continue in the IDG tradition of delivering quality for more than 30 years. You'll find no better book on a subject than one from IDG Books Worldwide.

John Kilcullen
Chairman and CEO
IDG Books Worldwide, Inc.

Steven Berkowitz
President and Publisher
IDG Books Worldwide, Inc.

IDG is the world's leading IT media, research and exposition company. Founded in 1964, IDG had 1997 revenues of $2.05 billion and has more than 9,000 employees worldwide. IDG offers the widest range of media options that reach IT buyers in 75 countries representing 95% of worldwide IT spending. IDG's diverse product and services portfolio spans six key areas including print publishing, online publishing, expositions and conferences, market research, education and training, and global marketing services. More than 90 million people read one or more of IDG's 290 magazines and newspapers, including IDG's leading global brands — Computerworld, PC World, Network World, Macworld and the Channel World family of publications. IDG Books Worldwide is one of the fastest-growing computer book publishers in the world, with more than 700 titles in 36 languages. The "...For Dummies®" series alone has more than 50 million copies in print. IDG offers online users the largest network of technology-specific Web sites around the world through IDG.net (http://www.idg.net), which comprises more than 225 targeted Web sites in 55 countries worldwide. International Data Corporation (IDC) is the world's largest provider of information technology data, analysis and consulting, with research centers in over 41 countries and more than 400 research analysts worldwide. IDG World Expo is a leading producer of more than 168 globally branded conferences and expositions in 35 countries including E3 (Electronic Entertainment Expo), Macworld Expo, ComNet, Windows World Expo, ICE (Internet Commerce Expo), Agenda, DEMO, and Spotlight. IDG's training subsidiary, ExecuTrain, is the world's largest computer training company, with more than 230 locations worldwide and 785 training courses. IDG Marketing Services helps industry-leading IT companies build international brand recognition by developing global integrated marketing programs via IDG's print, online and exposition products worldwide. Further information about the company can be found at www.idg.com.   1/24/99

Dedication

For this book on Help . . .

To the many who have helped me along the way

Anoraniyan mahato mahiyan

("Smaller than the smallest is bigger than the biggest.")

Acknowledgments

Talk about Help. This whole book is a testimonial to what help from others can do for an author. This book is a team project from start to finish.

I want to acknowledge, especially, my acquisitions editor, Sherri Morningstar, for knowing what I can do and giving me the chance to do it.

Thanks to my project editor, Jade Williams, for firm yet gentle guidance from start to finish. Thanks to an outstanding tech editor, Eric Butow, and to an all-star cast of copy editors: William (Bill) Barton, Stephanie Koutek, Darren Meiss, James Russell, and Suzanne Thomas.

I feel indebted to IDG's Steve Berkowitz, John Kilcullen, Mary Bednarek, and Leah Cameron. I would also like to thank the IDG sales force, whose skill and enthusiasm make IDG such a top publisher.

Blue Sky Software was great in providing the product and in giving support. Thanks to Kim Himstreet and to Premium Support (especially Matt Brown who spent endless hours with me). Also, I would like to thank Lori McDermeit — a former RoboHELP Help author, now a Help trainer — for sharing her experience and background.

Above all, I give all appreciation to my family, whose love is my support.

Publisher's Acknowledgments

We're proud of this book; please register your comments through our IDG Books Worldwide Online Registration Form located at `http://my2cents.dummies.com`.

Some of the people who helped bring this book to market include the following:

Acquisitions, Editorial, and Media Development

Project Editor: Jade L. Williams

Acquisitions Editor: Sherri Morningstar

Copy Editors: William Barton, Stephanie Koutek, Darren Meiss, James Russell, and Suzanne Thomas

Technical Editor: Eric Butow

Media Development Editor: Joell Smith

Associate Permissions Editor: Carmen Krikorian

Media Development Coordinator: Megan Roney

Editorial Manager: Leah Cameron

Media Development Manager: Heather Heath Dismore

Editorial Assistant: Beth Parlon

Production

Project Coordinator: Maridee V. Ennis

Layout and Graphics: Angela F. Hunckler, Dave Mckelvey, Barry Offringa, Brent Savage, Dan Whetstine

Proofreaders: Rachel Garvey, Nancy Price, Rebecca Senninger

Indexer: Richard T. Evans

Special Help
Blue Sky Software

General and Administrative

IDG Books Worldwide, Inc.: John Kilcullen, CEO; Steven Berkowitz, President and Publisher

IDG Books Technology Publishing Group: Richard Swadley, Senior Vice President and Publisher; Walter Bruce III, Vice President and Associate Publisher; Steven Sayre, Associate Publisher; Joseph Wikert, Associate Publisher; Mary Bednarek, Branded Product Development Director; Mary Corder, Editorial Director

IDG Books Consumer Publishing Group: Roland Elgey, Senior Vice President and Publisher; Kathleen A. Welton, Vice President and Publisher; Kevin Thornton, Acquisitions Manager; Kristin A. Cocks, Editorial Director

IDG Books Internet Publishing Group: Brenda McLaughlin, Senior Vice President and Publisher; Diane Graves Steele, Vice President and Associate Publisher; Sofia Marchant, Online Marketing Manager

IDG Books Production for Dummies Press: Michael R. Britton, Vice President of Production; Debbie Stailey, Associate Director of Production; Cindy L. Phipps, Manager of Project Coordination, Production Proofreading, and Indexing; Shelley Lea, Supervisor of Graphics and Design; Debbie J. Gates, Production Systems Specialist; Robert Springer, Supervisor of Proofreading; Laura Carpenter, Production Control Manager; Tony Augsburger, Supervisor of Reprints and Bluelines

◆

The publisher would like to give special thanks to Patrick J. McGovern, without whom this book would not have been possible.

◆

Contents at a Glance

Cartoons at a Glance

By Rich Tennant

"Hold your horses. It takes time to create a Help file for someone your size."

page 349

"Shoot, that's nothing! Watch me spin him!"

page 7

"Well heck, all the boy did was launch a search in RoboHELP and up comes Tracy's retainer, your car keys, and my bowling trophy here on a listing in Seattle!"

page 315

DAD ADDS LINKS AND GRAPHICS TO THE TRADITIONAL CAMPFIRE GHOST STORY

page 81

"It's another deep space probe from Earth seeking contact from extraterrestrials. I wish they'd just include a Help File."

page 129

"I tell him many times— get lighter tool kit. But him think he know better. Him have big ego. Him say,' Me Tarzan! You not!' That's why him vine break."

page 273

"This new Help program has really helped me get organized. I keep my project reports under the PC, budgets under my laptop and memos under my pager."

page 189

"What do you mean you're updating our Webpage?"

page 227

Fax: 978-546-7747 • E-mail: the5wave@tiac.net

Table of Contents

FOREWORD

Welcome to RoboHELP Office — The Industry Standard in Help Authoring. Blue Sky Software's RoboHELP Office 7 speeds and improves the development of high quality online Help systems and documentation, so software users can quickly and easily find answers to their questions — from within an application. If you are one of millions of frustrated software users who have waited on hold for technical support or tried in vain to get through to a Help Desk, then RoboHELP Office 7 can benefit you.

RoboHELP 7 For Dummies is a great introduction to the key features and functionality in RoboHELP Office 7. Not only will this book quickly teach you the basics of using RoboHELP to create application Help systems, it also provides some valuable insights and advice about technical writing in general. *RoboHELP 7 For Dummies* makes it easy for you to discover and use RoboHELP Office 7.

With the growing use of new HTML-based Help formats, RoboHELP Office is not only the world's most widely-used WinHelp authoring tool, it is embraced by the Help authoring community as the preferred solution for authoring HTML Help as well. So whether you have used previous versions of RoboHELP and now want to get up to speed on version 7, or you are completely new to RoboHELP or Help authoring, *RoboHELP 7 For Dummies* will be a useful tool. This book could even be your launching pad to a new career in technical writing! A recent search of Internet job postings for technical writers found that the vast majority of listings required RoboHELP expertise.

Take advantage of the trial version of RoboHELP HTML Edition and the Software Video Camera that Blue Sky has provided on the CD that accompanies this book. If you need more information or are interested in RoboHELP training, please call us at 800-459-2356 or 858-459-6365. You can also visit the Blue Sky Software Web site at `http://www.blue-sky.com`.

Happy Help authoring,

Jorgen S. Lien

Co-founder and CEO

Blue Sky Software Corp.

Introduction

• •

Don't tell anybody, but working in RoboHELP is really, really fun. In creating your Help files, you become a bit of a screenwriter, movie director, and all-around maestro. People may have the illusion that you're a hardworking writer. You, meanwhile, are the creative force behind text that informs, guides, cajoles, bails out, and otherwise leads some bedeviled reader to safety.

What fun you can have as you serve your future readers! People probably won't realize you've had all that enjoyment, and maybe you should keep the secret. After all, people do get paid for creating Help files. Employers shouldn't know that it's fun.

Whether you proceed as a fun-lover or something more serious, this book is a manic (though nonetheless deliberate and thoughtful) guide to the fun of RoboHELP. It's a companion as you go, and a rich compendium of tips, warnings, useful procedures, and silly asides.

About This Book

RoboHELP, at first glance, seems like some kind of a paradigm shift for the ordinary person. Help authoring is not conventional writing for print. Nor is it Web-page authoring, programming, page design, or graphic arts. It's a hybrid that includes something from standard writing, something from Web-page authoring, something from the graphic arts, and even (if you so choose) some programming.

Also, the perspective you take as the Help author, is unusual. You hide behind the scenes as someone uses a program, and you make help available when the baffled user turns to look for it. Being there for the reader seems to call for inordinate anticipation as well as comprehensiveness.

Unless you've done this kind of work before, Help authoring has a certain air about it of "I could never do that." The whole process seems to call for too many skills, from too many directions, in too many media. If you think you *can* do it, you may suspect that your company would never pay for all the training you'd need.

This book — conversational, down-to-earth, a little irreverent — looks to dispel the aura of "near impossibility" around help authoring while, at the same time, getting you quickly launched into help authoring yourself. This book breaks down the seemingly-difficult task of help authoring into digestible parts and makes them as friendly and approachable as your morning breakfast cereal (assuming, of course, that you eat and like one of the standard brands).

How to Use This Book

Take this book right around the middle and shake it. It's yours. Treat it that way. Grab what you want for now, and ignore the rest until you happen to want more.

First of all, I'd like to say that this is no "Bible." It covers all the main things you're going to want to do, yes. But it doesn't tell you all six ways to do something. It chooses one way — usually the easiest, fastest, and most fun way — and steps you through it quickly. In other words, this book is a great way to get started doing anything in RoboHELP.

Also, I have to admit that this ...*For Dummies* book is much more likely to tell you *what* to do than *why* you have to do it that way. Maybe, to get to a Web address, you may have to bow down in all kinds of ways to the great World Wide Web. This book tells you how to get to the Web address. You'll have to look somewhere else to find out why you do all the "bowing down" (all the special requirements that make you get there the way you do).

Strange as it may seem for such a friendly little book, this can be a reference book. That is, you can find things quickly and digest them quickly. I don't mean that it's some kind of unabridged tome. I mean that you should feel free to look in the Table of Contents or Index for something you want to know, and then go straight to that material in the book. No warm-ups. No qualifiers. Everything you need is right in that section. (If you need something specific from another section, I'll send you there briefly.)

Reference though it is, *RoboHELP 7 For Dummies* works as a narrative, too. You don't have to read from beginning to end, but you can. The book moves in a gently chronological sequence through RoboHELP tasks. If you want to know about everything, just read consecutively. You're welcome to do that.

This is your book. This is your friend. I'm your friend. The idea is to help you conquer a challenging subject quickly. Tame it. As I said, grab this book and shake. You own it and everything in it, or you will before long.

Foolish Assumptions

You probably know clearly what you want. You like your written material to be unpretentious. You'd rather spend your time doing RoboHELP tasks than slogging through paragraphs of hard stuff you don't really need to know.

You may be busy. People don't turn to RoboHELP as they do to word processing or Web-page authoring. That is, where anybody is likely to take on such mainstream computing, the people who turn to RoboHELP probably have business uses for the product. And the uses are probably immediate.

You may have an unreal deadline. You may well want training (which the company well may not provide). You probably want to get right to the gist of things, which leads you straight to a ...For Dummies book. You may not have time to get to know everything right now, but what you do need you want to have straight, fast, and clear.

Perhaps you tried just plunging into RoboHELP on your own and found yourself a little hung up. You want to be bailed out the fastest possible way with the least time wasted. Hence, a ...For Dummies book.

In spite of whatever real business pressures may be driving you to this book, you probably like a little chuckle now and then. You may turn to Comedy Central for your outright guffaws, but you appreciate a little lightheartedness now and then as you come to grips with a subject.

In any case, you apparently are interested in RoboHELP. If you're new to the subject, this book gets you started. If you're familiar with it already, this book is your reference book and quick refresher. If you're a trainer, this book is your ally.

How This Book Is Organized

In a way, the first chapter says everything. You can plunge into that chapter and find yourself well launched on RoboHELP. The rest of the first part expands on the first chapter. The other parts supplement the first chapter by giving you details on this or that of Help authoring.

The book tends to move chronologically, beginning with what you do to create a Help file and finishing with cleanup tasks you may perform as a finishing touch. Also, to some extent, you'll find easier tasks in the early chapters; somewhat harder ones are in the later chapters.

Here's a quick look at the parts of the book:

Part I: Zero to 60 in RoboHELP

Here you press the accelerator and take off in RoboHELP. You create an HTML application. You turn right around and create a WinHelp application. You closely examine your main building block — the topic. As you compose Help, you test and press the navigational tools you work with.

Part II: Getting Visual: Graphics and Links

If Help authoring were only about words, the whole process would be rather colorless and flat. But it's about typefaces, styles, images, and Hotspots. Here you have a good time thinking visually.

Part III: Setting Up Pointers: TOC, Index, Links

Help users are generally pretty exclusive in their thinking. They want to know about one thing. To get to that one thing and ignore everything else, they need a good table of contents, index, and links. Here you take up each of those subjects, one at a time, and gain remarkable proficiency in a short time.

Part IV: Being a Project Manager

You can get so carried away with your topics that you can forget that you're working inside a manageable whole — namely, the project. Here you step back, survey the whole, and see how to manage it to maximum effect. You manage the project, check into compiling, and find out about importing and exporting.

Part V: Doing Sexy Web Stuff

I'm not sure that you *have* to do many of the things in this section, but, boy, are they fun. (If you're having fun, your reader may have the same experience.) How about making your images dance on the page? How about having the steps in a procedure drop down before the user at a click? You find out about these things, tour the world of Web style sheets, and find out more than you really need to know about scripting (Web programming).

Part VI: Tidying Up at the End

All good things have to end, and your Help project is no exception. You probably want the end to be quick and painless (not prolonged and frustrating). Tools can help you clean up your work and avert future difficulties. Here you meet up with handy tools.

Part VII: The Part of Tens

These lists are mostly for fun. My list of ways to bribe a programmer for example, is offered in the lighthearted spirit. Some of these lists, though, ended up being business checklists. If you read 'em looking for a good yuk, then I apologize. If the lists make your life simpler as a Help author and save you some headaches, then no apology is necessary.

Part VIII: Appendixes

I like a glossary, just because there's no reason you should have to waste time on some unfamiliar term. Often, the concept itself isn't anything difficult; just the name is new. Here you can quickly fill in any terminology gaps you may have so that you can get straight at the meaning of things. Also, here you'll find a guide to the power-packed CD-ROM that comes with the book. For instance, you find that there's even a trial version of RoboHELP HTML Edition, so you can "try before you buy."

Icons Used in This Book

You can follow certain artistry by using icons. Yes, icons do break up an otherwise-humdrum page — but they also help you decide what to read and what to skip. If you know something but want to pick up helpful hints, look for Tip icons. If you're technical, linger on the Technical Stuff icons (which everybody else tends to skip).

Icons are a real navigational tool. Here are the ones I use in this book:

Once in a while, as a reader, you may think, "Gosh, I wish I had that myself." Sometimes the very thing is available for you in nice, electronic form on the CD. It helps to know it's there, and this icon points the way.

Sometimes I pass along a point that's worthy of particular attention. You're likely to encounter it again.

This icon means, most of the time, "skip this section." Sometimes there's background information or just fascinating explanations that you really don't need to know to get the task done. You can skip them. But you might like to know them. You might even scan through the book looking for them, if you happen to be a little technical yourself.

Often you can use a shortcut or try an alternative way to do something. You don't need the tip, but it will probably save you time in the future. Besides, a tip may show you a fun way to do something.

Things don't always go the way you expect. This icon shows a potential land mine; you can meet up with them. If you aren't careful, you may end up discombobulated or out of sorts. Warnings look to save you from dangers lurking nearby.

Where to Go from Here?

Hit the kitchen. Satisfy all those food cravings. Then, go wherever the spirit moves you. (The Index is definitely a popular place to start.)

Part I

Zero to 60 in RoboHELP

The 5th Wave   By Rich Tennant

RoboHELP
GADGET
CONTROLLER

NASA

NASA

SHUTTLE
CREW

"Shoot, that's nothing! Watch me spin him!"

In this part . . .

When you have a new toy, the fun is playing with it — pinching it, poking it, accidentally dropping it a little, and indulging in the joy of doing real things. In this part, you pinch, punch, and poke RoboHELP. That is, you start right in and do real stuff — a real RoboHELP HTML application and a real RoboHELP Classic application. You play around with the key ingredient in all the help — topics. And you tour all the buttons, zippers, bells, whistles, and cute little gadgets on the face of your RoboHELP screens. Irresistible stuff (just about).

Chapter 1

Jumping Right into HTML Help

- -

In This Chapter

▶ Starting up (because you can't do anything unless you do)

▶ Grasping the major differences between RoboHELP HTML and RoboHELP Classic

▶ Creating HTML topics (because Help is all about topics)

▶ Getting organized by dragging stuff around

▶ Putting in links (which make Web pages worth having)

- -

*W*elcome to RoboHELP 7 — a fancy, state-of-the-art, fun-to-use Help authoring environment. You use RoboHELP HTML to create the Help files that frenzied, desperate, or maybe just curious people turn to when using programs in Windows 98, 95, NT 4, and 2000. With RoboHELP Classic, a separate Help authoring environment within RoboHELP 7, you create Help for programs by using Windows 3.1 as well as (again) Windows 98, 95, and NT. (RoboHELP Classic is a little older than RoboHELP HTML.) With RoboHELP, you create all the things people see in their own Help windows when they click Help in a menu to get assistance on the program they're using.

You create an example of just such a Help file in this chapter. Here I show you how to create a fairly fancy HTML Help file as an example of what you can do in RoboHELP — one that contains books and topics and links that (surprise!) really work.

Books appear as icons in the Table of Contents that you can use to set up categories under Help files. *Topics* are the heart of everything — the main documents that you create. (They're the equivalent of documents in word processing, worksheets in a spreadsheet program, or brick walls in masonry.) *Links*, which often parade around in the fancy name *hyperlinks*, are the little areas that you click to jump straight to other topics. Links can be text (often blue-colored) or pictures.

Maybe you're not expecting to do so much so soon, but it's really pretty straightforward — so why not?

You start by starting up RoboHELP HTML. You create Help topics and, later, put words into them. You organize yourself in the *TOC Composer*, where you can just drag helpless topics around to your heart's content. (TOC Composer is an area on the left side of your screen for arranging and rearranging a Table of Contents. I discuss the TOC Composer big-time in Chapter 8.) You then link the topics and preview them (which I find kinda cool). Then, because you must, you compile and run the file.

You also get to see a comparison between the newer RoboHELP HTML 7 and its older sibling, RoboHELP Classic 7 (which you get to try out in Chapter 2). RoboHELP Office 7 contains both programs, so you can say that they're the same program if you want. (They're actually separate, however. You start each one individually, and the commands for using them vary somewhat, too.) In this chapter, you get a chance to try out RoboHELP HTML. (See Chapter 2 for your first dance with RoboHELP Classic.)

For several of the steps in this chapter, see the sample file musicians.mps.

Comparing RoboHELP Classic and RoboHELP HTML

RoboHELP Office 7 actually now comes with two programs in one — RoboHELP Classic 7 and RoboHELP HTML Edition 7.0. RoboHELP HTML is newer and, to be honest, is the one that most people are more likely to use if they are creating Help that will be deployed on Windows 98 or Windows 2000 applications. RoboHELP Classic, although older, has its uses as well.

The two versions are similar, as you may expect. You really need to keep only one fundamental difference in mind when you choose the RoboHELP version in which you're going to work: RoboHELP Classic specializes in preparing WinHelp; the HTML Edition specializes in creating HTML Help.

WinHelp is primarily for Windows 95, Windows 3.1, Windows NT 3.51, and Windows NT 4. Microsoft will continue to ship the older WinHelp display engine with Windows 98 and Windows 2000 to support Help systems on WinHelp. However, the format of the future appears to be HTML Help, which is the Help format that Microsoft plans to use for its future applications. WinHelp is, in a word, *older* (and in the fast-changing world of computers, older is rarely better).

HTML Help is the new Help standard for Windows 98, Windows 2000, and intranet systems. HTML Help is deployable on Windows 95. However, you need to ensure that your end-users have the special HTML Help display engine (because it isn't built into the Windows 95 operating system the way it is in Windows 98 and Windows 2000).

RoboHELP HTML is newer than Classic — and looks that way in some respects. The difference shows up right away, in fact, because RoboHELP HTML is a more WYSIWYG program than RoboHELP Classic. In other words, in RoboHELP HTML, the new information that you create on a page looks just like the final page. In RoboHELP Classic, you use Microsoft Word to create material that doesn't look quite the way it does in the final product. The Help material on the right side of the screen doesn't look exactly the way it does in the actual Help file — after you compile and run the page, you get to see how the page looks to someone who views it. (See Chapter 2 to view a Help file display.)

The two versions have lots of other little differences, too. RoboHELP HTML, for example, includes a neat preview feature that RoboHELP Classic doesn't have. RoboHELP HTML lets you write *scripts* (coded programs) where RoboHELP Classic doesn't allow scripts but only *macros* (which use code that's much more specialized). But those differences aren't immediately important as you get started. In fact, the differences don't become important unless you plan to work in both RoboHELP Classic *and* RoboHELP HTML.

If you're not sure which one to start with, find out what computing platform and operating system your audience uses — and then choose a Help format that can be viewed properly by all your end users.

You work in the version of RoboHELP that best supports the style of Help you're creating. More and more, you're likely to work in the HTML version, because so many new products on the market are for use in Windows 98, Windows 2000, and on the Web and intranets.

To help you compare the two versions, Table 1-1 summarizes the differences between RoboHELP HTML and RoboHELP Classic.

Table 1-1   Comparing RoboHELP Classic and RoboHELP HTML

RoboHELP Classic	*RoboHELP HTML*
Primarily prepares WinHelp (Windows 95, 3.1, NT 3.51 and NT 4)	Prepares HTML Help (Win 98, 2000 and intranet systems)
Older	Newer
What you see as you create isn't quite what you see in the final product.	What you see as you create is what you see after you display the finished Help.
Can't use scripts, such as VBScript.	Allows you to use scripts.

(continued)

Table 1-1 *(continued)*

RoboHELP Classic	RoboHELP HTML
Wouldn't know Dynamic HTML if it saw it face-to-face.	Lets you do lots of cool things with Dynamic HTML (explained in Chapter 17).
Makes you work with the Explorer on one side of the screen and Word on the other side of the screen.	Has a nice, single screen with an integrated HTML editor.
Has elaborate Image Workshop for working with images.	Has simple, quite effective tools for working with images (which you can check out in Chapter 6).
Older, kludgy, and, at times, complex (like the WinHelp format itself).	Newer, *funner*, jazzier, and sleeker.

Starting and Creating a New Project in RoboHELP HTML

RoboHELP HTML actually combines the process of starting up and creating the first topic. The program designers are just trying to make things easy for you and me — and to keep users from getting lost. It's nice of them, I think. In this section, you see how to start RoboHELP HTML by clicking its icon. Then I show you how to create a new *project* (a collection of Help topics that becomes a final Help file).

If you've ever started any Windows program (or even if you're doing it now for the first time), you're going to have no trouble at all starting RoboHELP HTML. Here's what you do:

1. **Locate the RoboHELP HTML Edition icon on the desktop and double-click.**

   You can also choose Start⇨Programs⇨RoboHELP Office⇨RoboHELP HTML Edition.

   The program window opens and a dialog box appears, asking whether you want to create a new Help project or open an existing one (as shown in Figure 1-1).

Figure 1-1:
You can
create a
new Help
project or
open an
old one
right after
starting
RoboHELP.

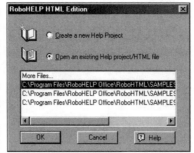

Figure 1-1:
You can
create a
new Help
project or
open an
old one
right after
starting
RoboHELP.

2. **Click the Create a new Help Project radio button and then click OK.**

   The New Project dialog box appears, as shown in Figure 1-2.

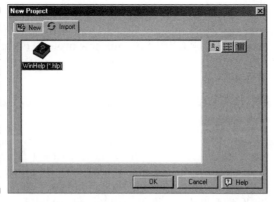

Figure 1-2:
The New
Project
dialog box
enables you
to import an
existing pro-
ject or click
the New tab
to create a
new one.

3. **Click the New tab to view your options for creating a new file.**

   The first choice in the Help Project Type list box — HTML Help — is
   already selected by default.

4. **For the current example, click OK to accept that choice.**

   The other choices are rather specialized. You might even call them
   advanced. A Custom project is a project based on a custom template
   (one that you make). An Intranet project is a one based on a special
   Intranet template. Special projects are projects using templates for slide
   shows and other fancy effects.

   The Create a New Project dialog box appears, as shown in Figure 1-3.
   Here you take the rather important steps of naming your project and
   giving it a filename.

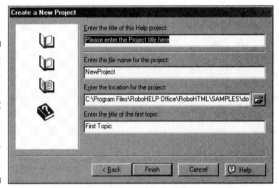

Figure 1-3:
In the
Create a
New Project
dialog box,
you can
name your
project.

Creating a new project is essentially giving the project a name and a filename that you will be working with. You probably want a descriptive name that means something to others, and that you can recognize yourself when you see it a few weeks later.

After the Create a New Project dialog box appears (as I explain in the preceding section), you're ready to type a title for your new project. (Whatever you type replaces the highlighted words `Please enter the Project title here`.) Here's how you name the project:

1. **Type a name for your new project in the Enter the Title of this Help Project text box.**

   For the current example, type **World Class Musicians**. After people open the project in the HTML Help viewer, they see this title. (The Help viewer, also known as a Help window, is the window that displays Help to the frenzied or curious person using the final Help system. Microsoft designed the window, which works quite a bit like an Internet browser.)

2. **Type a filename for the project in the Enter the File Name for the Project text box.**

   If you want to open the file again later, you can use this filename in the Open dialog box. For the current example, type **Musicians**.

3. **Enter or select a file location for the project in the Enter the Location for the Project text box.**

   This text box enables you to choose a location for the project on your hard drive by clicking the Folder button at the far right to access a list of folders.

   For the current example, click the Folder button to the right of the Enter the Location for the Project text box. Highlight `SAMPLES` in the Select the New Project Folder dialog box that appears. Then click OK.

This returns you to the Create a New Project dialog box. In the Enter the Location for the Project text box where the complete path name of the new project is `C:\PROGRAM FILES\ROBOHELP OFFICE\ROBOHTML\SAM-PLES\Musicians`

4. **Type a name for the topic in the Enter the Title of the First Topic text box.**

   For the current example, type **Beethoven** in this text box. (Topics, as I explain in the introduction to this chapter, are the building blocks in a Help system. As you work in the WYSIWYG Editor, you work on topics.)

5. **Click the Finish button at the bottom of the dialog box to start the project.**

RoboHELP starts your new project and displays the new topic in the WYSI-WYG Editor (the larger window in the right side of the RoboHELP program screen). The WYSIWYG Editor is the main program screen in RoboHELP HTML. In the smaller window at the left side of the screen, the Project Manager displays an open HTML Files folder with your topic file already selected. Figure 1-4 shows your opening screen at this point.

Project Manager   WYSIWYG Editor

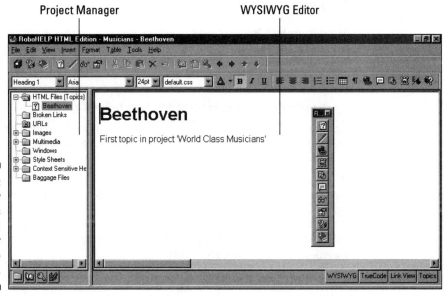

Figure 1-4:
Your new HTML file is open and ready for you to work on it.

Creating New HTML Topics

Topics are the heart of your HTML Help system. Topics are nothing more than topic titles until you put information into them. Once you fill them in, topics contain the information that people find whenever they use Help. (I mean, after all, they aren't using Help to see how pretty it is. They're using Help to, well, get *help*.)

If the Beethoven topic from the example in the preceding section is open in the WYSIWYG Editor, that's an invitation if I ever saw one for you to start creating the content for the topic. (If it's not open, you may want to check out that section before continuing. And if you don't even *have* a topic yet, you *definitely* need to see the preceding section to create one, whether you use the example or create your own from scratch.)

They call the *WYSIWYG Editor* by that name because what you see closely approximates what someone else really sees as they're displaying the topic in a browser. WYSIWYG stands for What You See Is What You Get (something all too rare in, say, buying items out of catalogs.)

To add content to your topic, follow these steps:

1. **Start RoboHELP HTML and create a project. In the WYSIWYG Editor, highlight the text that you want to replace.**

   For the example, you need to highlight the words `First topic in project 'World Class Musicians'.`

2. **Type your new text to replace the highlighted text.**

   The new text that you type automatically replaces the highlighted text on-screen, as is the case in most text editors. For this example, I type the following text:

   If you're going to talk world class, you just can't overlook Ludwig van Beethoven. He's the ultimate maestro. His Symphony No. 9 in D minor op. 125 may be the most famous piece of classical music of all time. He emulated the great J. S. Bach, and his music has influenced almost every Western composer after him. Even the Beatles and rock hero Chuck Berry paid tribute to him.

RoboHELP HTML comes with its own spell checker. To use it, choose Tools⇨Spelling from the RoboHELP menu bar. If you've used spell checkers before, you can readily put this one to use for yourself. (See Chapter 5 for information on RoboHELP's spell checker.)

Figure 1-5 shows the completed topic. Even in just starting RoboHELP HTML, you can get off to a roaring start by creating real content. In the following section, you create even more topics.

Figure 1-5:
Here's a
sample
topic.

Expanding Your Help Files by Adding More Topics

Help files must contain lots of topics. You aren't much help to anyone if you have only one or two. For the examples that I give you in this section, you create several topics quickly. You click the New Topic icon in the Project toolbar and use a Wizard to create topic titles. In another section, I show you how to create topics using the Tool palette — by clicking the New Topic icon in the Tool palette. Later in this chapter, in the section "Fleshing Out Those Topics," I show how to put text with your topic titles.

Creating topics by using the Wizard

You can create an initial topic when you create a new project, as I explain earlier in this chapter. Most of the time, though, you create a new topic from within an open project. Here you see how to create a topic from within RoboHELP, using the Create Topic Wizard to guide you.

To create a topic at any time while working in an open RoboHELP HTML project, the Create Topic Wizard guides you. Follow these steps:

1. **Start RoboHELP HTML and open or create a project.**

2. **Click the New Topic icon in the Project toolbar near the top of the screen.**

   The Project toolbar lies just below the menu bar — the third line from the top of the screen (counting the title bar). The New Topic icon is the fourth one from the left, displaying a page containing a question mark with a starburst in the top-left corner.

   The Create Topic Wizard appears to help you create your new topic (see Figure 1-6).

3. **In the Topic Title text box, type the name of a new Help topic.**

   Type **Bach** for the current example. You don't really need to do much else, because RoboHELP adds a filename and keyword for you. (Well, you do a little more.)

   You can't use some characters in filenames. (Techies like to know these things.) These forbidden characters are / \ : * ? < > | # " , . (The period at the end isn't one of the characters. It just ends the sentence.)

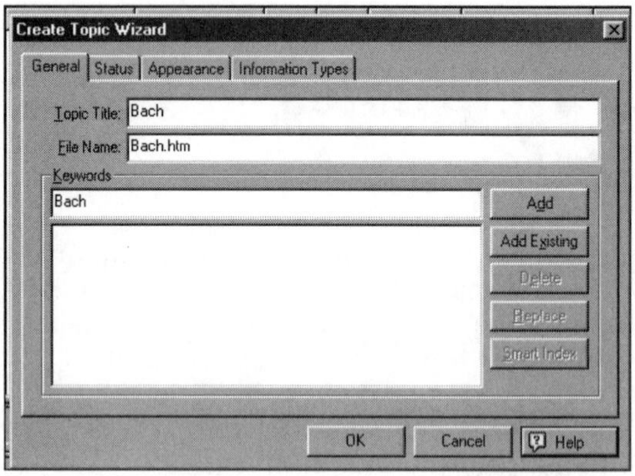

Figure 1-6:
The Create
Topic
Wizard
helps you
create new
Help topics.

> Create Topic Wizard
>
> General | Status | Appearance | Information Types
>
> Topic Title: Bach
> File Name: Bach.htm
> Keywords
> Bach
>
> Add
> Add Existing
> Delete
> Replace
> Smart Index
>
> OK   Cancel   ? Help

4. **Click OK.**

   Just as you do in creating any other topic, you find yourself in the WYSI-WYG Editor ready to type text. In the section "Fleshing Out Those Topics" in this chapter, you see how to put in text.

   You can create a number of topics and organize them. (See the "Gotta Get Organized": TOC Composer section later in this chapter.) In the following section, you see another way of creating topics.

Creating from the Tool palette

You can use the handy, floating Tool palette to create topics. The Tool palette is a movable bar with the most-used icons on it. To create a new topic from the Tool palette, you click the New Topic icon on the palette (significantly, the very top icon), then use the Create Topic Wizard.

1. **Start RoboHELP and create a new topic or open a topic.**

   For example, I open the project musicians.mpj. When you start RoboHELP, the Tool palette shows up in the same place you displayed it the last time you used it. In my example, the Tool palette is floating at the right of the screen, as I show in Figure 1-7.

   Notice in the figure that you see a single topic (Beethoven in my example) displayed in the main pane, where you often work in the WYSIWYG Editor. The topic is displayed in the Topic list. When you have multiple topics, they all show up in that list. You can work in your Topic list at any time by clicking the Topics tab — a tab at the lower-right of the pane. The tab looks kind of like a button, but it's a tab for opening a pane.

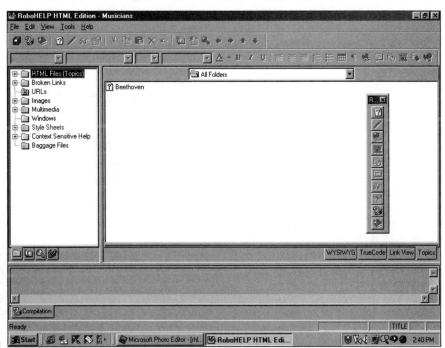

Figure 1-7:
My Tool palette is the one floating at the right of the screen.

2. **Click the New Topic button on the Tool palette (the button at the top in the figure).**

   If you're wondering, you can also click the New Topic button on the Project toolbar. Doesn't matter.

   The intent of the Tool palette is to make more readily available to you the buttons you're most likely to use in creating a project. You can read more about the Tool palette in Chapter 4.

   The Create Topic Wizard dialog box appears. (You can see it if you look at Figure 1-6.)

3. **Type a new topic name in the Topic Title text box and click OK.**

   Type **Beatles** for the example.

4. **Repeat Steps 2 and 3 to create more topics and click OK.**

   Name a second topic **Chuck Berry**.

5. **Click the Topics tab (lower-right) to see a list of your topics in the Topic list on the right.**

   You can also see the topics in the folder list in the Project Manager at the left side of the screen.

Figure 1-8 shows the four topics (most of which, of course, are only topic titles at this point).

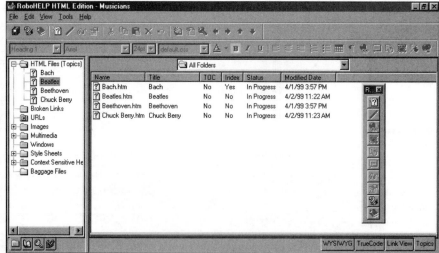

Figure 1-8: You can view your topics in the Topic list on the right side of the screen (or in the folder list of the Project Manager at the left).

"Gotta Get Organized": TOC Composer

If you work on your own, you're free to create topics first and then pull them into an outline later if you want. Often, however, you may want to plan your work in advance before plunging ahead. You can readily take either course. After you create a few topics that appear in the right pane of the RoboHELP screen, you can organize these topics into *books* on the left side. (Books are a traditional way of organizing Help files. They serve as "containers" for topics, but they're actually just a fancy name for regular folders.)

Books are folders in the TOC Composer, a pane you can display on the left side of your RoboHELP window. For an in-depth look at the TOC Composer, check out Chapter 8.

To organize your topics into books, open the TOC Composer on the left side of the screen, and use the New Book icon to create a book for the TOC.

1. **Start RoboHELP and create or open a project.**

   For example, I open Musicians.mpj.

2. **On the left side of the RoboHELP program window, click the TOC tab (which looks like an open book, at the bottom-left of the pane).**

3. **Click the New Book icon (on the Project toolbar menu, the third line down from the top of the screen). The icon is a picture of a book with a starburst in its top left corner.**

   The Book Properties dialog box appears, as shown in Figure 1-9.

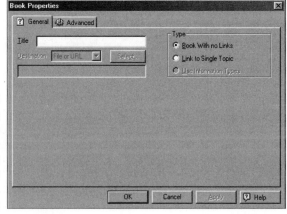

Figure 1-9: Create new books in the Book Properties dialog box.

4. **In the Title text box, type the title for the book and click OK.**

   For example, type **Classical Musicians**.

5. **Repeat Steps 2 and 3 to create a second book.**

   Call this book **Rock Musicians**. The TOC Composer pane now shows two book icons and the names of the two books after them.

After you have some newly created books and topics, you can put the two together. Here's what to do:

1. **In the main RoboHELP window, click the topic name in the right pane and drag it into the book in the left pane.**

   That's right. You just drag the item to where you want it. For the musical example, click the Bach topic in the right pane and drag it into the Classical Musicians book in the left pane.

2. **Repeat Step 1 for any other topics and books.**

   Drag the Beethoven topic into the Classical Musicians book and then drag the Beatles topic and the Chuck Berry topic into the Rock Musicians book.

   Notice that as you drag the topic from the right pane, it doesn't *leave* the right pane. But its name also appears in the TOC Composer on the left, wherever you place it.

Figure 1-10 shows the TOC Composer with its books and topics.

Figure 1-10:
You can
nicely
organize
your topics
into books
in the TOC
Composer at
the right
of the
RoboHELP
screen.

You can drag and drop your topics anywhere within the TOC Composer — not only from the Topic list to the TOC Composer. So you can think and rethink your project on the fly, which nicely accommodates your surges of creativity, your possible regrets at previous reorganizations, and any renewed surges of creativity.

Fleshing Out Those Topics

Adding text to a topic may be the most effortless of your activities as a Help author. You open a topic in the WYSIWYG Editor (the big pane on the right). You can double-click any topic in the topic list (on the right side of the screen) to open it. You use standard word processing procedures to type and edit text. If you have organized your topics into the TOC Composer (see the preceding section), you can start from there to open topics.

Following are some samples that show how to add text to topics.

1. **Start RoboHELP and create or open a project.**

   For example, open musicians.mpj.

2. **In the Topic list (the list of topics on the right side), double-click the topic to which you want to add content to display it in the WYSIWYG Editor.**

   For the example, double-click the Bach topic. If you don't see the Topic list on the right, click the Topics tab at the lower right to display it.

3. **Select the words** Type topic text here **and type your new text to replace it.**

   For the current example, type the following text:

   This 18th-century German composer greatly influenced successors, including Beethoven.

4. **In the TOC Composer (the left pane), double-click the next topic, select** Type topic text here, **and type in the text for its content.**

   For the example, double-click Beatles and type the following text in place of the selected type:

   Smashingly popular British rock group of the '60s, these four guys had 30 songs on the *Billboard Magazine* top-ten list between 1964 and 1969. Great admirers of Chuck Berry.

5. **Repeat Steps 1 and 2 to add content for other topics.**

   For the example, use the following text for content under the Chuck Berry topic:

   Regarded by some as the king, or at least the father, of rock and roll, he attained pop immortality with his songs "Roll Over Beethoven," "Rock 'n' Roll Music," and "Johnny B. Goode." "Maybelline" wasn't bad, either. The Beatles paid him the highest compliment: imitation.

Linking Topics

The Web is all about jumping around — *hyperlinking*, as people used to call it, or just *linking*. You just click a link and go directly to another site. You probably do it all the time. In the same way, you can set up links between Help topics. You can click a toolbar icon and set up the link, or you can drag and drop to set up the link (which is more visual and, I think, easier). In the following two sections I explain each method.

Using the Tool palette

You can use the Insert hyperlink icon on the Tool palette to open a Hyperlink dialog box, where you can set up a link from topic text to another topic.

Here's how to use the Tool palette to put links in your HTML Help documents:

1. **Start RoboHELP and open or create a project.**

   For example, open the project Musicians.mpj.

2. **Open the topic to which you want to add a link.**

   To open a topic, you can double-click the topic in the Topic list. For the example, open the Bach topic.

3. **Highlight the text that you want to serve as the link (the text that's to appear with a colored underline).**

   For the example, highlight Beethoven.

4. **Click the Insert Hyperlink button in the Tool palette. (It's the third button down and looks like chain links in front of a world globe.)**

   The Hyperlink dialog box appears, as shown in Figure 1-11.

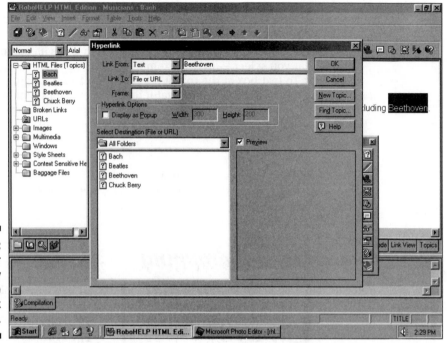

Figure 1-11:
Build your
hyperlink by
using the
Hyperlink
dialog box.

You can link to all kinds of cool stuff in this dialog box. If you click the downward-pointing arrow to the right of the Link To drop-down list box, you can see the possibilities — File or URL, E-Mail, FTP, News, Multimedia, and Remote Topic. Figure 1-12 shows the open Link To list. (In the figure, the link is set up to the topic Beethoven.) You can read about all these links in Chapter 11.

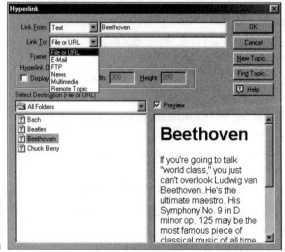

Figure 1-12:
You can
link your
topic text
to e-mail
addresses
and even
remote
topics.

5. **In the Select Destination (File or URL) drop-down list box, click your topic title.**

   For the example, click Beethoven. Make sure that the filename of the topic that you select — in this example, Beethoven.htm — appears in the Link To text box at the top of the dialog box, to the right of the Link To drop-down list box. Notice that if the Preview check box has a check mark in it, you can see the entire Beethoven topic in the large text box in the right half of the Hyperlink dialog box.

6. **Click OK.**

You're in business. You have a link from one topic to another. Try making another one. Just go back through the preceding steps and select new topics and text to link.

Dragging and dropping

You can also drag and drop text to create hyperlinks. You're probably going to prefer creating links this way, because it's faster and easier (and, generally, more fun). To drag and drop to create links, highlight the text in the topic that will appear as a colored link. Then drag a topic from the Project Manager on the left onto the highlighted text on the right. Follow these steps:

1. **Start RoboHELP and create or open a project.**

   For example, use the project musicians.mpj.

2. **In the Topic list, double-click the topic you want to work with.**

   For example, open the topic Beatles.

3. **In the WYSIWYG Editor (on the right side of the RoboHELP window), highlight the text where you want the link to appear.**

   For the example, open the Beatles topic and highlight Chuck Berry.

4. **On the left side of the screen, click the Project Manager tab (a folder) on the lower-left.**

5. **Click the plus sign next to the folder labeled HTML Files (Topics) to show your list of topics.**

6. **Click and then drag the topic that you want to use as a link.**

   For the example, click and drag Chuck Berry. As the topic moves across the screen, the cursor turns into a plus box showing where the link is to go.

7. **Drop the item on the highlighted text in the topic.**

   For the example, drop the topic on the Chuck Berry text. Voilá! The text becomes a link.

You can create many more hyperlinks, of course, but you always use one of the two procedures that I describe in this section — using the Tool palette or dragging and dropping (which is, don't forget, more fun).

Previewing Topics

In this chapter, you may have created links. But how do you know the links work? Compiling and running your program just to see whether the links work seems like a lot of trouble. Unfortunately, you may need to do just that in RoboHELP Classic. The RoboHELP HTML authors, however, came up with a better idea: You can *preview* your links and everything else you place on your Topic page.

To preview a link that you create for your Help topic, follow these steps:

1. **Start RoboHELP HTML and create or open a project.**

   For example, open the project musicians.mpj.

2. **Double-click the project's title in the Topic list to display the topic that you want to preview in the WYSIWYG Editor.**

   For the example, display the Beatles topic.

3. **Click the View button on the Tool palette (the button displaying a pair of glasses).**

   The topic appears on-screen in a preview window just as it appears to future readers, as shown in Figure 1-13.

Figure 1-13: You can preview your newly created topics in a preview window to make sure that your links work.

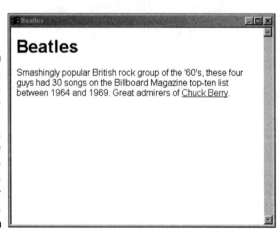

Beatles

Smashingly popular British rock group of the '60's, these four guys had 30 songs on the Billboard Magazine top-ten list between 1964 and 1969. Great admirers of Chuck Berry.

Next comes the part that's a little impressive.

4. **Click the link to your other topic.**

   For example, click the Chuck Berry link in this example. RoboHELP now displays the linked topic in another preview window, as shown in Figure 1-14.

   If the link doesn't display for some reason, you may not have put the link in correctly. Try the preview a second time by following Steps 1-3 again. Then, if the link still doesn't work, check the section in this chapter called "Linking Topics," and put your link in again.

5. **Click the Close box in the top-right corner to close the preview.**

Make note of that preview capability, because as you fool around with more and more capabilities, that haunting question's bound to come up: "Yeah, but does this *really* work?" The preview window can put your mind at ease or present you with the hard fact that "No, it doesn't really work." (But, of course, that's probably not going to happen.)

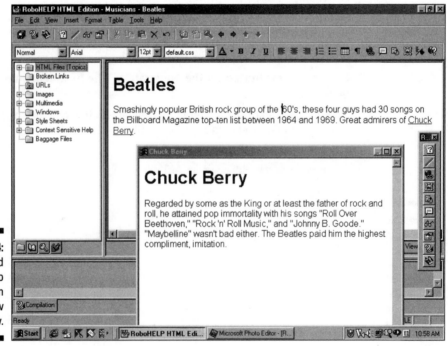

Figure 1-14: The linked topic also appears in a preview window.

Saving and Compiling Your HTML Help Topic

Thanks to the preview feature, the tasks of compiling and running topics aren't as critical in RoboHELP HTML as in RoboHELP Classic. (*Compiling* a project is producing an actual Help file from the topics, links, and so on that you create for your Help system. See Chapter 14 for more information on compiling.) You can test stuff on the fly as you work. Saving the file containing your topic is as important as in any other program; you must save it to securely place the document on the hard drive.

Here's what you do to save your project:

1. **Click the Save All icon (a picture of several floppy disks) in the Project toolbar.**

    RoboHELP saves the project under the name you gave it.

    "I thought I was just saving my project," you may wonder. "Why does the icon read 'Save all'?" I'm not sure that you *want* to know, but . . . Whenever you save the project, you're saving a lot of files at the same time — your HTML file, in compressed form, as the CHM file; style sheets, if you have any; your Table of Contents; your index; a file with the appendix HHP — all in a special project file that RoboHELP uses as it compiles a CHM file. And actually, you could save a bunch more files and possible files. Aren't you glad that all that effort goes on behind the scenes? (If you're really curious about them all, you definitely have programmer aptitudes.)

2. **Click the Compile button on the Project toolbar — the one displaying a question mark and a pen.**

    As RoboHELP *compiles*, it compresses all the pieces of your project into a compressed HTML file with the CHM extension. When you send out the Help project to users, you actually send the CHM file.

    You probably hear a little whirring as RoboHELP compiles the file, and then you see the message `Compilation complete` appear at the lower-left corner of your screen.

3. **Click the Run Help File icon on the Project toolbar to see your new project in the HTML Help Viewer (the tri-pane window designed by Microsoft and used in RoboHELP for viewing Help).**

    Your project appears as a "real HTML Help file." Figure 1-15 shows an open book displaying the topics with the Help file maximized to show you how a project is to appear in the viewer.

Figure 1-15:
A sample
Help file you
can create
by following
the steps
outlined in
this chapter.

I'm not sure that outlining, creating, linking, and displaying a Help file should really *be* so easy. (You may wonder at this point whether you even need the rest of this book. Well, yeah, I'm sure that I can find still find some useful stuff to talk about. So why stop?)

Chapter 2

Doing a Classic Little Help Application

- -

In This Chapter

▶ Starting and stopping RoboHELP Classic (and taking it on a little ride in between)

▶ Creating a big container (a project) and a smaller container (a book)

▶ Writing several classic Help topics

▶ Popping in a neat pop-up and putting a jump between topics

▶ "Compiling" and running the Help file

- -

*O*n first encountering the RoboHELP Classic environment, you may find it a little bewildering, and you may rightly wonder, "Where do I start?" You quickly find that you have so many possible menu choices to manipulate, icons to click, windows in which to work, and Help files to read that you can become lost quite easily. Your initial experience with the program can, in fact, turn into quite an information overload. (RoboHELP HTML, on the other hand, is a noticeably easier version of the program, as you can check out in Chapter 1.)

The experience may seem kind of like what happens after you first visit a new country. At first, you're disoriented, as in any new environment. But then you just hop aboard the tour bus and circle around the new city until you get a feel for things and, finally, get yourself oriented to the new locale. And that's what you're going to do in this chapter with RoboHELP Classic. (Minus the tour bus, of course.) You get the experience of the "whole" — that is, you create an actual classic Help file.

In this chapter, you create and test a simple, classic WinHelp file that actually works. In doing so, you find out how to start and stop RoboHELP (pretty basic, but helpful the first time). You also discover how to create a *project*, which contains the other pieces of your Help file, and another small container — a *book*, a folder in your Table of Contents. Then you put actual content in this book, in the form of *topics* (the main documents you create in RoboHELP).

To get a feel for creating a real Help file, you set up a topic with its own *pop-up Help* (Help that pops up in its own window) and then link two topics by using a *Jump* (Classic's name for a link). Finally, you run the Help file and try it out to make sure that it works.

If you're creating only HTML HELP, you can safely skip this chapter. I discuss both RoboHELP HTML and RoboHELP Classic in many of this book's chapters. This particular chapter, however, is here to give you a chance to see what good, old-fashioned RoboHELP Classic is all about (if, of course, you're interested). I think that the classic version is fun, too, and I hope that you look this chapter over to get a feel for it.

Starting RoboHELP Classic

Actually starting RoboHELP shouldn't prove too much of a challenge (as long as you first purchase RoboHELP, install it in Windows 95/98, and currently have Microsoft Word 95 or 97 installed, you're prepared to start rolling). Start RoboHELP Classic by following these steps:

1. **Locate the RoboHELP icon on the desktop and double-click it. Or click Start⇨Programs⇨RoboHELP Office⇨RoboHELP.**

   The icon looks like a purple book with a question mark on it, similar to the familiar Windows 98 icon, and has another question mark next to it. (The word RoboHELP also appears beneath the icon in case it's not clear enough otherwise.) The Open a Help Project dialog box appears, as shown in Figure 2-1. On the left is the RoboHELP Explorer (the portion of RoboHELP Classic where you work with files as a whole rather than creating text).

Figure 2-1:
After starting RoboHELP, you can open or create a new Help project in the Open a Help Project dialog box.

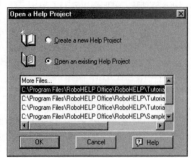

2. **To create a new Help project, select the Create a New Help Project radio button and then click OK.**

   If you're opening an existing Help project, you click the Opening an Existing Help Project radio button instead. Then locate your file by moving the left scroll bar up and down, click the file's name to highlight it, and click OK.

   The New Project dialog box opens.

Creating a Classic Help Project

To create a Help file in RoboHELP Classic, first you create a separate *project*. The project is actually just a file on your computer, but it's the file folder that contains all the other files in your Help file. If you think about the concept, you quickly realize that you start with some type of container for most undertakings in life. If you're building a house, for example, you first put up a frame. If you're collecting tennis balls, you generally start by picking up a pail in which to keep them. If you're building a Help file, therefore, you start with a project.

To create a *container* (a folder to hold everything else) for your Help project, you can either open an existing project or create a new one. You do so in the Open a Help Project dialog box.

After you have the Open a Help Project dialog box open on-screen, follow these steps to create a new project:

1. **Open (or create) the project you want to work with, click the <u>C</u>reate a new Help Project radio button, and then click OK.**

   The New Project dialog box appears, as shown in Figure 2-2. You can choose in this dialog box to set up a number of different kinds of Help files — Help for an application, Help for an online book, and so on.

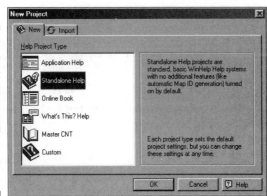

Figure 2-2:
The New Project dialog box allows you to choose the type of Help you want to create.

TIP

To view the other types of Help that you can create, click each Help project type listed in the New Project dialog box. A description of each Help project appears on the right side of the dialog box.

2. **To create a simple Help file, click the Standalone Help icon and then click OK.**

   Another New Project dialog box appears, as shown in Figure 2-3. This dialog box is for choosing the *target* for your Help file (that is, the operating system your readers will use). You may choose to create your Help system for WinHelp 4 (Windows 95, Windows 98, and Windows NT) or for WinHelp 3 (Windows 3.*x*).

Figure 2-3:
Choose the operating system for your Help project in this New Project dialog box.

3. **Select your operating system by selecting one of the three options in the New Project dialog box and then click Next. You can select either WinHelp 4 or WinHelp 3.**

   (If you chose WinHelp 4 by selecting the Only Allow WinHelp 3 Supported Features check box at the bottom, you create a WinHelp file that works for both WinHelp 4 and WinHelp 3.)

   You click the WinHelp 4 button, for example, if you're using Windows 95, Windows 98, or Windows NT. Another New Project dialog box appears in which you set up your project, as shown in Figure 2-4. In this dialog box, give your project a title and a name and designate a place to store the project on your computer.

4. **Type the new title for your project in the What Is the Title of This Help Project? text box, replacing the highlighted text** Please enter the Help Project title here.

Figure 2-4:
In this New
Project
dialog box,
type in a
name and
title for your
project.

5. **In the What Is the Name of the Project File? text box, select the word**
HelpFile **and type a new title.**

For the name of the project file, you may save yourself some grief later if
you use a filename with eight or fewer characters. If you later want to use
the same Help file in WinHelp 3 format, you must have an eight-character
name for that file (which is the only kind that WinHelp 3 recognizes).

6. **In the Where Should the Project Be Stored? text box, choose where
you want to store the file on the computer.**

You have the option of clicking the check box at the bottom that says
Create WinHelp 2000 Explorer view. If you select the choice, you
create a Help file that has the look and feel of HTML Help (the kind you
create with RoboHELP HTML).

You can accept the directory that RoboHELP suggests — C:\Program
Files\RoboHELP Office\RoboHELP\ — or you can choose another or even
create a new directory. Follow these steps to create a separate directory:

• **Click the Browse button.**

The Select the new Help project folder window appears.

• **Click New Folder to create a new folder.**

A New Folder dialog box opens.

• **Type a new name in the text box and then click the Create
button.**

You go back to the Select the new Help project folder window with
your new folder now selected.

• **Make sure that the Examples folder is selected and click OK.**

Figure 2-5 shows my completed New Project dialog box.

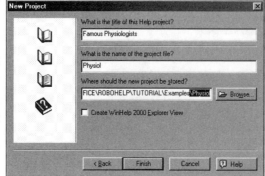

Figure 2-5:
Here's a
completed
New Project
dialog box
containing
all the infor-
mation that
you need for
a new
project.

7. **Click the Finish button at the bottom of the dialog box.**

   Your new Help project appears on-screen, as shown in Figure 2-6.

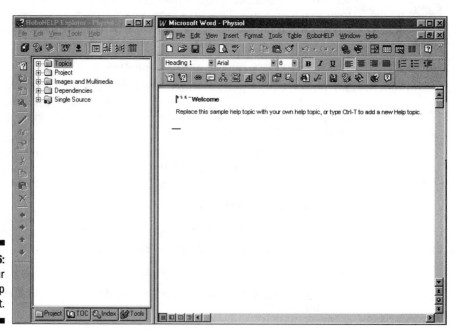

Figure 2-6:
Here's your
new Help
project.

Creating a Book

The preceding sections show you how to create a container for your Help file, known as a *project*. In this section, I show you how to create one more such container — a *book*. A book is a category within WinHelp. If you use various Windows programs, you may already be familiar with the concept of books. If not, you may want to see an example of a book in another application; just start WinHelp in any application by selecting Help⇨Content and Index. When the Help Topics dialog box appears, click the Contents tab. A Table of Contents for available Help files appear, and lists their titles. Notice the book icon that appears next to each topic. If you double-click one of the book icons, an expanded list of sub-topics appears beneath the title (with book icons next to them as well). Figure 2-7 shows an example of these books from Microsoft Word.

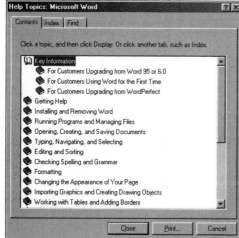

Figure 2-7:
Here you
see several
sample
books in
WinHelp.

As a Help author, you can create books that appear just the same as the books from Microsoft Word.

Here's how to create a book:

1. **With RoboHELP Classic open, click the TOC tab at the bottom of the left pane of RoboHELP Classic.**

   (Another name for the left pane, by the way, is the *RoboHELP Explorer*.) RoboHELP replaces the list of folders in your project with a blank pane — the *TOC Composer*, as shown in Figure 2-8. (When the left side shows the folder list, it's in Project Manager. When it shows the TOC pane, it's in the TOC.)

Figure 2-8:
Compose
your
Project's
TOC in the
handy left
pane of the
RoboHELP
Classic
window —
the TOC
Composer.

2. **Choose File⇨New⇨Book from the menu bar (or click the New Book icon on the RoboHELP Explorer Edit toolbar — it's the open-book icon just to the left of the pane in which you're working).**

The New Book dialog box appears, as shown in Figure 2-9.

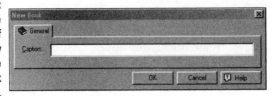

Figure 2-9:
Type in the
name of
your new
book in the
New Book
dialog box.

3. **Type the name of your book in the Caption text box and click OK.**

For this example, you can type **Historic Figures**. After you click OK, the new book appears in the TOC Composer, as shown in Figure 2-10.

Figure 2-10:
The new
book
appears in
the TOC
Composer.

As you create your own Help projects, you create multiple books and fill them in with information known as topics. To find out how to add topics to your newly created books, see the "Creating Classic Topics" section in this chapter.

Creating Classic Topics

The project and book that you create in preceding sections of this chapter are mostly containers. The real heart of any Help system is its *topics*. Topics contain the actual information that you want to communicate to struggling readers. This section shows you how to create topics for your Help project. To create a new topic, follow these steps:

1. **In the RoboHELP Explorer (the left pane), highlight the name of the book that appears in the TOC Composer and then choose File⇨New⇨Topic from the menu bar. (Or click the New Topic icon on the Edit toolbar at the left side of the screen — it's the icon displaying a question mark at the top of the toolbar.)**

   The New Topic dialog box appears with the words NewTopic 1 high-lighted in the Topic Title text box, as shown in Figure 2-11.

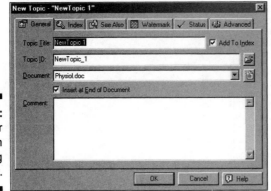

Figure 2-11:
Set up your
new topic in
this dialog
box.

2. **Type the name of your new topic in the Topic Title text box to replace the highlighted words.**

   RoboHELP automatically updates the Topic ID and Document text boxes for you.

3. **Click OK.**

   The new topic appears just below the name of your book in the TOC Composer on the left side of the screen (in the RoboHELP Explorer) and after a page break on the right side of the screen, as shown in Figure 2-12 (in Microsoft Word). Now you're ready to put in actual content for the topic.

   The funny characters that appear to the left of the topic title in the Microsoft Word portion of RoboHELP Classic are footnotes that RoboHELP uses (see Figure 2-12). These characters are codes that perform useful tasks, although they're somewhat annoying in appearance. Be careful, however, *not* to delete them — your topics won't display in your final Help file if you do.

4. **In the right pane, click below the topic title and then type your Help text.**

5. **Repeat Steps 1 through 4 to create additional topics with Help text.**

After adding topics to your Help file, you can run your Help file to see what your project looks like as a Help file. Or you can add some ingredients that are a little bit sexy — the kinds of things that automate Help (making it much more fun for users than just reading a book), such as *pop-ups* and *jumps*. (I describe these features in the "Adding a Pop-up" and "Adding a Classic Jump," sections later in this chapter.)

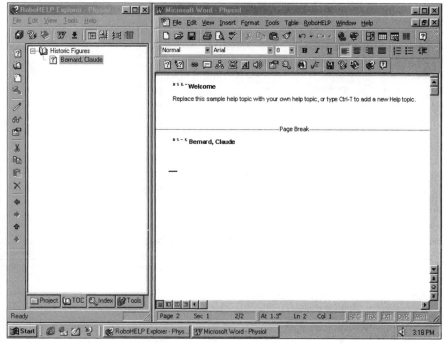

Figure 2-12:
Your new
topic
appears in
both the left
and right
panes of the
RoboHELP
Classic
window.

Adding a Pop-up

A pop-up is a temporary window that "pops up" to provide information about a Hotspot when the user clicks it.

I talk a lot more about pop-ups in Chapter 4. You've probably seen them a lot, however — little windows that just "pop up" on-screen after you click a word or phrase in Help. Try creating one by following these steps:

1. **Start RoboHELP Classic and open (or create) the project and topic you wish to work with. In the topic of your choice, double-click a word to select it.**

2. **Click the button for New Pop-up (a picture of text in a speech balloon, like you see in comics — it's the fourth button from the left) on the RoboHELP toolbar in Word (in the right pane on-screen).**

    The Insert Pop-up dialog box appears, displaying your selected word in the Hotspot Text text box, as shown in Figure 2-13.

3. **Select the text in the New Pop-up text box that reads** Type Pop-up Caption Here **and type your new caption to replace it.**

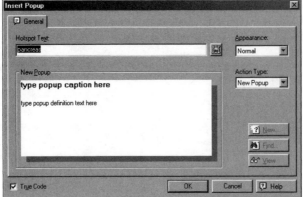

Figure 2-13:
Use this
dialog box
to create a
pop-up for
your Help
text.

4. **Select the text in the same text box that reads** Type Pop-up
Definition Here **and type your new definition to replace it.**

5. **Click OK.**

In Word under Topics, notice that the subject now appears in green type
with a single underline, which means that it's a *pop-up Hotspot*.

Adding a Classic Jump

Jumps are hyperlinks that offer a quick way of getting additional information.
You can click these links and find useful information much faster than you
can by leafing through the pages of a book. Whereas RoboHELP HTML just
uses links (see Chapter 1), RoboHELP Classic uses jumps instead. Links and
jumps are really about the same thing. Jumps, after all, are what make
WinHelp Help files fun and easy, just as links are all the rage on the Web.

Try adding a jump to your Help text by following these steps:

1. **Start RoboHELP classic and open the project you wish to work with.**

You can work directly in Word without double-clicking a topic in
RoboHELP Explorer if you want. Just scroll to the topic with the Word
scroll bars. After your Word files become very big, RoboHELP Explorer
can help you navigate to your topics more quickly.

2. **Double-click a word to select it.**

3. **Click the New Jump icon (the one that displays a chain-link symbol)
   on the RoboHELP toolbar in Word (at the top on the right pane).**

The Insert Help Hotspot dialog box appears, as shown in Figure 2-14.

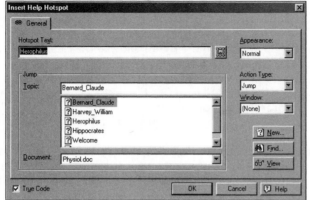

Figure 2-14:
Set up your
jump in the
Insert Help
Hotspot
dialog box.

4. **Select a topic by clicking its name in the Topic list box in the Jump area of the Insert Help Hotspot dialog box.**

   For additional information on using the Insert Help Hotspot dialog box to create jumps, see Chapter 4.

5. **Click OK.**

   You return to Microsoft Word, and your jump now appears in green with a double underline (meaning that it's a jump).

Saving, Compiling, and Running a Classic File

Even after you create a project, books, topics, pop-ups, and jumps, as the preceding sections of this chapter describe, you may wonder how you can see what this Help file really looks like as a true Help file? How do you get the reward for all your labors? You must *save, compile,* and *run* your Help file.

In creating a project (see the "Creating a Classic Help Project" section earlier in this chapter), you actually create a file to contain the Help information that you create in books and topics. For more information on books and topics in Help, see the sections on "Creating a Book" and "Creating Classic Topics" in this chapter.

As is the case with any computer file — any word-processing file, for example — saving the file regularly is always a good idea. To save a project, all you need to do is choose File⇨Save All from the RoboHELP Explorer menu bar (the one in the left pane of your program window).

That's it! You save the file — with any changes that you make — right to your hard drive. By choosing File➪Save All (instead of just Save), you save what you're working with in both panels, left and right — that is, any documents that you have open in Word in the right pane *and* the Help Table of Contents in RoboHELP Explorer in the left pane.

You can also click the Save All icon (it's the first icon on the left) on the RoboHELP Explorer Project toolbar (the one above the left pane) instead of using the menus. Save All is the icon showing a picture of a stack of disks.

Compiling has a definite techie ring to it. Usually, if you compile something, you translate the code in a C++ program (or some other collection of programming codes) into machine language to see whether those odd-looking hieroglyphics actually do what they're supposed to do.

In the case of RoboHELP, however, you're working with perfectly manageable English terms — projects, books, topics . . . . But however clear these terms may seem, behind the scenes actually lurks the dreaded . . . *code!* In the example that I show you in the section "Creating a Classic Help project" (earlier in this chapter), you choose a *target system* for the Help file at the time that you create the file — that is, you indicate that you want to create a WinHelp 4 file. After you compile the project, you put all those files together into a WinHelp 4 file that looks like a "real" Help file and not just a collection of topics with funny codes in the top-left corner.

Your WinHelp 4 file actually resides on the computer as a separate file in the HLP format. If you wonder what you're actually compiling (or *putting together*, as you may say in plain English), I can now confide that you're compiling various source files and components — the Table of Contents *(TOC)* has its own file, for instance — into one Help file.

For a more in-depth discussion on compiling, see Chapter 11. Programmers, I know, are likely to flip right to that section. Others may want to make a point right now to glue those pages together and never look at them.

To compile and run your Help file, follow these steps:

1. Choose File➪Compile from the RoboHELP Explorer menu.

As a short cut, you can also click the Compile icon on the Project toolbar (it's the third icon from the left) in the Explorer (left) pane or simply press Ctrl+M.

Your computer whirs and spins for a bit. (The length of time depends on the size of the file mainly and, of course, the speed of your computer. In the moment before the results appear, many people are known to pray to the deity of their choice or, at least, to hold their breath expectantly.) Finally, a Result dialog box, similar to the one shown in Figure 2-15, appears to show you how well RoboHELP put your pieces together into that one working Help file.

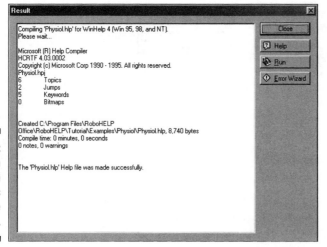

Figure 2-15:
A thorough
report on
your efforts
to compile
your file.

2. From the Result dialog box, *run* **the file by clicking the Run button.**

If the Result dialog box isn't currently open on-screen (or if you just want to run the file without opening the dialog box), click File⇨Run Help File, or press Ctrl+R, or click the Run Help File icon (it looks like a book with a question mark and an arrow tab in the top left) on the Project toolbar.

Your real Help file appears on-screen in a WinHelp window, and your book appears on its Contents tab. You can now try out the Help file if you want.

3. Double-click the book of your choice to view the topics within it.

Figure 2-16 shows my Famous Physiologists Help Topic with the Historic Figures book expanded to show its topics. The real fun, of course, is reading an actual topic.

4. Double-click a topic name in the Topics list to see the actual Help file that goes with it.

Figure 2-17 shows the topic in an actual WinHelp window.

For any project you undertake, you inevitably reach a final, culminating moment — the grand climax in a symphony, the denouement in a short story, the end of the decisive overtime in a basketball game, the moment that you take your chocolate chip cookies out of the oven. Such a moment comes in the world of RoboHELP as you run your file and can at last see it in all its grandeur as a real Help file. If you're new to this game, you may well find yourself saying, "I never thought that I could do that."

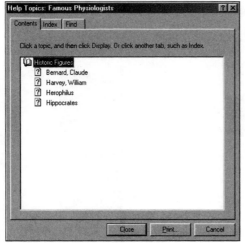

Figure 2-16:
After you compile and run the sample file, you can display its individual topics.

Figure 2-17:
You can view your topic in an actual WinHelp window.

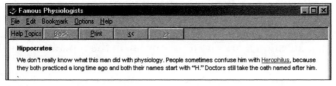

Follow these steps to test your new jump:

1. **Click the Help Topics button in the main Help Topic window.**

   A Help window appears displaying tabs for Contents, Index, and Find.

2. **Click the jump that appears as green, underlined text — double underlined before compiling.**

   You immediately jump to the Topic window that describes the underlined text — that's how you know that the jump works.

Follow these steps to try out your pop-up:

1. **Click the Help Topics button in the main Help Topic window.**

   A Help window appears, displaying tabs for Contents, Index, and Find.

2. **Double-click a topic from the list.**

   The topic displays in the Help window.

3. **In the Topic window that appears, click the pop-up text (green, dotted underlined text).**

   A pop-up appears, describing the topic. Pretty cool, really. Figure 2-18 shows you a sample pop-up Help file.

Figure 2-18:
Click to see
your pop-up
. . . well,
pop up.

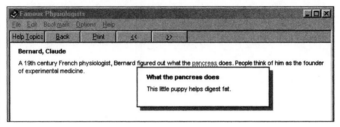

Shutting Down the Project and Exiting RoboHELP Classic

An important part of any chore, of course, is closing down for the day at the end. To shut down your project and exit RoboHELP Classic, follow these steps:

1. **If your Help Topic window is still open, choose File⇨Exit to close your file.**

2. **To close your project, choose File⇨Close Project from the RoboHELP Explorer menu bar (the one in the pane on the left).**

3. **To exit RoboHELP Classic entirely, choose File⇨Exit from the RoboHELP Explorer menu bar.**

4. **To exit Microsoft Word, choose File⇨Exit from its menu bar (the one in the right pane).**

Then go out and do something even more fun than creating a true Help file with jumps and pop-ups (if, indeed, you can find anything that's more fun to do).

Chapter 3

Taking Charge of Topics

• •

• •

*T*opics are *it.* Topics are your actual content — the substance of everything that you do in a Help file. You wrangle with all kinds of fancy tools and capabilities as you create your Help file by using RoboHELP. But where do you "get down to brass tacks" and get your message across to some poor soul who needs assistance? You do it by creating Help Topics. Topics are the heart of everything in a Help system, and that's why you find out about them at this early point in the book.

First, in this chapter, you create some RoboHELP HTML Topics and designate some links between them. Then you get down to the sometimes-tricky business of manipulating topics. In any project — building a boat, painting a picture, cooking lunch — you must be able to move things around or get unwanted stuff out of the way. In RoboHELP, renaming and deleting topics can prove challenging because of the links involved.

After showing you how to take charge of your HTML topics, I show you how to use RoboHELP Classic to look over some of the basic kinds of topics that people create — Procedure Topics, Reference Topics, and overviews. You use RoboHELP Classic the same way for each type of topic, but just knowing the kind of things you may do in Help is useful. I also show you how to put a couple special types of topics in your Help file — What's This? Style Topics and HTML Topics.

Finally, I show you how to rearrange and delete Classic Topics. You must be careful, however, in deleting topics. (You can delete something in Word, for example, and it still shows up in your RoboHELP Table of Contents, although nobody can access it any more.)

Here you find out about those useful capabilities that you're surely just going to use — rearranging and deleting classic topics.

For several of the steps in this chapter, see the sample files weather.mpj and physiol.hpj.

Getting "Manipulative" with HTML Topics

The real skill in working with your topics comes in bending them to your will. You want to be able to find them, rename them, view them, and (above all) delete them. In the following sections, I show you how to do such things. If you want to create topics of your own, follow the steps in Chapter 1 on creating topics, books, text, and links.

Finding an elusive HTML Topic

After you get down to serious work on your own in creating a Help file, you end up with lots of topics, and you need to know how to find individual ones amid all the rest. To find a topic, follow these steps:

1. **Click its icon to start RoboHELP HTML. Open a project. Choose Edit⇨Find Topic from the RoboHELP menu bar.**

   The Find Topic dialog box appears, as shown in Figure 3-1.

2. **Type any part of the title of the topic for which you want to search in the Topic Title Includes text box.**

   The topic title appears in the Found Topics window at the bottom of the Find Topic dialog box.

3. **Click OK to close the dialog box. In the Topic list (right side of screen), the topic you've been looking for is selected.**

   You've successfully used one of the most called-on capabilities of RoboHELP — the Find capability.

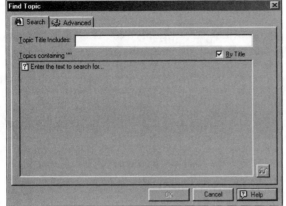

Figure 3-1:
Start with
the Find
Topic
dialog box
to find
topics.

Renaming an HTML Topic

I'm not sure that you need to rename topics all that often. You may decide
that renaming is not worth the trouble, because you may run into problems
with your links. Worse, you may confuse your reader. Still, at times, you
simply must rename a topic; follow these steps to do so:

1. **Make sure you're using the Project Manager, and check the View
   menu to make sure that you're displaying your files By Topic Title (the
   default method).**

   If you aren't viewing by Topic Title, click the check box next to Topic
   Title to select the option.

2. **Click the plus sign to the left of it to open the folder that contains the
   file that you want to rename.**

3. **Click the name of the file that you want to rename.**

4. **Right-click the selected name and, from the menu that appears, click
   Rename.**

   A box appears around the highlighted name (just as in the Windows
   Explorer).

5. **Type the new name and press Enter.**

   The name that you type replaces the selected text and the box disappears after you press Enter. The file now has a new name.

6. **Click Save All on the Project Toolbar to save the file (and your
   changes).**

You've now renamed a file. Fortunately, RoboHELP automatically updates all references to it so that you don't get any broken links. (For myself, though, I don't always trust RoboHELP to be equal to the task of tracking down all such links. Hence, I prefer to avoid renaming.)

You may have your own, more familiar ways of renaming files, such as by using Windows Explorer. If you rename your file that way, however, RoboHELP *doesn't* automatically update your references to it, and you may end up with some broken links. Users of your Help files may then click links that don't connect to anything.

Viewing a Topic

You may not want to just take my word for it that RoboHELP updates the links between topics after you rename those topics. You can view them yourself. As your project becomes increasingly complex, you may want to check links often. To do so, follow these steps:

1. **In the Project Manager (left side of screen; use the folder tab at bottom if it's not displayed), right-click the name of the topic for which you want to view links.**

2. **From the pop-up menu that appears, choose Show Topic Links.**

   The Link View that appears in the right pane shows links coming into the topic from the left and links going out from it to the right (see Figure 3-2).

Figure 3-2:
Incoming links appear from the left of the topic, outgoing to the right if you view the topic in the Link View.

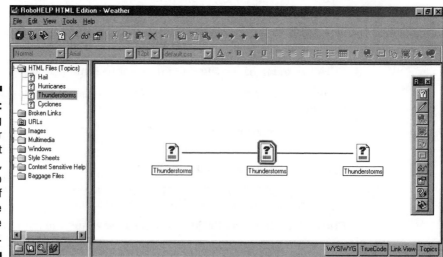

If you have any broken links (links that once worked but that now "connect" to a deleted topic), the links appear with a red line running between the links and the topic with red icons in the Link View.

Deleting HTML Topics

In creating your Help files, you're going to change your mind sometimes about what needs Help information. And if *you* don't change your own mind, a developer, manager, or somebody with authority is sure to change his. The result: You must change what you're working on. That's just the ephemeral nature of life.

If you delete your RoboHELP Topics, however, you affect not just the topic itself but topics that link to it. The following sections show you how to delete a topic without adversely affecting any links.

Deleting a topic that contains no links

If a topic has no links, you don't run the risk of creating broken links when you delete it.

Follow these steps to delete a topic that contains no links:

1. **Click the Topic list tab (lower-right) or Project Manager tab (picture of folder, lower-left) and then click the filename in the list to select the topic that's about to bite the dust.**

   If you're working in the Topic List (which you display by clicking the Topics tab on the right side of the screen), you can select multiple topics to delete. (You can't select multiple topics in Project Manager.) Just hold down the Ctrl key as you click each file's name.)

2. **Click the Delete icon (displaying an ominous red X) in the Project toolbar at the top of the screen.**

   A message box appears, cautioning you that you're deleting the file (see Figure 3-3).

Figure 3-3:
A message
cautions
you that
you're going
to delete
the file.

3. **Click Yes to delete the file.**

   The file disappears from your list and takes up temporary residence in the Windows Recycle Bin.

Restoring a deleted file

After you delete a topic, it's still not completely gone. Not exactly. The expunged topic takes up temporary residence in the Windows Recycle Bin (which you can empty at any time). For a topic, living in the Recycle Bin is a little bit like a squirrel deciding to live on the highway: Risky.

Changing your mind is a Help author's prerogative. You may need to put a deleted file back into operation. But you can't just undelete it. Here's what you need to do:

1. **Double-click the Recycle Bin icon on the desktop to open the Windows Recycle Bin and click its name in the list to select the file that you want to restore, as shown in Figure 3-4.**

   Notice from the little "e" icon to its left that the deleted file is an Internet Explorer file. You need that information later to import the file.

Figure 3-4:
You can restore a deleted topic from the Recycle Bin.

2. **Choose File⇨Restore from the Recycle Bin's menu bar.**

   Windows restores the topic, but you still can't see it in RoboHELP. You must now *import* the topic. To close the Recycle Bin, click the X in its top right corner.

3. **Back in RoboHELP HTML, choose File⇨Import⇨HTML File.**

   The Open dialog box appears, displaying HTML files, as shown in Figure 3-5.

Figure 3-5:
Locate the
file that you
want to
import back
into
RoboHELP
by using the
Open dialog
box.

4. **Click Hail in the Open dialog box to select it and then click the Open button.**

   RoboHELP restores the topic to your list of Topics.

Deleting a linked topic

If a topic links to other topics, you face more choices in deleting it than you do with a topic that contains no links. You have to decide whether to delete references to the topic (such as links to it from other topics). Follow these steps:

1. **In the Project Manager (the left pane), click the name of the linked topic that you want to delete to select it.**

2. **Click the Delete icon (a red X) in the Project toolbar.**

   A message box appears, as shown in Figure 3-6. This time, the message cautions you that references to the file are no longer going to work (naturally enough — after all, the file's not going to be there anymore).

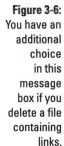

Figure 3-6:
You have an
additional
choice
in this
message
box if you
delete a file
containing
links.

3. **Click one of the three buttons in the message box.**

If you choose Yes, you delete both the topic and the references to it. If you choose No, you delete the topic but retain the references to it (causing broken links). You can also choose Cancel and not change anything.

For the example, click Yes. You delete both the file and the references to it.

4. **For now, exit from RoboHELP HTML by choosing File➪Exit from the menu bar.**

As a Help author, you're going to be creating topics and links and all sorts of other things. That much is fine. But you're also going to be changing things all around — renaming files, deleting files, restoring them, and then maybe even deleting them again. The right to manipulate is the basic right of the Help author, and this overall section shows you just how to do that for HTML Topics. The following sections show you how to perform some similar activities with WinHelp Topics, which at times can prove much trickier to work with than their HTML brethren do.

Reviewing Your Basic Topic Types

If you're creating Help for an application, you almost certainly have no shortage of subjects about which to write your Help. In fact, you probably have far too much to write about. Nevertheless, finding out about some of the most common categories of topics may prove useful. I show you some of the traditional topic types (which, of course, you can create in either RoboHELP HTML or RoboHELP Classic).

You don't need to think in terms of some fixed set of topic types or that you need to use all of them in creating your Help system. Still, knowing about some of the most common types of Help topics may give you ideas of the types of things you need to do as you create your own Help topics.

Some of the most common types of topics are *Task Topics* (or *Procedure Topics*), *Reference Topics*, *Overview Topics* (which you find useful as you're just getting to know a subject), and *Definitions*. I define each topic in this chapter.

The following sections guide you in preparing samples of each of the common types of topics. Just for the fun of it, I use RoboHELP Classic. You can create the same types of topics in RoboHELP HTML (except that, in RoboHELP HTML, you don't have the same pop-up windows as in Classic and might want to use expanding text instead of pop-ups. You can read about RoboHELP expanding text in Chapter 15).

Whatever the category of your topic, you need to follow one cardinal rule: Make the topic answer a single question about a single subject for a single purpose (such as, to show people how to use that one thing).

Opening a Classic Project and creating a new Book

For the examples in the following sections, you can use the sample physiol Help file that I create in Chapter 2. (If you haven't read Chapter 2, you can quickly review the material there and the sample Help file.) To open your Project, follow these steps:

1. **Double-click the RoboHELP icon on the desktop to start RoboHELP.**

2. **In the Open a Help Project dialog box that appears, make sure that the Open an Existing Help Project radio button is selected.**

3. **In the list box in the dialog box, select the physiol.hpj file and click OK.**

You should now see the RoboHELP Explorer in the left pane of the screen and Microsoft Word on the right, with the Explorer displaying the topics for `physiol.hpj`.

You can, of course, add more topics to the Historic Figures Book that I show you how to create in Chapter 2. For the examples in this chapter, however, I'm going to have you create a new Book. Just follow these steps to create the Book:

1. **Click the TOC tab at the bottom of RoboHELP Explorer.**

   The TOC Composer opens and displays your existing Books (including the Book Historic Figures if you go through the exercises that I describe in Chapter 2).

2. **Click the New Book icon in the RoboHELP Explorer Edit Toolbar (the icon that looks like an open book with a starburst in the corner).**

3. **In the New Book dialog box that appears, type the name of the new Book in the Caption box and then click OK.**

   Type **Physiological Systems** for the example. The new Book appears in the TOC Composer, which now occupies the left pane of the RoboHELP window, as shown in Figure 3-7.

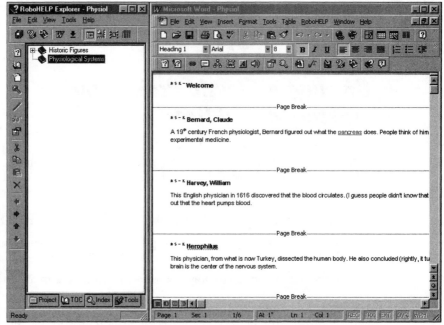

Figure 3-7:
Your new
Book now
appears in
the TOC
Composer.

Getting nitty-gritty — Task Topics

People using Help systems often want to find out how to do something. You show them by creating *Task Topics* (also known as *Procedure Topics*). Task topics are topics that describe the procedure for performing a certain task. You just lead them step by step through the procedure that they need to know.

To create a Task Topic, follow these steps:

1. **With the Book in which you want to create the topic highlighted in RoboHELP Explorer (the left pane), click the New Topic icon — that is, the icon displaying a question mark in the Edit toolbar on the left.**

   For the example, that's the Physiological Systems Book. The New Topic dialog box appears.

2. **In the Topic Title text box, type the name of your new topic.**

   Type **Measuring Body Temperature** for the example. RoboHELP automatically completes the Topic ID and Document fields for you.

3. **Click OK.**

   The new topic appears in Word (in the right pane of the screen).

4. **Now type the text for the procedure that the user must follow.**

   For this example, you can type the following text:

One way to ascertain the state of a system is to measure its temperature. Follow these steps to measure temperature in the human body:

1. **Locate an accurate mercury thermometer.**

2. **Insert the thermometer well beneath the tongue.**

3. **Leave the thermometer in the mouth for at least one minute.**

4. **Remove the thermometer and read it right away.**

Notice that a Task Topic leads the reader step-by-step. You want to focus on a single topic. And you may want to be careful to limit yourself to a small number of steps — perhaps fewer than six. If you want to add additional steps, see whether you can break up your Task Topic into two separate topics.

Adding Reference Topics

Sometimes you want to provide dry, technical information that's not in a step-by-step format. (Although it doesn't *have* to be dry, of course.) You may want to supply information "for reference," such as lists of commands, a collection of useful values, a set of variables that people may want, or a list that's just good for the reader to know.

To create a *Reference Topic*, follow these steps:

1. **Click the New Topic icon (a page with a question mark and a starburst at the top) to create a new topic in your Book.**

   Use the Physiological System Book for the example.

2. **In the New Topic dialog box that appears, type the title of your new Reference Topic in the Topic Title text box and then click OK.**

   Type **Systems of the Human Body** for this topic in the example.

3. **Type the following text and list in Word (in the right pane):**

   You find the following systems in the human body:

   > **Circulatory system**

   > **Digestive system**

   > **Endocrine system**

   > **Immune system**

   > **Lymphatic system**

   > **Musculoskeletal system**

> **Nervous system**
>
> **Reproductive system**
>
> **Respiratory system**
>
> **Urinary system**

You can use Help Topics to store such collections of information so that readers can access the reference information on demand.

Creating Overview Topics

People who are new to subjects need an orientation to the topic. Often, almost nothing's more useful for getting them started than an *Overview Topic*. In an Overview, you usually begin with what people do know and then lead them gently into the new information they're about to read. Follow these steps to create an Overview Topic:

1. **Click the New Topic icon in RoboHELP Explorer.**

2. **In the New Topic dialog box that appears, type the title of your new Overview Topic in the Topic Title text box and click OK.**

   For the example, type **Overview** (what else?).

3. **Type the text of your Overview in your word processor (the right pane).**

   For the example, type the following text:

   Physiology studies physical and chemical processes in the body. Organ systems contribute to such processes as digestion, reproduction, and growth.

   Here you can find out about how to work with organ systems in such activities as measuring temperature. You also can see a listing of each major system, with descriptions of the activities in those systems.

In Chapter 2, I show you how to add a pop-up window, and I give you more information about pop-ups in Chapter 4. Just remember that you often aid your reader by using pop-ups for yet another form of topic — Definitions of new or difficult terms.

Chapter 4

Exploring Your Working Environment

- -

In This Chapter

▶ Getting an overall view of your RoboHELP HTML main windows

▶ Seeing how to handle your main tabs (Project, WYSIWYG, and so on)

▶ Playing your HTML toolbars for all they're worth

▶ Getting a grasp on the two RoboHELP Classic main windows

▶ Getting a feel for Classic's RoboHELP Explorer

▶ Feeling out the hybrid world of RoboHELP inside Microsoft Word

- -

*R*oboHELP HTML and RoboHELP Classic look almost identical after you
open either one. Both display a main window, tabs, toolbars, and
menus. Each, however, has capabilities tailored to the kind of Help it's
preparing — HTML Help, in the case of RoboHELP HTML, and WinHelp, in the
case of RoboHELP Classic. In this chapter, you look in detail at both environments. (Of course, if you know you're only working in one of the
environments, you can skip or skim the sections about the other one.)

Chapters 1 through 3 enable you to get your hands on RoboHELP and try it
out without pausing to look over all the tools at your disposal. Jumping right
in like that is the modern way, I think. (Why start out by studying a bunch of
tools that mean nothing to you until you have some reason to use them?)

After you have worked in RoboHELP a bit, however, you may start looking for
efficiencies and short cuts of various sorts. (And if you like to study your
tools at the outset, you can always read this chapter first. After all, this text is
a *book*, so of course you can go through it in any sequence that you want.)

Personally, I like to pause and briefly handle each of the tools at my disposal,
and this chapter enables you to do just that. Such hands-on activity just
makes me feel more at home with my environment.

For several of the steps in this chapter, see the sample files weather.mpj and physiol.hpj.

Looking Over Your HTML Environment

You may face the danger of "icon shock" as you look at any window similar to one of those in RoboHELP. The effect is kind of like looking over the control panel on an airplane: Where do you start — and how do you know what *not* to touch? The following sections provide you with an introduction to what you see in the RoboHELP HTML main window so you can turn the stuff to your advantage instead of being overwhelmed by it.

Checking out the big picture — the RoboHELP main window

The idea of a main window in any program is to put all the right capabilities at your fingertips so that you can get right down to work without much fuss. You need, therefore, an interface that's "intuitive" — one that you can use by applying common sense.

Check out your RoboHELP HTML main window by following these steps:

1. **Double-click the RoboHELP HTML Edition program icon to start the program.**

2. **In the RoboHELP HTML Edition dialog box that appears, click Open an Existing Help Project/HTML file, select a file from the list, and click OK.**

   You can select any file. For this example, I select the file weather.mpj that appears on the accompanying CD-ROM.

   The main Window appears, as shown in Figure 4-1.

The biggest organizing principle in the main window is that you edit your topics in the right pane and manage them in the left pane.

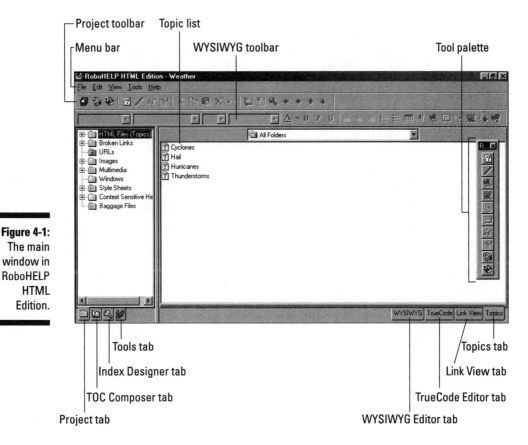

Figure 4-1:
The main
window in
RoboHELP
HTML
Edition.

Touring the tabs

Each tab in the left or right pane opens a key capability you're likely to use often. A tab doesn't simply accomplish a task; it opens an arena in which you can work. You can get a good overview of every work arena available by clicking the tabs at the bottom of each pane. The following sections give you a quick tour of the tabs.

Going over the Project Manager

To begin a tour of the main window's tabs, first click the Project tab. The Project Manager is visible at the bottom of the left pane of the main window that you see in Figure 4-1. It has an icon of a folder on it. You can use the Project Manager in very much the same way that you use the Windows Explorer. (Notice the similarity between the two: The Project Manager stores files in folders that look just like Windows Explorer folders.) You can create and delete folders in the Project Manager, just as you can in the Windows Explorer, and you can click to expand or collapse folders the same way, too, by following these steps:

1. **Click the plus sign next to the HTML Files (Topics) folder to expand it.**

2. **Click the Style Sheets folder and the Context Sensitive Help folders.**

   Figure 4-2 shows the Project Manager with its folders expanded.

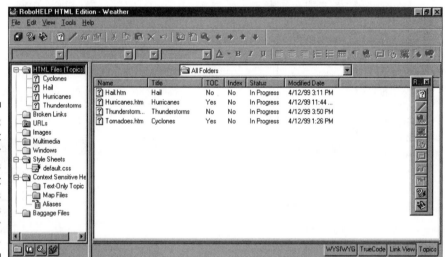

Figure 4-2: Project Manager folders function just the same as Windows Explorer folders.

 Don't expect to use the Windows Explorer to create new RoboHELP subfolders or to perform other tasks that rename, move, or delete folders. If you work on files outside of RoboHELP HTML Edition, RoboHELP doesn't recognize what you do. If you rename a folder in Windows Explorer, for instance, you won't rename it automatically in RoboHELP.

 To get Help on any tab, click the tab and then press F1. Context-sensitive Help for that tab appears on-screen.

Glimpsing TOC Composer

A table of contents is vital in a Help system. After all, people are trying to make their way around the system to find the topics on which they need information. A table of contents *(TOC)*, therefore, is a big . . . well, *help*. (See Chapter 8 for additional information on creating a TOC.) To view your Help system's table of contents, click the TOC Composer Tab (on the left, at the bottom, a picture of an open book) to open the TOC Composer in the left pane of the main RoboHELP window.

As is the case with the Project Manager, you can work in the TOC Composer much as you do in Windows Explorer. You can drag and drop topics to move them around, and you can drag in topics from the Topic List in the right pane of the main window.

You also can right-click anywhere in TOC Composer to open a handy pop-up menu that enables you to perform the most common tasks that you do in the TOC Composer.

Figure 4-3 shows the TOC Composer with the right-click pop-up menu and its submenu open to enable you to create a new book, page, or topic.

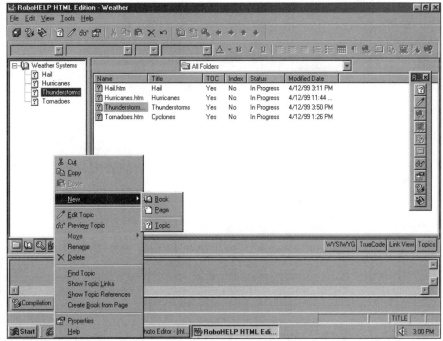

Figure 4-3: Right-click in the TOC Composer to access your most common tasks.

You can right-click in all kinds of places to open a pop-up menu of the most-frequently-used commands. The choices on these right-click menus change depending on the part of the RoboHELP window you're in, which is precisely what makes them so handy. You may not even know what you're most likely to do in a certain place. Often, however, you can simply right-click to find out.

Viewing the Index Designer

If a TOC is important in a Help File, an index is probably even more important. The RoboHELP Index Designer enables you to easily create an index for your Help system. (I talk in detail about the Index Designer in Chapter 9.) To access the Index Designer, simply go to the row of tabs at bottom of the left pane and click the Index Designer tab (the one displaying the image of a key). The Index Designer panel now opens in the left pane of the RoboHELP main window, as shown in Figure 4-4.

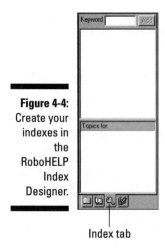

Figure 4-4:
Create your
indexes in
the
RoboHELP
Index
Designer.

Index tab

You can add and delete keywords, rename them, and sort your index entries. When you're ready for it, your Index Designer usually proves itself a key tool (so to speak) for creating a workable Help system (which is why it deserves its own tab and panel on the left side of the RoboHELP main screen).

Understanding the Tools tab

You may not guess what the *Tools tab* does right away, so a brief explanation here may help. You click the Tools tab to display a panel of handy programs and documents. Some come with RoboHELP initially, and you can add other icons of your own for programs you may want to use along with RoboHELP. To access these tools, just click the Tools tab at the bottom of the left pane (the one that displays a little toolbox). The Tools panel opens, as shown in Figure 4-5. (You can read in-depth about the Tools tab in Chapter 19.)

The Tools tab initially contains such tools as Software Video Camera, Web Graphics Locator, and several others.

To add other icons to your Tools panel, you can drag and drop them from the Windows desktop or the Windows Explorer.

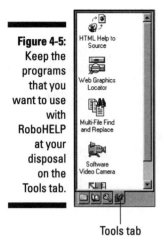

Figure 4-5:
Keep the
programs
that you
want to use
with
RoboHELP
at your
disposal
on the
Tools tab.

Tools tab

Touring the Topic tabs

Tabs in the larger pane on the right side of the screen — down in the bottom right corner — enable you to open the capabilities you're most likely to use in actually creating your topics.

Applying the WYSIWYG tab

You work in the *WYSIWYG Editor* on the right side of the screen an awful lot of the time. You can probably figure out that the WYSIWYG Editor is something relatively new to RoboHELP, because the program makers still refer to it as WYSIWYG. (People don't get overly excited anymore if a word processor comes in a what-you-see-is-what-you-get format, because you no longer need to concern yourself with on-screen codes or other bygone stuff.)

Well, now you are free from those pesky codes in RoboHELP HTML Edition. The topic you're creating appears on-screen, just as it will to your viewer, as a Help topic. All you need to do is click the WYSIWYG tab at the bottom right of the right pane and the WYSIWYG Editor shows you what's what!

The WYSIWYG Editor is doing some hard work behind the scenes, however, because it's actually creating HTML (*Hyper*Text *M*arkup *L*anguage) code — the code that Web browsers read.

Aside from that, the WYSIWYG Editor is a full-featured editor, with its own spell-checker, the capability to create tables, complete formatting options, and all kinds of other capabilities — in short, everything that you need to create your Help system without needing to resort to your word processor!

Examining the TrueCode tab

As I mention in the preceding section, the WYSIWYG Editor actually does generate HTML code. If you're a programmer (or just have a knack for such things), however, you can edit the HTML code directly by using the TrueCode Editor. To peek at the TrueCode Editor, you simply click the TrueCode tab. The TrueCode Editor appears in the right pane, displaying all the HTML code for the topic on which you're working, as shown in Figure 4-6.

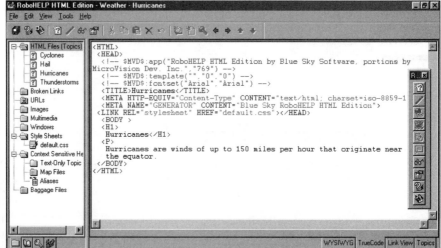

Figure 4-6:
You can work directly on HTML code in the TrueCode Editor.

You can type new HTML tags (codes), delete them, and copy them in the TrueCode Editor. You can even insert scripts from JavaScript or VBScript (if you know how to work with scripts, that is). The point is that the TrueCode Editor allows you to do it all if you want.

Checking out Link View

Navigating through Help topics is all about links, and from time to time, you're certain to want to check out the links in any file you're creating. Click the Link View tab to do just that. Link View shows you the links between topics in a graphical format, displaying incoming links (if any) on the left and outgoing topics on the right, as shown in Figure 4-7. (The figure shows only an outgoing link.) You can drag and drop any topic that you want from the Project Manager into Link View. (You can try it out — just drag any topic from the Project Manager into Link View.)

The displayed topic may link to several other topics. You can also double-click any topic in Link View to see the links for that topic.

Appreciating the Topics tab

You can use the Project Manager on the left to manage your topics, but you can also use the Topic List in the right pane to organize your topics. You can create new topics and delete ones you don't want from this list. Check it out by clicking the Topics tab and then right-clicking anywhere in the right pane to open a pop-up menu containing the most common tasks to perform on that tab. Figure 4-8 shows the Topic List with its right-click menu open.

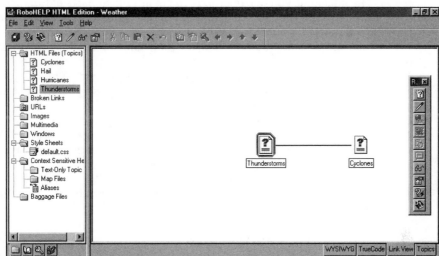

Figure 4-7: Check out the links to your topics by clicking the Link View tab and then dragging a topic into the Link View pane to view its links graphically.

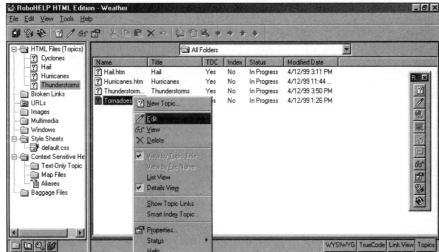

Figure 4-8: Here's a menu of common tasks to perform in Topic List.

You can view your topics in Details View, which gives information such as Title and Modified Date. Or, if you prefer, you can use List View and see the topics in a list sorted by their titles or their file names. Just choose the appropriate command from the Topic List pop-up menu.

Getting a handle on your toolbars

The tabs offer you one main way to get at crucial parts of RoboHELP HTML. The toolbars provide you with another way to speed up your work. You don't need to use the toolbars; you can access the same capabilities by using the menus. But using toolbars is faster than using menus because toolbar commands require only a single click. RoboHELP's designers also put on the toolbars all the capabilities you're most likely to use. (They *may* be wrong, but on the other hand, they should have a good idea about what average RoboHELP users do as they work.)

RoboHELP HTML offers more toolbars than you may know about. You can look them all over by clicking View➪Toolbars from the menu bar. The Toolbars submenu offers you the following choices: You can choose to display the *Project toolbar* and/or the *WYSIWYG toolbar* (or neither if you want). Just make sure that a check mark appears on the submenu next to the toolbars that you want to display.

The View menu is your main weapon for setting up your work environment to suit your needs. Just click to the appropriate command on that menu to select any view or toolbar that you want to display. (And you can click commands on the menu to deselect stuff that you don't use that's just getting in the way. Any time that you see a check mark next to the command, clicking the command removes the check mark and the feature from your screen.) Figure 4-9 shows the open View menu.

Figure 4-9: The View menu is where you can customize your work environment.

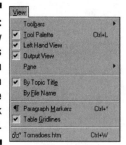

The *Tool palette* (which you access by clicking the second command on the View menu) provides you with a particularly handy way to get at the buttons you use the most. And you can drag it to wherever you want it in the window. When you first display it, it appears on the right side of the screen (or wherever it was the last time you or someone else displayed it).

You find lots of other capabilities as you use the menus and move around in RoboHELP HTML. If you understand the tabs, toolbars, and menus, however, you're pretty much off to the races — soon you'll be working quickly and efficiently in RoboHELP HTML.

Exploring Your Classic Environment

RoboHELP Classic is the "older sibling" of RoboHELP HTML. Although the Classic version is streamlined and sleek compared with its own predecessors, it isn't as streamlined and sleek as RoboHELP HTML. Above all, it doesn't have the WYSIWYG HTML Editor of RoboHELP HTML. If you're preparing Help for Windows 95 or Windows 3.1, however, RoboHELP Classic is your working environment. Many of the capabilities of RoboHELP Classic are almost identical to those of RoboHELP HTML, but several differences do remain, so looking over the Classic environment in detail is worth the effort.

Examining the two main windows

If you start RoboHELP Classic after first viewing RoboHELP HTML, you notice right away that RoboHELP Classic has a separate pane on the right that contains Microsoft Word (instead of the WYSIWYG HTML Editor and other tabs of HTML). RoboHELP Classic works in concert with Word. Although both the Classic and HTML versions contain right and left panes, the two are more integrated in the HTML version (where you have the feeling of working almost in a single, albeit split, pane). In Classic, on the other hand, you work with what amounts to two separate main windows — a RoboHELP window and a Word window.

To view these two main windows, follow these steps:

1. **Double-click the RoboHELP Classic icon on the desktop to start the program.**

2. **In the Open a Help Project dialog box that appears, make sure that the Open an Existing Help Project radio button is selected, select a file to work with, and click OK.**

Figure 4-10 shows the two main RoboHELP Classic Windows and labels the key parts of each.

Project toolbar

RoboHELP toolbar

RoboHELP Explorer

RoboHELP inside Microsoft Word

Microsoft Word toolbar

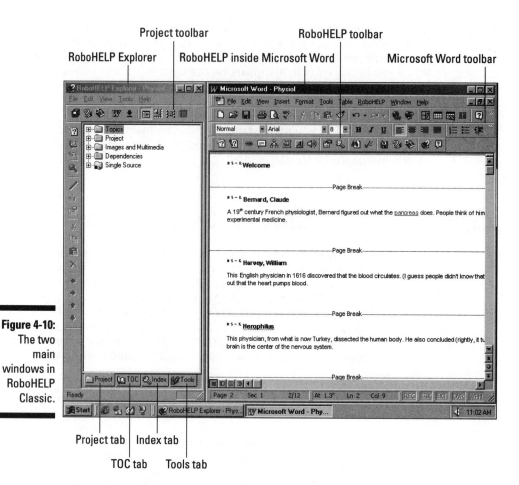

Figure 4-10:
The two
main
windows in
RoboHELP
Classic.

Project tab | Index tab

TOC tab | Tools tab

Examining the RoboHELP Explorer

In RoboHELP Classic, you use RoboHELP Explorer to work with your project as a whole (just as you use the Project Manager in the left pane in RoboHELP HTML for the same task). You use RoboHELP Inside Microsoft Word (the formal name for the right pane) to create your actual topics. The following sections explain the parts of the RoboHELP Explorer.

Sometimes the RoboHELP Explorer takes up the entire screen (in two panes), which means that both the left and right sides of the screen contain the Explorer. If you click the Show Topic List button in RoboHELP Explorer, for example, Explorer takes up the whole screen and displays the Topic List on the right side. If you don't see Word at all, click the Show Word icon (which displays a big *W*) on the RoboHELP Explorer toolbar (on the left side of the screen).

See the following section, "Looking into Classic's Project Manager," to find out how RoboHELP works inside Microsoft Word. Classic also has a Project Manager (just as RoboHELP HTML does), but the Classic Project Manager is a part of the RoboHELP Explorer. HTML doesn't have the Explorer as a separate entity.

Looking into Classic's Project Manager

The main resource for working with your overall project in RoboHELP Classic, as is also the case in RoboHELP HTML, is the *Project Manager*. To use the Project Manager in Classic, you click the Project tab (at the bottom of the left pane — the first tab in the row). The Project tab is selected by default when you open RoboHELP Classic. Follow these steps:

1. **Click the Project tab (at the bottom-left of the left pane).**

2. **Click the plus sign next to the Project folder to expand it.**

   You see a number of additional folders appear under the Project folder, some designed particularly for working in the WinHelp Environment, as shown in Figure 4-11.

Figure 4-11:
Your Project folder contains useful WinHelp folders.

Glimpsing the Classic TOC Composer

You use the TOC Composer to create your Help system's table of contents — a much-valued resource for any WinHelp user.

Click the TOC tab in the row of tabs at the bottom of the left pane (the second tab from the left) to view the Classic TOC pane.

Figure 4-12 shows the TOC pane. See Chapter 8 for additional information on RoboHELP Classic's TOC pane. You discover how to create, drag and drop, and arrange your topics in your table of contents in that chapter.

Figure 4-12:
You can
create a
table of con-
tents in the
RoboHELP
Classic
TOC pane.

Looking at Classic Index Designer

You use the RoboHELP Classic Index Designer to create the most valuable of all tools for locating useful Help — the index. As I explain in Chapter 9, you build a *keyword list* in your index, and you can use drag and drop to rearrange it.

To display the Index Designer, click the Index tab in the row of tabs at the bottom of the left pane, as shown in Figure 4-13.

Looking over Classic's Tools tab

Just as you do in RoboHELP HTML, you can click the Tools tab to open a window containing useful programs to use with RoboHELP Classic. You can add additional icons of your own to the standard tools if you want. You can read more about it in this chapter in the section "Understanding the Tools tab." I also talk about it extensively in Chapter 19.

Understanding Explorer's Project toolbar

Across the top of RoboHELP Explorer, just below the menu bar, lies a toolbar containing special tools for working in the RoboHELP Explorer. You may particularly want to note the following three icons on that toolbar.

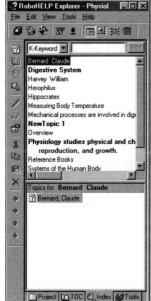

Figure 4-13: Create your index by using the Classic Index Designer.

✔ **Link View.** As you do in RoboHELP HTML, you use Link View in Classic to navigate through the linked topics in your Project. The icon is a question mark with lines coming from it. Figure 4-14 shows a typical Link View in RoboHELP Classic. You can read all kinds of things about Link View in Chapter 11.

✔ **Topic List.** The Topic List, which opens in the right pane, is a great tool for viewing a list of all your topics at once. You can even drag them from the Topic List to the TOC Composer to build your Table of Contents and the Index Designer to build your Index if you want. Figure 4-15 shows the Topic List. You can read more about the Topic List in the section "Appreciating the Topics tab" in this chapter.

✔ **Image Workshop.** You can click the Image Workshop icon (third from the right in the RoboHELP Explorer Project Toolbar) to turn the right pane into an image work area where you can resize images, crop them, and otherwise doodle with them to your heart's content. I talk about working with images in Chapter 5.

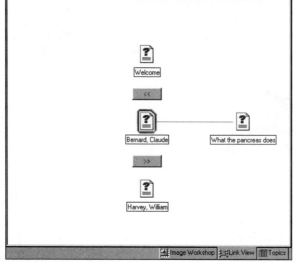

Title	Topic ID	File	Comment
?	Chewing	Physiol.doc	
? Bernard, Claude	Bernard_Claude	Physiol.doc	
? Harvey, William	Harvey_William	Physiol.doc	
? Herophilus	Herophilus	Physiol.doc	
? Hippocrates	Hippocrates	Physiol.doc	
? Measuring Body Temperature	Measuring_Body_Temperature	Physiol.doc	
? Mechanical processes are in...	Mechanical_processes_are_inv...	Physiol.doc	
? Overview	Overview	Physiol.doc	
? Reference Books	Reference_Books	Physiol.doc	
? Systems of the Human Body	Systems_of_the_Human_Body	Physiol.doc	
? Welcome	Welcome	Physiol.doc	
? What the pancreas does	What_the_pancreas_does	Physiol.doc	

Point to any icon for pop-up Help on the button. If the Help doesn't appear, click the title bar (the top line of the window) to make RoboHELP Explorer the active window — and then point again to the button for pop-up Help.

Reviewing Explorer's Edit toolbar

The Edit toolbar (initially down the left side of the RoboHELP Explorer screen unless you move it somewhere else) contains icons for the tasks you perform most commonly while editing your Help system — such as creating a new topic or editing an existing topic.

To make sure that the Edit Toolbar appears on-screen, choose View➪Toolbars➪Edit Toolbar from the Explorer menu bar. Make sure that the Edit Toolbar command on the Toolbars submenu has a check mark next to it. If it doesn't, click in the check box to add the check mark.

You can click and drag any RoboHELP toolbar wherever you want to place it anywhere on-screen. Just click the toolbar between the icons on one of the lines separating the tools, then hold down the mouse button and drag the toolbar where you want it.

Understanding RoboHELP inside Microsoft Word

To create topics in RoboHELP Classic, you don't have the advantage of a complete WYSIWYG Editor. Your topics in RoboHELP don't look the way they do for viewers until after you actually *run* the Help file.

But you do have a powerful environment for creating the content of your topics — inside Microsoft Word. You use Word in RoboHELP just as you use Microsoft Word on its own, with its full panorama of capabilities, but you also use special Help-authoring capabilities within Word, such as creating topics, adding jumps, and much more. The following sections explain the special RoboHELP capabilities you find within Microsoft Word.

Checking out the RoboHELP menu in Word

On the right side of the screen in RoboHELP Classic, you find Microsoft Word. If you're one of the many who uses Microsoft Word as your word processor, notice that the familiar Word menu has an added menu choice — RoboHELP.

Click the RoboHELP menu on the Word menu bar to display its list of commands, as shown in Figure 4-16.

You perform all kinds of tasks by using the RoboHELP menu within Word — even *compile* and *run* your Help document. (See Chapter 2 for compiling and running RoboHELP Classic.)

In certain cases, like compiling or running, you can choose commands either from RoboHELP Explorer on the left or RoboHELP within Word on the right.

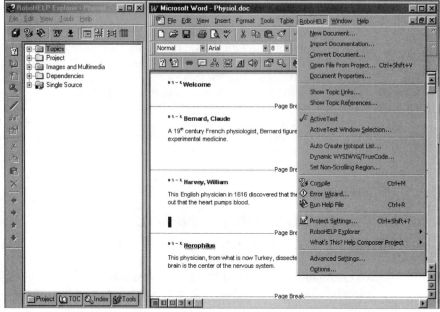

Figure 4-16:
You now
find a
RoboHELP
menu within
Word.

Reviewing the RoboHELP toolbar in Word

Another quick way to get at RoboHELP's capabilities is by using the RoboHELP toolbar in Word — the one that initially appears as the bottom toolbar in the Word pane, just below Word's standard Formatting toolbar. The toolbar duplicates some of the icons from RoboHELP Explorer on the left while adding its own icons (the ones you use in creating a topic, such as New Topic or New Jump). You can use the RoboHELP toolbar in Word to perform your common Help-authoring tasks, such as creating a topic, adding a jump, or just crying out, "Please, please, somebody Help me!" (No, wait — that last one isn't real. At least we can hope not.)

Glimpsing the RoboHELP Explorer toolbar in Word

You also have a separate toolbar that enables you to access the RoboHELP Explorer capabilities from within Word — the Project, TOC, Index, and Tools tabs, as well as a couple other capabilities. (I discuss those RoboHELP Explorer capabilities in the section "Understanding Explorer's Project toolbar" in this chapter.)

"But I can just click those on the left side of the screen," you may protest — well, you can, but you may want to move them even closer to you while you're working in Word.

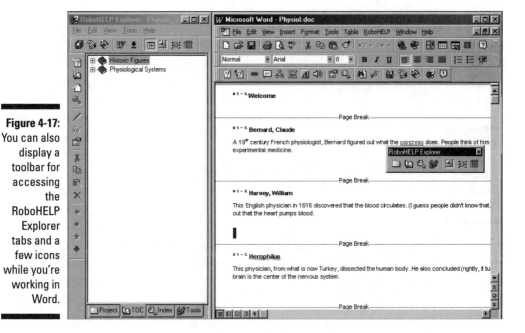

Figure 4-17:
You can also display a toolbar for accessing the RoboHELP Explorer tabs and a few icons while you're working in Word.

If you're not displaying this toolbar already, just choose View⇨Toolbars⇨ RoboHELP Explorer from the Word menu bar to make the RoboHELP Explorer toolbar appear on-screen in Word. Figure 4-17 shows the RoboHELP Explorer toolbar open on the right side of the screen (in Word). (As with all toolbars, you can click and drag it where you want, or you can drag it to the top or side and anchor it.)

You can click the RoboHELP Explorer toolbar and drag it to wherever on-screen proves most convenient for you (or to wherever it isn't blocking something you're trying to read). You can drag any toolbar, but this one in particular is "born to be dragged."

Looking at the RoboHELP Gallery toolbar in Word

The RoboHELP Gallery toolbar, which you use in Word (in the right pane), is similar to the standard RoboHELP toolbar in Word (the one at the bottom of the Word toolbars). In fact, it's almost identical. It does, however, offer a few icons for activities more advanced than you usually perform by using the standard RoboHELP toolbar (such as the New Mini button to create buttons on your Help topics and the New Graphical button to put graphical buttons into your Help topics). To review the standard RoboHELP toolbar in Word, see the section "Reviewing the RoboHELP toolbar in Word" in this chapter.

To display the RoboHELP Gallery toolbar in Word, choose <u>V</u>iew⇨<u>T</u>oolbars⇨ RoboHELP Gallery from the Word menu bar to open it in Word. (If you haven't removed the toolbar previously by using the View menu, then the toolbar is already displayed.)

Figure 4-18 shows the RoboHELP Gallery toolbar open in Word.

Figure 4-18:
The
RoboHELP
Gallery tool-
bar in Word.

Analyzing the Floating RoboHELP Palette in Word

The Floating RoboHELP Palette enables you to access RoboHELP Explorer capabilities while you're working in Word — from the New Topic to the Run Help File tab. (You may wonder why you need this toolbar if you already have the RoboHELP toolbar in Word, which is almost identical. Truth is, you really don't need this extra one. If you like to have a floating toolbar to drag around as you work various places on the screen, you can use the Floating RoboHELP Palette. You can even anchor the so-named Floating palette. It's enough to cause "toolbar overload" for you or me.)

To display this palette on-screen in Word, choose <u>V</u>iew⇨Toolbars⇨Floating RoboHELP Palette from the Word menu bar.

Although the Floating RoboHELP palette has the word *floating* in its name, you can anchor it in one spot on-screen the same way that you do any other toolbar (by clicking and dragging it).

Part II
Getting Visual: Graphics and Links

The 5th Wave   By Rich Tennant

DAD ADDS LINKS AND GRAPHICS TO THE TRADITIONAL CAMPFIRE GHOST STORY

In this part . . .

Help files aren't just for telling people useful information. They're for *show*. And what's the best way to make something stand out in a crowd? Pretty it up. Here you indulge yourself in handling color and formatting. You put in pictures — nifty, fun, colorful ones. Heck, you even put in one of those moving marquees. Stopping at virtually nothing, you put in clickable images and multiple hotspots. Phew!

Chapter 5

Dressing Up Your Text for a Night on the Town

- -

In This Chapter

▶ Adding color and formatting to paragraphs

▶ Using the "hidden power" of HTML to create inline styles

▶ Putting fun little boxes around text

▶ Making sure you don't mess up your spelling

▶ Creating fancy text using RoboHELP Classic

- -

*T*he text you create with RoboHELP isn't just for people to read; your text has entertainment value. Therefore, you'll want to know every possible trick for having the text charm the reader by its sheer looks. (Appearances do matter.) After all, for RoboHELP HTML at least, people look at these files in their Help viewers (which are very much like Web browsers). They want to be amused, pleased, entertained, impressed, or something good. They want a little magic.

In this chapter, you find out how to add a little of that magic to your RoboHELP HTML text. You see how to do some basic formatting like adding that much-needed color to fonts. You can also find out about some fun things that look cool and that aren't really hard to do — like putting in a background for a paragraph or putting a cool box around a paragraph.

I talk, too, about formatting in RoboHELP Classic using Microsoft Word, which gives you the advantage of using Word's elaborate, powerful formatting (at least some of which you probably know how to use already).

Examples of steps in this chapter are available on the accompanying CD-ROM under fishing.mpj and flowers.hpj.

Doing Quick, Neat WYSIWYG Formatting

You can format text the same way you would in your familiar word processor — by highlighting text and then choosing a format from a menu or from a toolbar. In RoboHELP HTML, you choose formatting primarily from the WYSIWYG Toolbar (the one right above your topics).

The left side of the WYSIWYG Toolbar has drop-down lists for choosing paragraph styles and fonts. In the middle, you find formatting buttons to make text italic, bold, or a different color. A little further right are buttons for creating lists and tables, and at the far right are buttons for advanced things like numbered lists and bulleted lists (also discussed in this chapter). Figure 5-1 shows the WYSIWYG Toolbar.

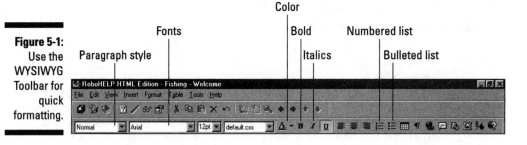

Figure 5-1: Use the WYSIWYG Toolbar for quick formatting.

The following sections show how to use paragraph styles, add color, put in italics (always a favorite), and center text.

Giving your paragraphs new styles

You can apply a number of pre-established styles to your paragraphs by selecting styles from the drop-down list on the far left of the WYSIWYG Toolbar.

Suppose, for example, that you want to apply the Heading 2 style to the topics listed in the Welcome topic — Bass Fishing, Catfish, and so on. Follow these steps:

1. **Start RoboHELP and create or open a project. Open a topic.**

2. **Select the text whose paragraph style that you want to change.**

   For example, drag the mouse across them to select the subjects.

3. **Click the arrow next to the Paragraph Styles list box to display the drop-down list of styles.**

4. **Click the style that you want to use.**

   For example, select Heading 2.

   That's it. Just highlight, point, and click and the text takes on the designated paragraph style.

Experimentation is welcome when choosing styles. If you choose one and don't like what you see, click the Undo button on the Project Toolbar. (You can also press Ctrl+Z to undo.) You better make up your mind right away, though, because RoboHELP only allows one level of undo, not several like popular word processors. There is, though, a nice Redo capability if you want to keep trying a look one way and then the other.

Adding real color

You apply formatting and colors the same way you apply paragraph styles: Select the text you want to change; then click a button. Suppose that you wanted to change the color of the word Welcome. Try it out:

1. **Select the word that you want to work with.**

2. **Click the arrow next to the Change Font Color box to show the list of possible colors.**

   Figure 5-2 shows the Default color list.

Figure 5-2:
Choose a
color from
the Default
color list.

3. **Click the color that you want.**

   For example, click Green (because it creates a vision of fishing waters in the mind of the reader).

You can readily define colors of your own. Click the Custom choice at the bottom of the color drop down list to see the Define Color dialog box, as shown in Figure 5-3. You can experiment with hues, saturation, and other factors shown in the box, and preview the result right within the dialog box.

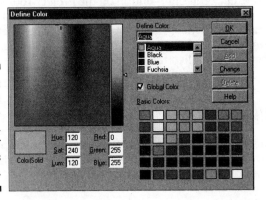

Figure 5-3:
If you're adventure-some, define your own colors here.

Adding those curly italics

Everybody loves some occasional italics (but don't italicize words too often or the italics will lose their effect).

Try adding some italics:

1. **Select the text that you want to change.**

2. **Now click the button that says Apply Italic Style.**

   The text turns to italic style.

Getting your text really centered

Apply line positioning in the same way as other formatting; select text and then click the positioning you want. Follow these steps to center text:

1. **Select the text that you want to change.**

2. **Click the Align Center button (an icon with a picture of centered lines on it).**

   RoboHELP centers the text.

   Experiment with styles on your own. Just select text, point, and click.

You can, of course, use the menus to do your formatting instead of pointing to and clicking buttons on the WYSIWYG Toolbar. Myself, I find that if I'm in a reflective mood and want to check out the options available to me, I like to use menus (and the dialog box that often goes with them).

Enjoying the Power of HTML Inline Styles

In RoboHELP HTML, you can work with *inline styles* — styles that you create at any given spot without using the style sheet. (See Chapter 16 for complete coverage on applying and using style sheets.)

In creating HTML Help topics, you are of course working in the world of the Web. Therefore, you can operate in other ways than the familiar selecting and formatting that you do in your desktop word processor. By using inline styles, you can define a look (a style) for selected text that may even be fairly elaborate if you want.

The term inline styles applies to the world of HTML code that is going on behind the scenes as you create your RoboHELP HTLM topics. In HTML, an inline style uses the STYLE attribute within an HTML tag. Attributes are codes you use in HTML coding. The code is within the line of the HTML code. The name makes perfect sense within the HTML coding world. (Tags, in HTML, are codes at the beginning of elements. They often just refer to the whole coded element.) In HTML coding, you apply the style right within the line. You don't have to name the style, nor do you have to apply a current named style from your style sheet. See Chapter 16 for additional information on style sheets.

Defining your own inline style

Suppose you wanted to dress up a phrase using a more elaborate style than you would readily get from the WYSIWYG Toolbar. For my example, I use the words "the most popular sport fish." Here's what to do:

1. **Select the text that you want to change.**

   You can move the words on a line by themselves to make your task a little easier.

2. **Choose Format⇨Character.**

    The Character dialog box comes up.

3. **Click the In-Line Font tab.**

4. **In the Font Family box, click the selection arrow to the right to see all your choices.**

5. **In the Size box, click the selection arrow to the right to see all your choices.**

6. **In the Color box, click the selection arrow to the right to see all your choices.**

7. **In the Style area, click the check box for whatever style you would like.**

    Figure 5-4 shows my completed Character dialog box with the In-Line Font tab clicked.

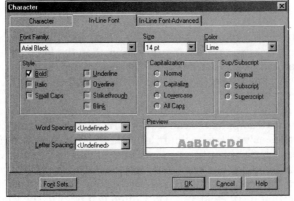

Figure 5-4:
Design your inline character style here.

7. **Click OK to apply the inline style.**

    The line appears on the Help page in green with the other style attributes you have selected.

Putting in a paragraph background

Inline styles make it easy to apply neat style effects like backgrounds to text — colors that appear just behind a certain paragraph. Try it out:

1. **Click inside the line that you want to change.**

2. **Choose Format⇨Paragraph.**

    The Paragraph dialog box opens.

3. **Click the In-line Bkground tab.**

4. **In the Background Color box, click the color you want.**

   Figure 5-5 shows my completed In-line Bkground tab in the Paragraph dialog box.

5. **Click OK.**

   The title of the Welcome box now appears with a neat, navy blue background behind it, as I show in Figure 5-6. (Oops. You're reading in black and white. Trust me, it's blue.)

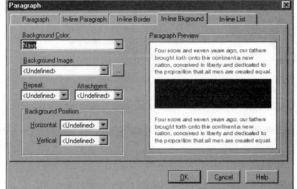

Figure 5-5:
Use this dialog box to put in a background color for a paragraph.

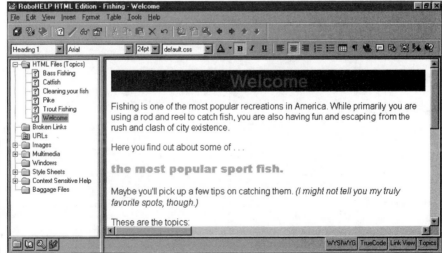

Figure 5-6:
"Welcome" now has a nifty background behind it.

Now that you've applied a number of styles to the title of this topic, you may (or may not!) want to see how those styles show up in the code.

Click the TrueCode tab. The styles you've inserted are in the line that starts out like this: `<H1 STYLE=background-color navy>`. And so on. RoboHELP does all that coding for you as you work with styles.

Putting in a text box

Inline styles give you a lot of power and flexibility in dressing up your text. For my example, I want to put a box around the quotation from Izaak Walton at the bottom of the Welcome topic. Here's how to put text in a box:

1. **Select the text that you want to put inside a box.**

2. **Choose Format⇨Paragraph.**

3. **Click the In-line Border tab.**

4. **In the Style box, select the type of border you want.**

5. **In the Thickness box, choose the degree of thickness you want for your border.**

6. **In the Color box, choose the color that you want for your border.**

   Figure 5-7 shows the completed In-line Border tab in the Paragraph dialog box.

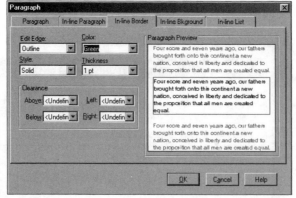

Figure 5-7:
Set up
a box
around
text here.

7. **Click OK.**

   My text now displays inside a cool-looking box, as shown in Figure 5-8.

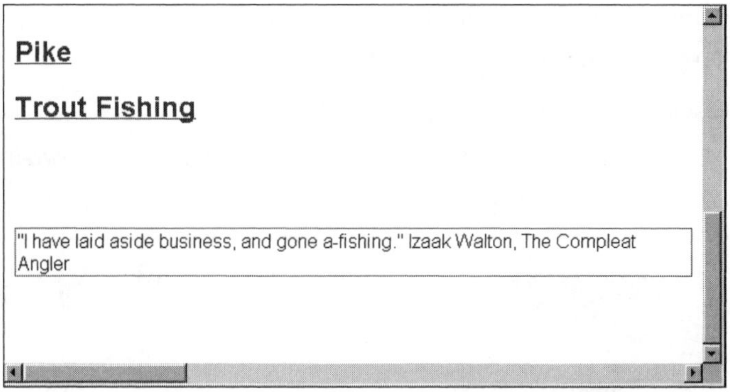

Pike

Trout Fishing

"I have laid aside business, and gone a-fishing." Izaak Walton, The Compleat Angler

Figure 5-8:
A neat
green box
around
some text.

Enumerating with a Numbered List

Suppose you want steps to appear as a numbered list. RoboHELP makes creating numbered lists easy. Here's what you do:

1. **Select the text that you want to appear as a numbered list.**

2. **Click the numbered list icon in the WYSIWYG toolbar for creating a numbered list.**

   Your text appears as a numbered list, as shown in Figure 5-9.

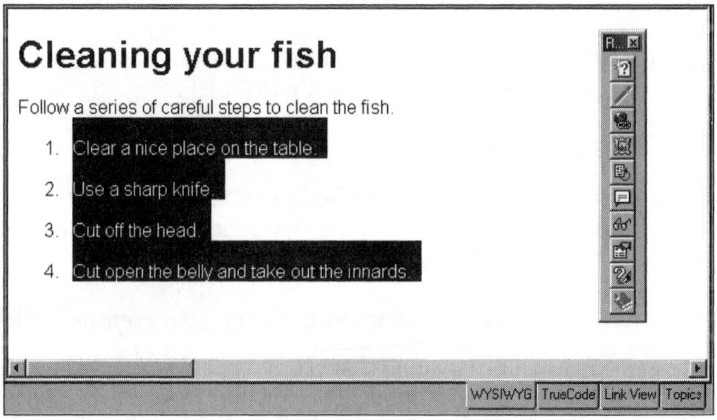

Cleaning your fish

Follow a series of careful steps to clean the fish.

1. Clear a nice place on the table.
2. Use a sharp knife.
3. Cut off the head.
4. Cut open the belly and take out the innards.

WYSIWYG | TrueCode | Link View | Topics

Figure 5-9:
RoboHELP
creates a
numbered
list for you.

Getting Staccato: Making a Bulleted List

Creating a bulleted list is as easy as creating a numbered list. You select text and click the bulleted list icon. Make sure that you select a number of paragraphs (at least two). You can try it out:

1. **Open a topic in a project.**

2. **Select two or more paragraphs.**

3. **Click the tab for creating a bulleted list.**

   The tabs appear with neat bullets in front of them, as shown in Figure 5-10.

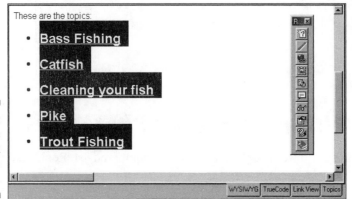

Figure 5-10:
Add bullets
with a click
of the
mouse.

Verifying and Adjusting Your Spelling

Misspellings just can't be tolerated in your Help documents. People probably ought to realize that what matters is the meaning of the word, not the particular characters used to place it on the page. But they don't think that way. They tend to see bad spelling as a lack of attention on your part. But never fear; this section tells you how to use the RoboHELP spell checker.

1. **Choose Tools⇨Spelling.**

   A dialog box opens (see Figure 5-11) where you choose whether to check the whole document, the document starting at the cursor, or just the word at the cursor.

2. **Make sure the Whole Document option is selected and click OK.**

   Spell check highlights the first word it doesn't recognize and presents you with a number of choices, as shown in Figure 5-12. Here are the choices in the Spell Check dialog box:

   • **Change:** Changes the spelling of the word to the suggested spelling in the Change To box.

   • **Change All:** Replaces the spelling of the word wherever it appears in the project.

   • **Ignore:** Pays no attention to the word — skips the word.

- **Ignore All:** Skips the word everywhere it appears (which saves you from having to skip it each time).

- **Stop:** Terminates the spell check and closes the dialog box.

- **Add Word:** Puts the word in your RoboHELP custom dictionary.

- **Undo Last:** Allows you to change your mind and not make a correction you've already made (particularly helpful if you've made a change that occurs multiple times).

3. Continue spell checking the entire document.

Figure 5-11:
Choose how
much you
want to
spell check.

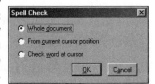

Figure 5-12:
Check your
spelling
using this
dialog box.

If you're in the habit of working directly with your spelling dictionaries, you can open and work with your RoboHELP dictionary. You find it as ROBO-HTML\USER.DIC.

Formatting with RoboHELP Classic

When you format in RoboHELP Classic, you use the formatting capabilities in Microsoft Word. That is, you format the same way you would in Word. Now, Word certainly does have all kinds of formatting possibilities. Up to a point, at least, you can do just about anything that you can do with HTML formatting. (If you find it hard to do some of the dynamic things that you can do with HTML, see Chapter 20 for help.) In this section, I look at how to do a few common formatting tasks using RoboHELP inside Microsoft Word.

To try out formatting, you need some sample text to work with. Go ahead and type in your own if you like or use the flowers.hpj sample file on the CD-ROM located in the back of your book.

Centering Classic text

Centering text, as in RoboHELP HTML, is a matter of selecting text and then clicking an icon. To try it yourself:

1. **Select the text that you want to center.**

   For my example, I select the word Welcome.

2. **Click the Center tab on the Formatting toolbar (the tab with centered lines on it).**

   RoboHELP centers your text.

Actually, in Word, you don't even have to select the line you want to center. You can just put the cursor there. Either way works.

Of course, to fully appreciate the effect in a non-WYSIWYG program, you have to compile and run it. Once you compile and run the file, you view it as an end-user views it — that is, what you see is what you get.

On the RoboHELP toolbar in Word, click the icon for Compile and then the one for Run. (That is, work on the right side of the screen, though actually you can compile and run from either side.) You can see your compiled file. Figure 5-13 shows my sample file with the title centered.

Adding Classic color to text

Adding color within Word in RoboHELP Explorer is identical to doing so in RoboHELP HTML. (See the "Adding real color" section for additional information.) Try it once to see for yourself.

To add color:

1. **Select a word.**

2. **Click the arrow next to the Font Color tab.**

   You may have to maximize Word to see the Font Color button (or click the right arrows (>) at the end of the button bar) to see the Font Color button.

3. **Click the box for a color.**

If you don't see the icon right away, because Word doesn't take up the full screen in RoboHELP, click the Maximize button in the right corner of the Word window so it does take up the full screen.

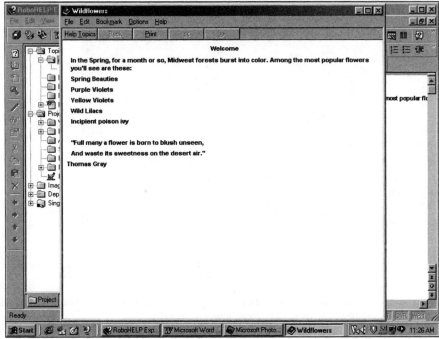

Figure 5-13:
Your file
looks nice
after you
compile and
run it.

Putting a box around Classic text

Quotations always look nice with a box around them. You can readily put a box around your own text. Here's what to do:

1. **Put the cursor in the paragraph that you want to put the box around.**

2. **From the Format menu, choose Borders and Shading.**

3. **Click Box.**

4. **Click OK.**

Figure 5-14 shows my completed Borders tab.

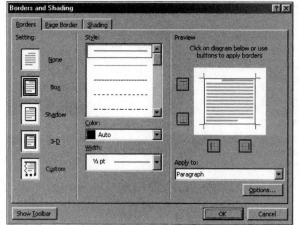

Figure 5-14:
Use this to
put a box
around text.

Creating a Classic bulleted list

Creating bulleted lists is pretty much the identical process to doing the same thing in RoboHELP. Here's what you do:

1. **Select the text that you want to set off.**

2. **Click the Bullets button.**

   Word adds in bullets.

3. **Click the Compile and then the Run buttons to see what your file looks like in Help.**

Life isn't completely simple when using Microsoft Word in RoboHELP. Not everything you format with Word actually gets compiled. It can be scary if you don't know it's not your fault. For instance, if you put in a nice background color for a paragraph, it shows up nicely in Word itself, but it doesn't show up when you compile the file. Yikes! It's a reality, though. It's not RoboHELP's fault. It's the Microsoft Help Compiler's fault. The outcome is the same, though. What you want to do doesn't quite work, and it can be frustrating.

Chapter 6

Pleasing with Pictures

● ●

In This Chapter

▶ Importing pictures onto the Help page

▶ Manipulating graphics in RoboHELP (without mangling them too badly)

▶ Adding cool backgrounds, impressive lines, or even a marquee to your Help pages

▶ Examining the image capabilities in RoboHELP Classic

● ●

*P*eople like to look at pictures. People are increasingly visual. For the comic book/television generations and beyond, pictures can be the whole deal, with words being decidedly secondary.

This chapter guides you in inserting and manipulating images in your project by simply creating a border, changing the size of a graphic, adding a background, inserting a horizontal line — I even throw caution to the wind by showing you how to put a marquee on the page. You can also try out images in RoboHELP Classic and see how to add, resize, and delete them.

Copying Images to Your Project Folder

You can add images into any project of your own. The examples in this chapter are available on the accompanying CD-ROM under brickwall.gif and pets.mpj.

You can compile images from all kinds of sources. You can scan images in or use your own; you can copy images from clip art libraries on the Internet; or you can find images in clip art libraries in software that you have purchased, such as Microsoft Office or RoboHELP Office. For examples, the images in this chapter are from RoboHELP Office.

Here's how to find images and copy them into your Project Folder, from which you can then insert the images into your Help topics.

1. **Start RoboHELP HTML and open the file that you want to work with.**

2. **In the WYSIWYG Editor, display the text that you plan to work with.**

 3. **Click the Tools tab on the left side of the screen to display the programs on the Tools pane.**

 4. **Double-click Web Graphics Locator.**

 The Graphics Locator dialog box opens, as shown in Figure 6-1.

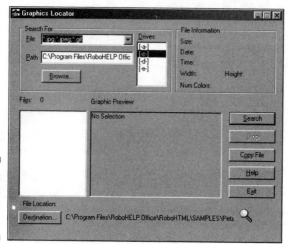

Figure 6-1:
Start here
to find
images.

You use the Graphics Locator to find, look at, and copy graphic files.

 5. **For the Path box, you may click the Browse button, choose a path, and then click OK.**

 For my examples, I use the path `C:\Program Files\RoboHELP Office\RoboHTML`.

 6. **Click the Search button.**

 If you accept the suggested file types in the File box at the top (.jpg, .jpeg, .gif) of the window, RoboHELP locates all files of that type in the path you've provided and lists them in the Files list box at the left side of the file. Click Exit to close the Graphics Locator.

Now that you have graphics to choose from, follow these steps in the Graphics Locator to make your selection:

 1. **Click once in the Files list box to make it active.**

 2. **Click the Destination button at the bottom of the window to show where you want to place the graphic. Click OK when you're satisfied.**

 3. **Use the down-arrow key to go over the files one at a time.**

 When you select a file, you can see a preview of it in the Graphic Preview box on the right.

4. **When you see a file that you want, click the C̲opy file button on the right.**

   RoboHELP places the file in the folder of your choice.

5. **After choosing the images you want to work with and inserting them accordingly, click the E̲xit button to close the Graphics Locator.**

Trying to find graphics can be annoying and a real time waster. This Graphics Locator can be a big help (unless you end up wasting even more time fiddling around with it).

Adding an Image into HTML Help

Once you have images in your Project folder, getting them into RoboHELP HTML involves just a couple steps:

1. **Place the cursor in the document where you want to put your picture.**

   For example, click at the end of the topic called The Elephant and then press Enter to place the cursor just below the last line of text.

2. **Click the Insert Image button (an icon of a picture frame in the WYSIWYG toolbar).**

   The Image dialog box appears, displaying whatever images you have placed there, as I show in Figure 6-2.

3. **Click the image you want.**

   If you don't see the image you want, you need to press the folder button and go browse for it on your computer.

   If you have the Preview Image box checked, you can see the image there. For myself, I always like to have that box checked. Weird things can happen. The file name may say `elephant`, but the picture may show a rocket ship or something.

   At the bottom of the dialog box, you can choose lots of things about the size of the image if you want. Graphic designers will do so. You can just accept the suggested settings, though.

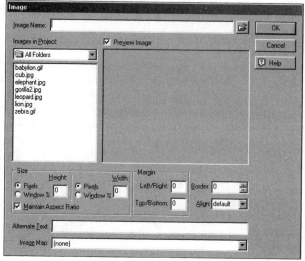

Figure 6-2:
Here you
can choose
and insert
pictures.

The Alternate Text box at the bottom of the Image dialog box is kind of cool for techies, because such people like to help out other techies who do things like use a low power PC and turn off the graphics capability in their browsers. The text you type here will display in a browser with its graphics turned off. It also appears over the image when people just point to it — I mean, if they can't tell that it's an elephant or something.

4. Click OK.

RoboHELP HTML puts the image right where you say to put it, as shown in Figure 6-3.

5. Save your project.

RoboHELP saves the image in the Images folder in the Project Manager.

Figure 6-3:
With any
luck, your
picture
shows up
where it's
supposed to.

The Elephant

The elephant makes a great city pet. Dogs are commonplace, and a Zebra often gets overlooked as just another horse. But few of your neighb[ors are] going to overlook an elephant walking down the street with you, unless you li[ve in] Delhi or areas where elephants are really common.

Dragging and dropping images

After you have an image in a topic, you can drag and drop it into other topics. Drag and drop from the Images folder on the left. With drag and drop, you can readily experiment with images in your folders and then delete them if you wish.

Here's what you do:

1. **Place the cursor in the document where you want the new image.**

2. **Click the Project tab on the left and then click the plus sign next to the Images folder to open the image.**

3. **Click and drag the image from the Images folder to its new location.**

The image goes to the new location. Dragging and dropping images is handy. If you want to try out several looks for a topic, you might put several pictures into the project and then drag them into the topic to see how they look. Of course, you have to delete the pictures you don't want. I show you how to do that in the "Deleting an image" section.

Deleting an image

Images often just don't live up to expectations, and you have to get rid of them. If you're experimenting with different possibilities, try things out and then delete images you don't like. Here's what to do:

1. **Click the image to select it.**

   For this example, I select the elephant in the Welcome box.

2. **Click the delete button (a big red X) in the Project toolbar.**

   That's it. The picture goes away.

After you delete the image from a topic, it stays in your Images folder. I think this is really considerate of RoboHELP. That way, if you want to use the image later, you can.

Adjusting an Image

Images don't always immediately conform to your expectations. You think they are just right and then you look at the actual product and stammer something like, "Oh, phooey, this doesn't look right." You don't have to take the extreme measure of deleting the image altogether, though. You can work with it. In this section, I show you how.

Adding a border to an image

Images and frames just go together. It's a time-honored tradition. Pictures need something to set them off from the surrounding text (which isn't nearly as royal and dignified as a picture).

Here's how to put a frame around a picture.

1. **Double-click the image that you want to work with.**

   For example, double-click the elephant in the topic The Elephant.

2. **In the Border text box (lower-right), put in a value for the Border box. You may either type or use the arrow keys.**

3. **Click OK.**

   A border appears around your picture.

The value you enter for the border is a *pixel,* which is a dot on the screen. It has its origins, I've heard, from the term picture element, and it's the smallest little dot a screen can display.

Resizing an image

When you're working with visuals, you often want to "eyeball" something as you work with it instead of using precise measurements. My favorite method for resizing an image is just to drag it to the size that I like. Try it yourself.

1. **Click the image to select it. (It will display with red borders.)**

2. **Slide the mouse over to the border until the cursor turns into a double arrow.**

3. **Drag the border until you get the look you want.**

If you drag by a corner, the picture maintains its original proportions. Get into the habit of dragging that way. Once you drag a side and mess up your proportions, it can be hard to restore the original look. (That is, you can end up with a long, skinny elephant or something.)

Resizing by percentages

You might want to make sure that your picture doesn't overwhelm your Help page (or, contrarily, maybe you want to make sure that the picture is big enough on the page to show up nicely). You can try it by following these steps.

1. **Double-click the image that you want to resize.**

   The Image dialog box opens.

2. **Click the Window % button for both Height and Width.**

3. **Type a value in the text box for Width and the one for Height. For example, type 50 (for 50 percent) for both width and height.**

4. **Click OK to see the results of your rash actions.**

5. **Click the View button to see how the picture looks in the Help window.**

   Figure 6-4 shows an image taking up 50 percent of a Help window.

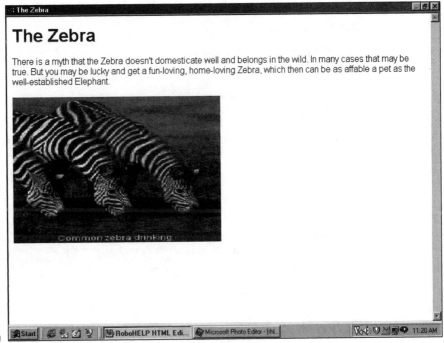

Figure 6-4:
You can specify that a picture takes a certain percentage of the Help window.

Discovering Other Graphic Tools

Graphics are more than just putting in pictures and fooling around with the size and shape of your pictures. You can quietly influence the reader by inserting lively backgrounds (which create a mood for a topic) or horizontal lines (which can focus the reader's attention on part of the screen).

Finding a background image

Backgrounds give definite texture and feel to your Help pages. You may want to use them occasionally to reinforce the message on a page to create a mood, or simply a pleasing effect. To insert a background image you must have one available in your image file.

Here's how to put a background onto a topic:

1. **In the topic that you want to work with, click Insert Image to open the Image dialog box.**

2. **Click the button of a folder at the right side of the Image Name box.**

   This is a neat shortcut for opening the Graphics Locator.

3. **Choose a path.**

4. **Click Search.**

5. **Click the image that you want to use as a background.**

   For example, click brickwall.gif.

6. **Click Select.**

   The Graphics Locator closes, and the name of the file you've selected appears in the Image Name box.

   A dialog box appears stating that the file will be copied to the project folder.

7. **Click OK.**

   RoboHELP places the image in your destination folder (the folder for the topic you're working in, unless you've changed the destination).

8. **Click Cancel to close the Image dialog box.**

Inserting a background image

You can assign an image as a background in a topic. You may have to experiment with the various looks. You don't want the image to take over the page altogether but, rather, to reinforce the message of the page. Here's how to insert a background image:

1. **In the Project Manager (left side of screen), click the Topics folder.**

2. **Click the topic that you want to format.**

3. **Right-click the topic to display the Topic Properties dialog box.**

4. **Click the Appearance tab.**

   Figure 6-5 shows the Appearance tab in the Topic Properties dialog box.

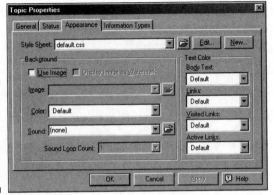

Figure 6-5:
Use this
tab to
add a
background
image.

5. **Click the Use Image box.**

6. **Click Display Image as Watermark.**

7. **In the Image box, click the arrow to select the image you want to use as a background image.**

8. **Click OK and then click the WYSIWYG tab.**

    The image displays as a background.

    Click the View button to see what the background will look like on the Help page. Figure 6-6 shows my sample background.

I don't know about you, but the term watermark tends to confuse me. It sounds like about the last thing I want on my Help page. The best I can glean from my research is that paper manufacturers sometimes impress a mark that looks like a mark made by water. They do it on purpose, and it looks nice. And that's where the somewhat odd term watermark comes from. A watermark in an HTML document differs from a standard background in that with backgrounds, text and background scroll as one, whereas with a watermark the text will scroll over a stationary background. (As of this writing, watermarks only work in Internet Explorer — in Netscape Navigator the watermark functions as a standard background.

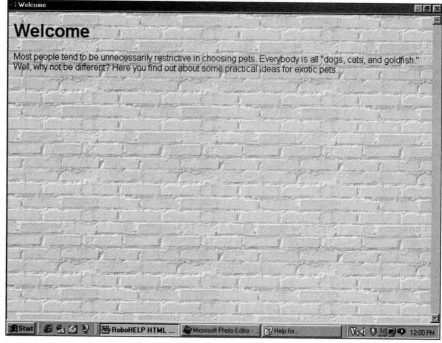

Figure 6-6:
You can
add a neat
back-
ground to
any
page.

Inserting a horizontal line

Lines are the great, classic dividers. If you're going to put one on the page,
why not have RoboHELP assist you so that you can put in a really nice looking line? Here's what to do:

1. **Put the cursor on the page where you want the line.**

2. **Choose Insert⇨Horizontal line.**

   RoboHELP inserts a line on the page.

Of course, the line that RoboHELP puts in is a little thin for my tastes. Here's
how to modify the line:

1. **Right-click the line.**

   A red box appears around the line after you right-click.

2. **Click Horizontal Line Properties.**

   The Horizontal Rule Properties dialog box appears, as shown in Figure 6-7.

3. Click the up arrow next to the Height box to change the Height to 2 and then click OK.

The line looks thicker and, to me, a whole lot better. I mean, if you're going to put in a line, put in a *line*.

Figure 6-7:
Use this
dialog
box to
shape the
line up
the way you
want it.

You may want to change the line color, and I don't blame you. To do it, you have to unclick the 3D Look box in the Horizontal Rule Properties dialog box. (The 3D feature insists on gray as the line color. It's just a quirk of that feature.)

Going all the way, with a Marquee

The marquee (text that scrolls across the screen) is one of the great tricks of the trade that have come from the world of HTML. That is, HTML creators have created a MARQUEE tag (command), which means that anybody can put a marquee on the page with that single command.

To someone who doesn't know how simple it is to put in a marquee, that little dramatic effect looks downright impressive but can also be distracting, sometimes outright annoying, and even completely maddening. Use a marquee once in awhile, but don't overuse them. I'd say, use them once in awhile for your introductory topic and, unless you have some creative new use for them, leave them alone otherwise.

Choose a topic where you want to insert the marquee (named after movie marquees) and follow these steps:

1. Put the cursor where you want the marquee.

2. Choose Insert⇨Marquee.

The Marquee Properties dialog box (shown in Figure 6-8) appears.

3. Click OK.

The box for the marquee appears at the top, but it isn't active until you put something in it.

Figure 6-8:
You can set
up the
appearance
of your
marquee.

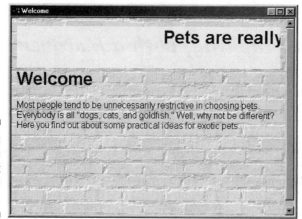

4. In the box, type the text that you want to scroll across the marquee.

5. Click the View button to see your animated classic.

Figure 6-9 shows my marquee. (This book only allows a freeze frame, but you get the idea, I think.)

Figure 6-9:
Here's
my text
scrolling in
a marquee.

Chances are that you'll love your marquee at first and then find yourself less and less infatuated with it over time. To delete a marquee, select it and then press the Delete key.

Working with Classic Images

RoboHELP Classic has some quite powerful tools for working with images (even if, to be honest, WinHelp isn't the truly visual environment that HTML Help is).

Adding a Classic image

To add in a Classic image, you just locate the image and then put it into the text. You can try this yourself by following these steps:

1. **Start RoboHELP Classic and locate a topic to work in.**

2. **Type some sample text if you like.**

3. **Put the cursor where you want to put the image, and click the New Help Image button.**

   The Insert Help Image dialog box opens, shown in Figure 6-10.

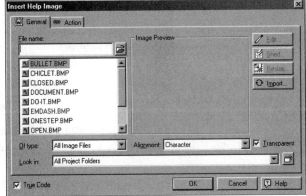

Figure 6-10: Start here to insert a Classic image.

4. **Click the arrow in the Look in box.**

5. **Click the folder that says Misc (Clip Art).**

6. **In the File name box, click the file SAIL.BMP to select it and then click OK.**

   RoboHELP Classic puts a code for the image on the page.

   To see what the image looks like, compile and run the file. Figure 6-11 shows the sample file with the inserted image.

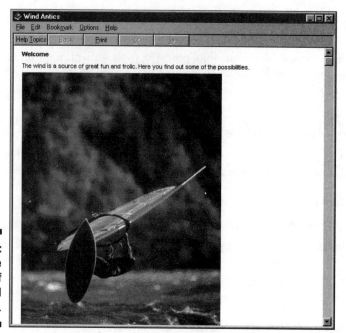

Figure 6-11:
Here's the
display of
the inserted
image.

To resize a Classic image, work in the Image Workshop.

Opening Image Workshop

Image Workshop gives you lots of capabilities for doing probably more than you've ever wanted to do with an image.

Here's what you do:

1. **From RoboHELP Explorer (left side), choose View⇨Pane⇨Image Workshop.**

   The right side of the screen displays the Image Workshop.

2. **Click the Open button to help you locate the image you want to work on.**

   The Open Image from Project dialog box appears.

3. **Click the file that you want to work with and click OK.**

   The image displays in the workshop. Now you can resize it.

Resizing the image

After you have the image displayed in the Image Workshop, you're ready to work with it. Here's how to resize the image:

1. **Click the button for resize mode (a box with a two-headed arrow inside).**

   Arrows appear on the sides of the image. The arrows follow the usual conventions for resize arrows: Dragging the sides increases or decreases the width; dragging the top or bottom works on height; dragging the corner maintains proportion for the image while changing its size.

2. **Drag the arrows to change the size.**

   For example, drag the corners in the lower-right to make the image a less overwhelming size. (You probably have to use the scroll bar at the right to scroll down to the bottom of the image.)

   Figure 6-12 shows the resized image.

3. **Click the Save button to save the resized image.**

Figure 6-12:
Cut an image down to size.

Cropping an image

Perhaps you start out with an image that isn't quite what you want. Often you can adapt an image by cropping out just the part you do want. Here's how:

1. **Open the image that you want to work with in Image Workshop.**

   See the "Opening Image Workshop" section earlier in this chapter.)

2. **Click the Select Mode button (the button with the black arrow) and then drag over the section that you want to use.**

3. **Click the Crop button (the one with two + signs).**

   RoboHELP keeps only the portion you've selected.

4. **Click the save icon to save the image.**

   To go back to the topic, click the Word button in RoboHELP Explorer.

Deleting an image

Images are fun, but they can drive you batty. Often they just don't look on the page the way you envisioned them in your mind. What's the solution? Delete them and start over.

Here's how to delete a Classic Image.

1. **With the topic open that contains your unwanted image, select the image.**

   You can drag across the code, or you can triple click it (which is fun — how often in life do you get to *triple* click?) Note that you're working with the code in your Word topic, not with the image itself.

2. **Press the Delete key.**

   RoboHELP Classic deletes the image. (See the "Opening Image Workshop" section earlier in this chapter.)

Chapter 7

Turning Up the Heat with Graphics

* *

In This Chapter

▶ Clicking an image to leap to fascinating details about it

▶ Inserting Hotspots in an Image Map for faster travel (linking) to your next destination

▶ Using sound and video clips to mesmerize your viewers

▶ Inserting *point-and-click* Hotspots in a Classic image

* *

After you begin to think visually, you begin to think of more and more things that you can do with graphics in your Help files. People love to look at pictures, listen to music, point, click, and daydream. Visuals help you create a magical world for your Help viewers.

In the section "Inserting Hotspots by Using the Image Map," you discover how to use an image as a link (because, as I mention elsewhere, most people prefer to click an image than text) and explore the potent world of *Hotspots*, where a viewer can move to another topic by clicking a special place in a picture.

Also fun — and quite visual — are *buttons*, and you find out in this chapter how to add Related Topics buttons at the end of a topic. (Even if, for some reason, you don't use other images, you're sure to add some Related Topics buttons to help your readers.)

Multimedia is a nice, supercharged word, and I tell you how you can add moving pictures and sound to your Help files in this chapter, too.

Because it's a WYSIWYG program, RoboHELP HTML is particularly useful for working with images and sound. RoboHELP Classic also enables you to work with sound and visuals. In this chapter, therefore, you see how to insert a Hotspot into a Help topic by using RoboHELP Classic.

For several of the steps and figures in this chapter, see the sample files islands.mpj, boat.jpg, and entertain.hpj files.

Linking to Fresh Topics by Clicking an Image

Linking through an image means clicking a spot on a picture to go to another topic. To link from an image, you designate a Hotspot in the image and set up the topic with which to connect. For example, you might click Boston in a map of Massachusetts to go to a detailed street map of Boston.

Many people prefer to click an image than a word while searching for something. I don't know of a study proving that concept, but it just seems natural from a visual perspective. Whenever you see a picture, you want to participate in the event it displays. If you see an object on a page, you want to reach out and touch it, which you can actually do on-screen by using the mouse.

Whenever you see an image, you usually instinctively want to click and see more.

To use an image as a link in RoboHELP, follow these steps:

1. **Start RoboHELP HTML and open the project of your choice.**

2. **Double click the topic in the Topic List to open the topic where you want to insert your link.**

   Figure 7-1 shows an initial topic.

3. **Click the image in which you want to add the link.**

4. **Choose Insert⇨Hyperlink from the RoboHELP HTML menu bar.**

   The Hyperlink dialog box appears, as shown in Figure 7-2.

5. **In the Hyperlink dialog box, check to make sure that the selection in the Link From drop-down list box reads** Image **and that the filename of the image that appears in the drop-down list box, to the right of Link From, is the one you want. (If they are not the ones you want, click the arrow to the right of the Link From list box to choose Image. Click the Select button to the right of the list box where the image names appear to navigate to the image name you want.)**

6. **Make sure that the selection in the Link To drop-down list box reads** File or URL. **(If it doesn't, click the arrow to the right of the box to select File or URL.)**

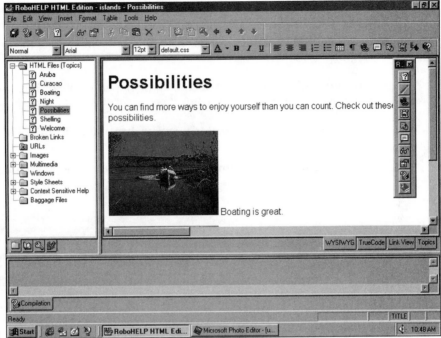

Figure 7-1:
Start with a
topic — one
containing
an image —
from where
you want to
create a
link.

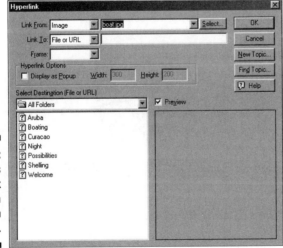

Figure 7-2:
Use this
dialog box
to set up a
link from
your image.

7. **In the Select Destination (File or URL) list box, click the name of the Help file (topic) to which you want the image to link and click OK.**

   RoboHELP now sets up the link between the image and the destination file.

If the Preview check box is selected in the Hyperlink dialog box, you can use the Preview feature to test the link if you want. Just follow these steps:

1. **With the topic you want to preview displayed, click the View button (a pair of glasses) in the Tool Palette.**

2. **In the preview window, click the linked image of your choice.**

   See Figure 7-3 for an example of a linked topic.

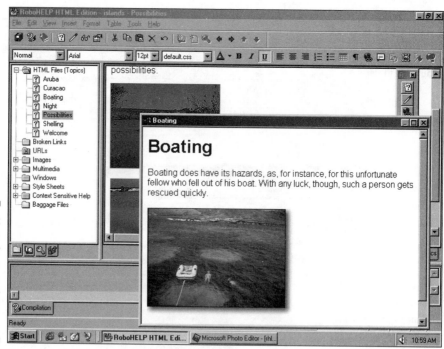

Figure 7-3:
Use the Preview feature to determine that your link indeed does work.

Inserting Hotspots by Using the Image Map

Images make great links that enable Help viewers to jump to numerous places through a single image. You can insert a picture of a house into your Help file, for example, and have people click a part of the house to view its insides. Or, in perhaps the most common example, you can add a map to the file so that people can click different parts of the map for more information about a specific destination. These areas that help viewers click in images are "Hotspots."

When you set up your clickable portions on an image, RoboHELP creates an Image Map for you — an HTML file that defines the areas of the image users can click and tells where those clickable areas connect.

Starting up the Image Map

Clickable places on an image are known *Hotspots*. You can insert images into your Project by using the Image Map. First, you need to start the Image Map and get it set up. To do so, follow these steps:

1. **Start RoboHELP HTML, open a project, and open a topic. Right-click the image on which you want to create Hotspots.**

2. **Choose Image Map from the pop-up menu that appears.**

   The Select Image Map dialog box appears, as shown in Figure 7-4.

Figure 7-4:
Use this dialog box to create a Hotspot on an image.

3. **Click the Edit Map button.**

   A prompt appears, asking whether you want to go ahead with creating the Hotspots.

4. Be bold and click Yes.

RoboHELP saves the current topic and opens its HotSpot Studio (a special program within RoboHELP for creating Hotspots), displaying the image that you right-clicked in Step 1, as shown in Figure 7-5.

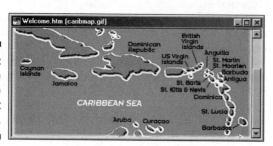

Figure 7-5: Your image opens in the HotSpot Studio.

Adding Hotspots

You designate certain areas on an image as clickable areas. To do so, you start HotSpot Studio (described in the preceding section).

After you have an image open in the HotSpot Studio, you can designate your Hotspots for that image. Just follow these steps:

1. **Click the Rectangle tool (the icon with a rectangle on it) on the HotSpot Studio toolbar.**

   When you click the Rectangle tool, the cursor changes to a + with a rectangle next to it.

2. **Click the image near the spot that you want to enclose. Drag to enclose by drawing a rectangle around the image.**

   After you release the mouse button, the Set HotSpot Target dialog box appears, as shown in Figure 7-6.

3. **Click the target topic in the Topics in Project list box to select and then click OK.**

4. **With the Rectangle tool still selected on the HotSpot Studio toolbar, click and then drag another rectangle around the next part of the image that you want to designate as a Hotspot.**

   For example, draw a rectangle around the image.

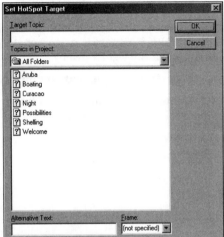

Figure 7-6:
The Set
HotSpot
Target
dialog box
enables you
to specify
where you
want the
Hotspot link
to appear in
the image.

5. **In the Set HotSpot Target dialog box, which again appears, click the next target topic in the Topics in Project list box and then click OK.**

    You now have multiple Hotspots set in a single image. Visitors can now link multiple places in the same image and, from there, jump to multiple topics that link to those Hotspots.

6. **Choose File⇨Save from the HotSpot Studio menu bar to save your image and Hotspots.**

7. **Choose File⇨Exit to close the HotSpot Studio.**

Trying out the multiple Hotspots

To try out any multiple Hotspot images that you set up as links, you need to *compile* and *run* your project. (Compiling the image means pulling together all the topic files and any other files needed to make the project a Help file. Running the project is displaying it as a Help file the way a viewer would see it.) To do so, follow these steps:

1. **In RoboHELP HTML, choose the File⇨Open from the menu bar to open your Project.**

    If you haven't been working with other Projects since adding Hotspots (or working otherwise in a Project), your Project appears at the top of the list of recent files, which is at the bottom of the RoboHELP HTML File menu when you start RoboHELP. You can just click the name there instead of going through the standard procedure for opening a Project. The project opens in RoboHELP.

2. **Click the Compile button and then click the Run Help File button.**

   You see your Help file as it appears to Help viewers of HTML Help. Make sure that the topic containing your Hotspots is on-screen. (If it isn't, choose it from the Contents tab in the Help viewer.)

3. **Slide the cursor over the image in this topic that contains Hotspots.**

   As the cursor passes over a Hotspot, the pointer turns into a pointing finger. Figure 7-7 shows a compiled file with the multiple Hotspots.

4. **Click a Hotspot to display the linked topic.**

   See Figure 7-8 for an example of a linked topic.

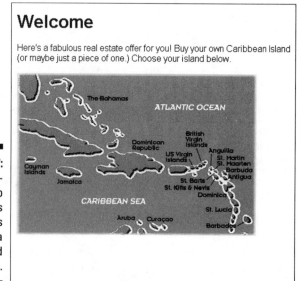

Figure 7-7:
This compiled Help file contains Hotspots over Aruba and Curacao.

Hotspots, therefore, offer you a powerful way to integrate images and related information. From a single image, you can point your reader to multiple related topics.

Aruba

This particular location went down in a small windstorm last year, but that doesn't happen very often. You can get one just like this one at a reasonable price.

Figure 7-8:
After you click a Hotspot on an image, the linked topic appears.

Inserting Related Topics Buttons

As a Help author, your job is to save your reader as many mouse clicks as possible. You want to put information right at that person's fingertips. Related Topics buttons (buttons that appear in the Help file to allow the Help user to click and go to related topics) provide you with a great way to do just that. To add them to your Help file, follow these steps:

1. **Start RoboHELP. Open a topic. Double-click a topic in the Topic List to open it.**

2. **Click at the end of the topic and press Enter at the end to place your cursor on a new, blank line.**

3. **Click the Insert Related Topics Control button on the Tool palette.**

   The Related Topics Wizard – Button Options dialog box appears, shown in Figure 7-9.

4. **Click Next in the dialog box to accept all the suggested settings.**

   The Related Topics Wizard – Related Topics Section dialog box appears. Here's where you do the real work of adding your Related Topics button.

5. **Click the first topic in the Topics in Project scroll box that you want to designate as a Related Topic.**

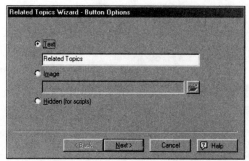

Figure 7-9:
Set up your
Related
Topics but-
tons in this
dialog box.

6. **Click the A_dd button in the middle of the Related Topics Wizard - Related Topic Selection window.**

   The topic appears in the Related Topics list box in the left area of the dialog box.

7. **Repeat Steps 5 and 6 for any other topics that you want to add to your list.**

   You now can choose a few other options if you want.

8. **After you complete your list of Related Topics in this dialog box, click _Next.**

   The Display Options dialog box appears. You can just accept the suggested settings by clicking Next. (If you want to check out the options, click the Help button in the Related Topics Wizard - Display Options box.)

9. **Click _Next again.**

   The Font Options dialog box appears.

10. **Click the Finish button.**

    A Related Topics button appears at the bottom of your topic.

You can try out any Related Topics button that you create to see whether it works by following these steps. Open any topic containing a Related Topics button.

1. **Click the View button on the Tool Palette.**

2. **Click the Related Topics button.**

   For example, I click the Related Topics button in my Shelling topic. A Topics Found dialog box appears for this topic, displaying its Related Topics for your readers, as shown in Figure 7-10.

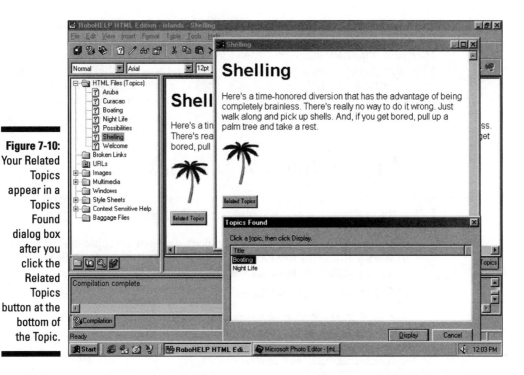

Figure 7-10:
Your Related
Topics
appear in a
Topics
Found
dialog box
after you
click the
Related
Topics
button at the
bottom of
the Topic.

Bombarding the Senses: Multimedia

Multimedia is often a slightly confusing name. The term reminds me of certain happenings I used to see in college, where a band would be playing, while slides appeared on the wall, theater troupes performed, and light shows flashed on and off . . . all at the same time. Multimedia doesn't need to be quite so confusing, however. A television, for example, is a more easily understandable multimedia platform. In RoboHELP, using multimedia simply means inserting movies and sounds into your topics.

You don't need to limit yourself to just text and pictures in your Help files any more. You can now add motion pictures and sound to your files, much to the delight of your audience. You can, in fact end up spending a lot of time deciding on the right musical and video effects to add. Yet the procedures for adding sound and video to your files isn't all that much different from those for adding plain old text or pictures.

The sound and movie formats that you can use in your Help files include AVI, AU, MID, RMI, and WAV. *AVI* (which stands for *Audio-Video Interleave*) is Microsoft Windows' standard video format. Similarly, *WAV* is the native Microsoft Windows sound format. *MID* files are those synthesized from electronic instruments. *RMI* files, likewise, contain synthesized sounds from electronic instruments. *AU* is a format for sound files common on UNIX platforms, but Windows and HTML Help support it as well.

Adding multimedia to topics

Suppose that you want a sound to play whenever a particular topic opens. Follow these steps to add the sound to your Help Topic file:

1. **Start RoboHELP HTML, open a project, and open a topic that you want to work with. Click the mouse at the point in your topic where you want to put the effect to set the cursor there.**

2. **Choose Insert⇨Multimedia from the RoboHELP HTML menu bar.**

   The Multimedia dialog box appears, as shown in Figure 7-11.

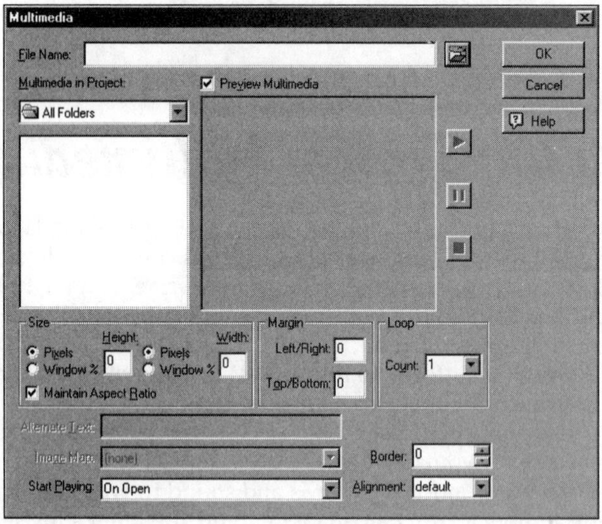

Figure 7-11:
Use this dialog box to insert your multimedia effect into a topic.

3. **Click the downward-pointing arrow of the Multimedia in Project drop-down list box, and then click the file from the list that you want to add to your topic.**

If you want to look for a multimedia item to add, you can click the Folder button to the right of the File Name text box and navigate to the file that you want. (An Open dialog box appears when you click the Folder button. Double click to open folders, and click the file that you want to select.) For my example, I use a sample file from the folder `C:\Program Files\RoboHELP Office\VideoCam\Sample32`.

4. **From the Start Playing drop-down list box at the bottom of the Multimedia dialog box, select when you want the effect to play and then click OK.**

   For example, you can accept the default selection — On Open. RoboHELP inserts a multimedia box into the topic to show where you added the multimedia clip.

5. **Click the View button in the Tool Palette to test out the effect.**

Modifying multimedia by changing properties

Suppose that you want to change something about your multimedia item after you add it to your topic. Perhaps you want to change the music theme that plays with a topic. You use the Multimedia dialog box to do it. You can modify the effect by following these steps:

1. **Right-click the object.**

2. **From the pop-up menu that appears, click Multimedia Properties.**

   The Multimedia dialog box opens (refer to Figure 7-11 in the preceding section).

3. **Make whatever changes that you want in this dialog box and then click OK.**

   You may, for example, want to change your sound effect to a different WAV file. For the example, open the Start Playing drop-down list box and click the choice that says On Open and Mouse Over.

   Preview the changes, as I described in the preceding section "Adding multimedia to topics."

Removing multimedia effects from topics

You may decide not to have a multimedia effect in a file at all.

You don't need to apply any special tricks to delete your multimedia objects from your Help files. Just follow these steps:

1. **Start RoboHELP HTML. Open a project. Double-click a topic in the topic list. Click the multimedia object to select it.**

2. **Click the Delete button (an icon of a bold, red X) on the Project toolbar.**

   RoboHELP deletes the object.

Adding a Classic Hotspot

In RoboHELP Classic, you also have good tools for placing and manipulating advanced graphics in your Help files. They're not quite a streamlined as the ones that you use in RoboHELP HTML. In fact, they can seem a little clumsy at times. But if you need to use them, they can get the job done.

Try inserting a Hotspot (a clickable area) into a Help file by using RoboHELP Classic. To add the Hotspot, you need to use Image Workshop. (See Chapter 7 for additional information on Image Workshop.)

Converting a Classic image into a Shed image

In Classic, you must first convert the image into a Shed Hotspot image, which is a type of image that can contain Hotspots. The main benefit for you in performing the conversion is that RoboHELP then allows you to create the Hotspots. To perform the conversion, follow these steps:

1. **Click anywhere inside the image command in Word on the right pane of the screen (that is, inside the code that reads something along the lines of** `bmct Sail.bmp`**).**

2. **Click the Properties icon on the RoboHELP toolbar (fourth line from the top) in Word.**

   The Help Image Properties dialog box appears.

3. **Click the Shed button.**

   The Create Shed File dialog box appears, as shown in Figure 7-12.

Figure 7-12:
You can
create your
Shed file in
this dialog
box.

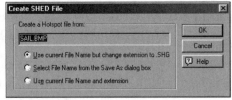

4. **Click OK to accept the radio button for the default selection in this dialog box — to keep the current filename but change the extension.**

   RoboHELP converts the file to the format that enables you to add Hotspots to the image. (Obviously, you almost certainly have no interest at all in the file type or the conversion. In RoboHELP HTML, you don't even need to make the conversion. In Classic, however, you unfortunately do . . . if, of course, you want to add Hotspots to your files.) The new (now fully usable, trainable image) appears in the Image Workshop sporting its new SHG file extension.

Inserting Hotspots in images

Hotspots in images allow your Help viewers simply to click a picture to go to a new topic.

After you have your image in a SHG format, as I describe in the preceding section, you can add a Hotspot to it. Just follow these steps:

1. **Click the mouse pointer near the spot in the image to which you want to add a Hotspot and then drag the cursor around that area.**

   The Insert Hotspot dialog box appears, shown in Figure 7-13.

Figure 7-13:
In this
dialog box,
you can set
up the jump
from the
Hotspot of
the image to
a related
topic.

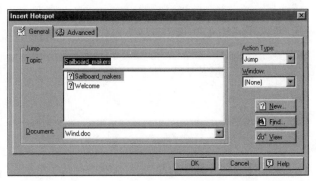

2. In the list below the Topic text box, click the name of the target topic.

3. Make sure that Jump is the selection appearing in the Action Type drop-down list box and then click OK. (If it isn't appearing, click the list arrow next to the box and click Jump.)

4. Back in the Image Workshop, click the Save icon (picture of a diskette) and then click the Close icon (a folder with an arrow at the top right).

You return to the Help Image Properties dialog box. Click OK.

Experimenting with your Hotspot

Having made something new, you can have the pleasure of testing it out. If you build a glider in your back yard, you want to fly it. When you create a clickable Hotspot, you naturally want to click it.

After you have your Hotspot in place, you can test it by following these steps.

1. Click the Compile icon in the Floating RoboHELP Palette to compile the project and click the Run icon in that same palette to run it.

2. Click the Hotspot. (To find it, slide the mouse pointer over the image. When the pointer changes to a hand, the pointer is over the Hotspot.)

You jump right to the new topic.

So, as you can see, RoboHELP Classic also enables you to insert those neat little Hotspots into your Help files. You must work with codes a bit, however, instead of merely seeing your image before you all the time. But with a little determination, you can get the job done quite handily.

Part III

Setting Up Pointers: TOC, Index, and Links

The 5th Wave   By Rich Tennant

"It's another deep space probe from Earth seeking contact from extraterrestrials. I wish they'd just include a Help File."

In this part . . .

*L*et's say you've put all kinds of brilliant, tantalizing, enlightening content into your Help file. What good is it if people can't find the Help file (preferably easy)? Here you master the tools for the "Department of Helping Readers Find Stuff." You discover yourself creating tables of contents, indexes, and smart indexes in no time, while taking charge of the easiest and funnest of all navigation methods — the link.

Chapter 8

Crafting and Shaping Your Table of Contents

In This Chapter

▶ "Getting there" in the first place, by auto creating a TOC

▶ Playing with your choices if you auto create when you already have a TOC

▶ Putting in the key parts of a TOC — books and pages

▶ Fiddling, rearranging, and doing what you do in real life with a set of ideas

▶ Finding out some of what makes for a good TOC

*Y*ou pretty much cannot overstate how important your Table of Contents is to your Help project. People use the Table of Contents (and the Index, of course) to find what they need. Usually, they're in a state of semi- to full consternation as they look. (I mean, they are admitting that they need *help.*) If they can't find the Help, that assistance might as well not exist at all. The TOC can get them to the help they need, even in their agitated state.

The Table of Contents is like the door of your house. People go in and out of it all the time. (If they can't find that door, anything in the house is useless to them.) It's like a flashlight on a dark night — the TOC lets you find things that otherwise you couldn't. The TOC is just essential, and here you find some nice ways to make it work best for you and your readers.

The Table of Contents feature works almost identically for RoboHELP HTML and RoboHELP Classic. In this chapter, I use RoboHELP HTML for the examples, but you can create, click, drag, and otherwise work in RoboHELP Classic the same way.

In this chapter, you see how to make an automatic TOC. (RoboHELP doesn't make one for you unless you ask.) You see how to work by hand in the TOC — creating books and pages, moving them around, deleting them. Basically, you gain an intimate familiarity with a valuable tool — the Table of Contents. In Chapter 1, you get a quick introduction to setting up and fiddling around with a TOC. You find enough there to get you started nicely.

For several of the steps and figures in this chapter, see the sample file amerlit.mpj (a Help file on the subject "American Literature").

Making an Automatic TOC (Presto!)

You can have RoboHELP generate a TOC for you automatically. The process is pretty basic if you don't have a TOC already. If you do have a TOC, you have to make some choices (still reasonably basic). Here's a look at both processes.

Making a quick TOC (when you don't have one)

TOC Composer doesn't display any books and topics until you actually put some in there yourself. You'd think it might know you made some topics and would just display them as pages, but it doesn't. It's empty until you work in it directly. Here's how to "fill it up."

Figure 8-1 shows a list of topics with a blank TOC Composer.

Figure 8-1:
Start with a
list of topics.

Here's how to create your TOC automatically:

1. **Click the TOC tab (the open book, on the lower-left side of the screen).**

   The empty TOC Composer appears.

2. **Right-click anywhere on the TOC Composer and click Auto Create TOC.**

   RoboHELP creates the TOC, as I show in Figure 8-2.

Auto creating is simple; of course, the initial result isn't all that much either. But once you autogenerate, you have a TOC in the TOC Composer, which you can then modify as suits your needs.

There is a certain interplay between the HTML Help viewer your viewers use and the Microsoft Internet Explorer Browser. The viewer will synchronize the page on the left side with the topic content on the right, but it might have trouble if you have words on the left with spaces between them. You can make RoboHELP automatically put in underscores when you need them. Here's how:

1. **Choose Tools⇨Options.**

2. **On the General tab, be sure you have selected Use Underscore in Filenames from the pop-up menu.**

Figure 8-2:
RoboHELP
creates your
TOC auto-
matically.

Making a quick TOC (when you already have one)

Life can get a little more interesting for you if you auto create when you already have a TOC. (Now, as I think about it, how often are you going to do such a thing on purpose? I mean, you already *have* it. You might do it by accident, or you might do it for some special reason of your own. Perhaps you want to work with a duplicate list at the end of your TOC.)

You can try it out (or, better, you can skip to the next section):

Choose Tools⇨Auto Create TOC.

A dialog box politely asks, Do you want to delete current TOC before creating new? (See Figure 8-3.)

Figure 8-3:
You get
these
choices if
you auto
create when
you already
have a TOC.

If you click Yes, the effect is simple enough. RoboHELP deletes the old TOC and replaces it with the new one. (Be careful about doing that if you have invested a lot of thought and energy into arranging the existing version.)

If you click No, though, RoboHELP appends an alphabetical list of all topics to your current list.

You can use a couple of methods to undo your work if curiosity gets the better of you and you append an extra set of items to your TOC. You can just click the Undo button (the ordinary person's best friend). You can also press Ctrl+Z to undo if you are so inclined. The Undo button is the easiest way to get back to where you were before. Chances are, you may never face the hard choices that come up when you have an existing TOC and auto create another one. Engineers are the types who would wonder, "Yeah, but what if I did do that?" Nevertheless, you might decide to play with the options, and knowing more is generally better than knowing less about how to work with the TOC.

Crafting Your TOC by Hand

Many things are just better off once you go over them by hand, and a Table of Contents is such a thing. You have to go lovingly over it to make sure that it is the way you want it. Waxing your car is the same way. Sure, you can get the auto wax at the car wash. Your car looks a lot better, though, if you get out the Turtle Wax once you get home and massage some of your favorite spots by hand.

Putting books into your TOC

If you auto create the TOC, then initially, it's just an alphabetical list of topics. That is, it's not that useful. You can also create the TOC by dragging topics over to it, but, again, you need to find ways to put those topics into classifications. A TOC is most helpful when it has a few categories and subcategories (called *Books* in HTML Help and WinHelp).

Books are a good bit of what the TOC is all about. Readers want you to save them work by taking them directly to what they want to read about, and books do just that.

Here's how to add a book:

1. Click the tab for TOC in the main RoboHELP window.

2. On the Project Toolbar, click the New Book button.

The Book Properties dialog box comes up, as shown in Figure 8-4.

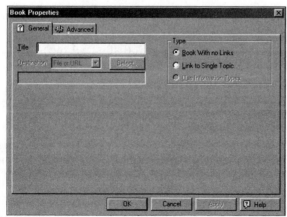

Figure 8-4:
Name your
book here.

3. **In the Title text box, type the title.**

4. **In the Type box, accept the suggested setting — Book with No Links.**

RoboHELP allows you to link a book to a single topic, but I would advise against it. In Windows 98 Help from Microsoft and lots of other programs, the books are containers of Help pages. I think that's a good use for them, and, besides, people get used to seeing them that way.

5. **Click OK.**

RoboHELP creates the book and puts it in your TOC. Figure 8-5 shows a TOC with the book near the top.

To insert additional books, repeat Steps 1-5.

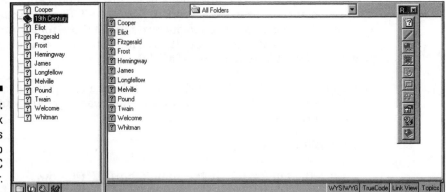

Figure 8-5: The book appears near the top in the TOC Composer.

Putting books inside books

The idea in a TOC is to create a hierarchy; that is, put the important stuff at the top level and put less important stuff within that. Here's how to put books within books.

1. **First, create the books that you need, following Steps 1–5 in the previous section.**

2. **Use the arrow buttons on the toolbar to position the items. Click the Up arrow to move the book beneath another book. Click the Move Right arrow to place the book inside the first book.**

You can also rearrange by clicking and dragging in the TOC Composer. It's quite visual, it's easy, and it lets you slip and slide around until you get what you want.

You have to put at least one book in your book before you compile your project, or RoboHELP will summarily drop the empty book when it compiles your project. Nobody has much use for an empty book, I guess.

Putting in pages

Pages actually coincide with topics, for the most part. The duplicate terminology may cause unnecessary confusion. (At least, the dual names troubled me a bit at first.) When you're working with a topic within TOC Composer, you call it a *page*.

Here's how to create a new page in the TOC:

1. **In TOC Composer, click the book where you want to insert the page. On the Project Toolbar, click the New Page button.**

   If you don't want to try to keep all your toolbars and button names straight, just right click anywhere on the TOC composer to show the pop-up menu, then choose New⇨Page to create your new page. The Page Properties dialog box comes up, as shown in Figure 8-6.

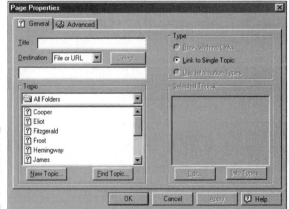

Figure 8-6: Create a new TOC page here.

2. **In the Title text box, type your title for the page.**

3. **If you don't already have a topic to link to the page, click the New Topic button, type the topic the Create Topic wizard, and click OK.**

4. **Be sure that the topic you want shows up in the Destination box. Then click OK.**

Linking a page to the Net (or to some other wild place)

For the Destination for a Page in the Page Properties dialog box, you can choose several possibilities. Click the list arrow next to the Destination box, and you see that you can link to these things:

✔ An URL (Internet address)

✔ An e-mail

✔ An FTP site

✔ A News site

✔ A Multimedia item

✔ A Remote topic

If you click either Multimedia or Remote Topic, the Select button becomes active so that you can select your multimedia item or topic.

You can also link a Classic Book or Page to a number of possibilities. To do so in Classic, you use the Action Type box in the New Page dialog box. From the Action Type box, to link to the Internet, choose HTML Jump.

A topic doesn't automatically appear as a page in the TOC. If you want to be sure that a topic appears in the TOC as well, create the topic initially as a TOC page.

Note that in the topic list, the topics that have associated TOC pages have their topic icons (the icon of a ? in the box) in cyan instead of white. Use the color-coding to identify pages not yet in your TOC.

Rearranging the TOC

You can use the arrow keys on the Project Toolbar to rearrange your TOC. If you're feeling methodical, the toolbars are a good method. If you're in an impulsive mood, though, use drag and drop.

You can also use drag and drop to place topics from the Topic List into the TOC. Just watch the yellow arrow as you move the item, and you can tell where the item will go when you drop it.

Drag and drop all your pages into the books where you want to place them. Figure 8-7 shows my rearranged, quite nice-looking (in my opinion) TOC.

If you have trouble positioning a book using the somewhat finicky yellow arrow in drag and drop, use the direction arrows on the Project Toolbar. They're more precise, I find.

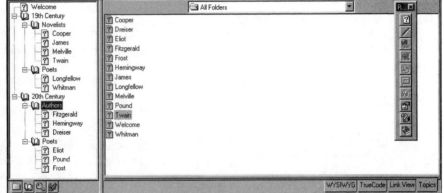

Figure 8-7:
Here's my
TOC after I
drag and
drop it into
shape.

Deleting a book or page

Don't be shy about taking stuff out. As I mention in the sidebar about "Planning a good TOC," you should weed stuff out of your TOC . . . even good stuff, at times.

Here's how to delete a book or page:

1. **Click TOC Composer (if it's not open already).**

2. **Select the book or page that you want to delete.**

3. **Click the Delete button on the Project toolbar.**

    That's it for your item — it goes away.

Be careful in deleting from the TOC. You can delete many items at once by clicking a book that contains multiple books and pages.

If you delete a page from the TOC, the topic for that page still remains in your project. That can be annoying if you want to get rid of the topic, too. To delete both, delete the topic from the Topic List (right side of the screen). Deleting a topic also deletes the reference to it in the TOC.

Planning a good TOC

You may find that the greatest good you can do for your reader is to have a good Table of Contents. Readers will thank you again and again if they can readily find stuff. (Well, they may completely take a nice TOC for granted, but they'll say unpleasant things if they can't find stuff quickly.)

Here are a few things to keep in mind in building any TOC:

✔ Remember that the TOC is a hierarchy. Plan so that you have containers of larger categories with smaller categories inside.

✔ Always have at least two items in any container, such as at least two pages in any book or at least two "books within a book."

✔ Don't have too many containers. Three levels in any TOC is fine — top level, second level, and pages.

✔ Have a logical flow to your topics.

One good organizing principle is chronology, like the 19th and 20th Centuries books you see in the figures in this chapter. You also might use simpler to more complex. When in doubt, you can always arrange alphabetically.

✔ Weed stuff out. Particularly, do your best to limit the number of main books. You're trying to simplify the reader's life, not impress her with how many choices are available.

Renaming a book or page

Brainstorming doesn't end with arranging and rearranging topics. Sometimes you want to change the name for one of your books or pages. You can do it. Here's how:

1. **In TOC Composer, select the book or page that you want to rename.**

2. **Right-click the selected book or page and choose Rename from the pop-up menu.**

3. **Type the new name and then click anywhere outside the selected name.**

You don't even have to use the menus to rename your item. Just click on the item and then slide the pointer a little until just the characters are selected. Then retype.

By renaming a book and not a page, I sidestepped an issue. If you rename a page linked to a topic, you don't rename the topic as well. You end up with a page that doesn't exactly match the topic. I don't know of a one-step way to accomplish the renaming. You have to rename the page, then rename the topic as well. You can rename a topic in the Topic Properties dialog box.

Fiddling with TOC Properties

You can have fun making your TOC look cool in various ways. You can decide to include a border and a number of other possibilities (such as a scroll bar on the left instead of on the right, as is most familiar). You can choose a font to display in the Help file. You can use a custom window to display TOC items to the user. You can put a frame around the topic when it appears. You can even choose a "Custom Image File," which allows you to choose special icons for your book and page icons.

Most of the time, you probably won't want to put in any of these properties, but you may be glad to know that you can. A special situation may come up where you decide to do it.

You don't see these special properties when you work in the TOC Composer. You could say that these properties are not WYSIWYG. To see the effects of choices you make in the TOC Styles tab of the Project Settings dialog box, you have to compile and run the project.

Check out the properties you can work with:

1. **Choose File⇨Project Settings.**

2. **In the Project Settings dialog box, click the TOC Styles tab.**

   You see a tab showing lots of possibilities for you to play with, as shown in Figure 8-8.

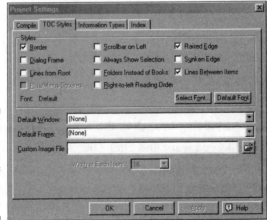

Figure 8-8:
Here you
can change
the look of
your dis-
played TOC.

To see the effect of any one of the changes, first you may want to see the TOC in its default form. Then you can make some changes and, by contrast, see the effect.

1. **Click Cancel to close the Project Settings box.**

2. **Click the Compile button on the Project Toolbar, then click the Run Help File button.**

   The Help file and its all-important TOC display as the viewer will see it, as shown in Figure 8-9.

Figure 8-9:
Here's the look of a standard RoboHELP TOC and topic.

3. **Close the Help viewer.**

Now try out some changes in the TOC Properties.

1. **Choose File⇨Project Settings.**

2. **In the Project Settings dialog box, click the TOC Styles tab.**

3. **Make the choices that you want and click OK.**

   For example, click Folders Instead of Books.

If you want to use some of the properties RoboHELP HTML offers for your Help file, you have to wait for the Microsoft HTML Help compiler to catch up. It can't display Raised Edges, Sunken Edges, Scrollbar on the Left, Border, and Custom Image File. I'm not so sure it does so well displaying some of these other capabilities either.

4. **Compile and run the program to see the effect of the changes you made to your TOC.**

   Figure 8-10 shows my Help file, now displaying folder icons in the TOC instead of books.

Figure 8-10:
Changed
properties
show up
in the final
TOC (if
they're
supported).

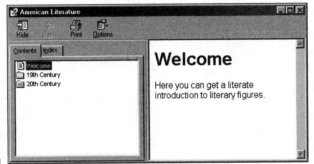

Most of the time, to be frank here, you won't be changing the properties of your TOC. People are used to seeing certain conventions, and if you change them you just risk confusion. (Those folders in Figure 8-10 could easily confuse people, for instance.) I just thought, though, that I'd show you the possibility . . . mostly for fun.

Chapter 9

Indexing Your Material "The Old-Fashioned Way"

*T*he *index* is the main switchboard of the Help file. Almost everyone goes there to find topics. You just *have* to get your index right. At the same time, the index is a much more challenging undertaking than the Table of Contents. You can easily overload it, "underload" it, or put in duplicate entries where you need a single entry. Also, in terms of your own time and efficiency, your index can become a "black hole" where you spend more time than you do in creating the content for your actual topics. With a little common sense and a little restraint, though, you can build good indexes that help your readers out a good bit.

In this chapter, using RoboHELP HTML, first you master the key procedure in the whole world of indexing — getting entries into the index in the first place. You see more ways to get that accomplished than you ever wanted to know. You see how to cross-reference using See Also references. You master the simple but essential technique of sorting your index alphabetically. And you go over the techniques for deleting, renaming, moving, and things like that. (All of which are easy enough to do, but you can go nuts trying if you don't know how to do them.)

For examples in this chapter, see the sample file inventrs.mpj.

Collecting the Words in Your Index

To create an index, you use the Index Designer and arrange the *keywords* (the words people look up in the index). When people actually use your Help file, they see the keywords in a dialog box and can select topics that go with them.

The Index Designer has three main parts, as shown in Figure 9-1. First is the Keyword text box at the top, which you use to type in keywords. Next to the text box is the Add button for inserting keywords. Just below the text box is the Keyword pane, which shows all the keywords in your project. Below that is the Topics for: pane, which lists all the topics linked to the keyword currently displayed.

Adding in keywords by right-clicking them

Keywords are the words people look for in an index. If you don't have a keyword for a subject you want to place in the index, then that subject isn't *in* the index.

Most of the time, you add keywords to your index by reading through topics and saying to yourself, "Oh, yeah, this has to be there in the index." Then, the easiest thing to do is highlight the term and put it into the index right then and there. Here's how:

1. **Open the topic file that you plan to work in.**

2. **Double-click the word you want to index.**

   Figure 9-1 shows a sample file with the new keyword *telephone* highlighted.

3. **Right-click to show the pop-up menu, then click Add Keyword.**

   RoboHELP places the keyword in the list in the Index Designer.

4. **To see the new keyword, click the Index Designer tab (the tab with a key on it) on the lower-left side of the screen.**

Really, the process of indexing is mostly doing what you just did in the previous steps, over and over again. Read through topics and add the right words to the index.

You may prefer other methods of adding keywords, so I go over some of those here. You add keywords in RoboHELP Classic the same way. Highlight and use the right-click menu.

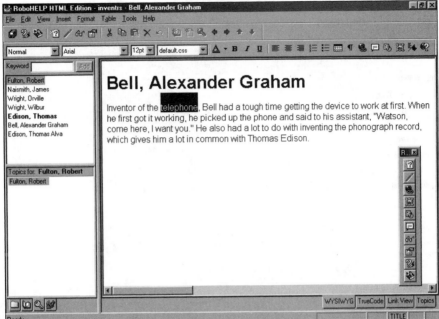

Figure 9-1:
Highlight
the word
you want
to index.

Adding keywords when you create a topic

When you create a new topic, you have the chance to put in keywords for the topic. In fact, you add your topic title automatically unless you delete it from the Keywords box in the Create Topic Wizard. You can try it out again, if you like:

1. **Start RoboHELP HTML and open the project you're going to work in.**

2. **Click the New Topic button.**

   The Create Topic Wizard comes up, as shown in Figure 9-2.

3. **Type the topic title.**

   Notice that when you type the title, it also appears in the Keywords box.

4. **Click the A̲dd button to add the keyword to your list and click OK.**

   The Add button allows you to work in the box without closing it. You can continue to put in keywords by clicking Add for as long as you want until you click OK. If you just click OK and don't click Add, the title appears as a keyword anyway.

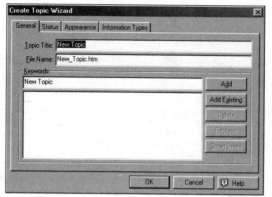

Figure 9-2:
You can add
keywords
when you
create a
new topic.

Inserting keywords with the Properties button

If you want to add keywords after you've already created a topic, you use the Properties tab. You can try it out:

1. **Click the Topics tab to display your topic list.**

2. **Click the topic that you want to work with and then click the Properties icon.**

3. **In the Keywords box in the Topic Properties dialog box (shown in Figure 9-3), type the new keyword and click Add.**

4. **Don't click OK yet. Type another keyword into the Keywords box and click Add.**

   You can continue to add keywords using the Topic Properties dialog box and the Add button.

   Use your basic Windows techniques to display both your topic and the Topic Properties dialog box so that you can see the text in the topic while working in the dialog box. Figure 9-3 shows this strategic placement of windows.

5. **When you finish adding keywords, click OK to close the dialog box.**

   RoboHELP puts the keywords into the Index Designer.

Smart Indexing is a convenient way to put in keywords. It's a fairly elaborate capability. See Chapter 10 for more information on this RoboHelp feature.

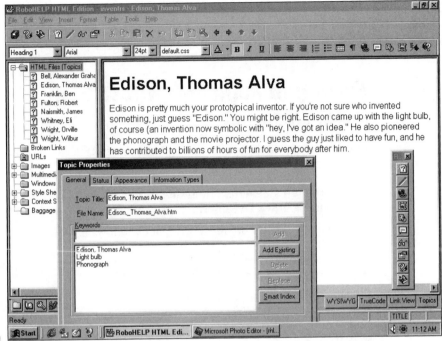

Figure 9-3:
Get set up
so you can
see your
topic as you
work in the
dialog box.

Dragging and dropping titles

You can also drag and drop titles directly from your Topic List into the Index Designer. (Of course, in many cases you have already added the title when you created your topic. So you may not use this capability as often as you might at first think.) Here's how:

1. **If you don't already have a topic title that's not in the index, create one. In the Create Topic Wizard when you create the topic, in the Keywords box, delete the title (so you can see how to add it by drag and drop in just a moment). Then click OK.**

2. **Click the Topics tab to display your topic list.**

3. **On the left side, click the Index Designer tab (tab with a key on it) to display the Index Designer.**

4. **Click and drag the topic from the Topic List to the Keyword pane in the Index Designer on the left.**

   RoboHELP adds the title to the keyword list.

Now, personally, I wish you could drag and drop keywords from anywhere in a topic, instead of just dragging a title. You can't do that, though. You can only drag and drop titles.

Putting in keywords directly in Index Designer

You can also decide to work directly in the Index Designer and add your keywords there. Check it out:

1. **On the left side, click the Index Designer tab (tab with a key on it) to open the Index Designer.**

   Figure 9-4 shows the Index Designer window.

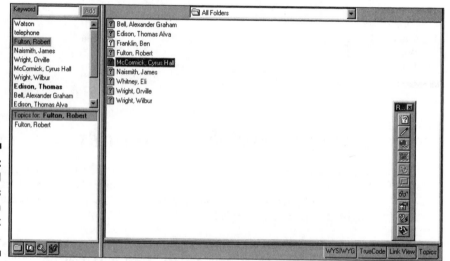

Figure 9-4:
You can add keywords directly in the Index Designer.

2. **Optionally, you may want to open a topic containing keywords you wish to add (so you can refer to the topic as you type in the Index Designer).**

3. **Click in the Keyword text box at the top of the Index Designer and type in the word you want to add.**

4. **Click the Add button.**

   RoboHELP adds the topic to the list.

When you first create a keyword in the Index Designer, it appears in bold to indicate that it has no topics associated with it. In other words, it isn't worth much yet, because it doesn't point the reader toward any Help topic. In the next section, you see how to associate the keyword with a topic.

Referencing a topic from a keyword

When you first create a keyword in the Index Designer, it has no topic associated with it. You have to add the topics.

An advantage of creating your topics in the Index Designer, though, is that you can readily associate multiple topics with a keyword if you wish.

Here's how to add a reference to a topic:

1. **In Index Designer, click the keyword where you want to add a reference in the Keyword section (top half).**

2. **Click the Topics tab on the right side to display the topic list.**

3. **Drag the Topic into the Topics For pane on the left side.**

   For example, Figure 9-5 shows *Edison, Thomas Alva* in the left pane.

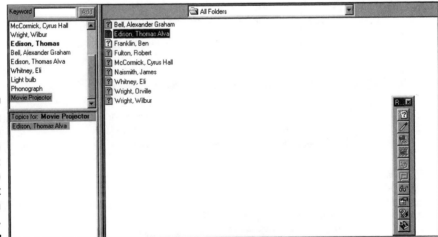

Figure 9-5: Drag a topic to the Topics for: pane to associate it with a keyword.

If a topic in your topic list has no keywords associated with it, the topic icon in the Topic List appears in white when you're in Index Designer.

You can also use the Smart Index Wizard to add topics and do all kinds of other things to your Index. The Smart Index is the latest in index automation, but it's comprehensive enough that I talk about it all by itself in Chapter 10.

You'll probably come up with a favorite way to work that suits you — right-clicking, using the Topic Properties dialog box, working right in the Index Designer, or whatever combination suits you or suits the moment. For myself, I guess I'm just as happy to be "all over the place," using whichever method I happen to be in the mood for at the time.

Creating See Also References

Using a See Also reference, you can point people from one keyword to another keyword. For example, under a keyword *Phonograph,* you could enter a See Also reference to *Alexander Graham Bell* to point the user to additional information. Here's how to do it:

1. **If you're not in Index Designer, click the Index tab.**

2. **Select the keyword that you want to use as a See Also reference.**

3. **Click the Properties button to display the Keyword Properties dialog box.**

4. **If it's not already displayed, click the General tab. In the Keyword Properties box, click See Also.**

   The drop-down list box becomes active.

5. **Click the List arrow at the right of the drop-down list and then select a topic to associate with the See Also topic.**

   Figure 9-6 shows a completed Keyword Properties dialog box.

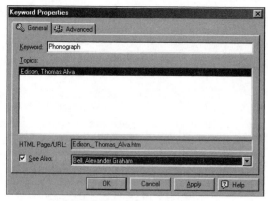

Figure 9-6:
Set up your
See Also
reference
here.

6. **Click OK.**

   The topic appears as a See Also reference in the Topics For pane, as shown in Figure 9-7.

RoboHELP Classic calls See Also references "A-keywords" and the regular references "K-keywords." The program designers must have decided the distinction caused more confusion than anything else, so they don't make much of it for RoboHELP HTML. I have to say I agree with their decision. (You can still use the terms if you're used to doing so.)

Figure 9-7:
Here's an
example of
a See Also
reference.

Going "Multilevel" in the Index

Like a Table of Contents, an index is actually hierarchical. Often, you can save your reader some time and effort if you put smaller subjects inside bigger ones. As with the Table of Contents, you can put keywords inside others by using the arrow buttons or by dragging and dropping.

Arranging by using arrow keys

The best way to get used to the arrow keys is to click them and see the result. Just click to move items to where you want them. For example, click the Move Up arrow to move a keyword up in the index (for example, you might move Light bulb to appear under Edison, Thomas Alva).

Click the Move Right arrow to move a topic to the right and make it a subkeyword of another keyword (for example, you might make Light bulb a subkeyword of Edison, Thomas Alva).

You can move other keywords around to where you want them. For instance, I put telephone as a subkeyword of Bell, Alexander Graham.

TIP

Any directional arrow that is inappropriate at a given time is grayed out. For instance, if a keyword is already as far left as you can move it, then the left direction arrow is grayed out.

Arranging by dragging and dropping

Dragging and dropping is hard to beat as a way to arrange things. Just use the blue arrow to show you where the topic will be appearing as a keyword, the yellow arrow to see where it will appear as a subkeyword. Simply drag the keyword and drop it where you want it.

Figure 9-8 shows an index in its hierarchical form.

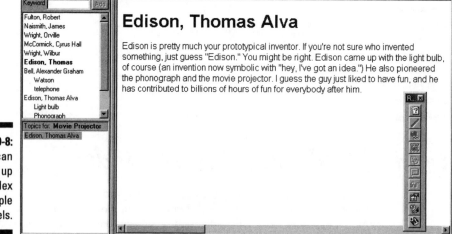

Figure 9-8: You can set up your index in multiple levels.

Sorting Your Index

Indexes follow one nearly universal organizing principle; it is "A, B, C." Indexes are alphabetical. In electronic indexes, people can find a term just by typing it into a search box, but people still expect to see lists in alphabetical order.

Here's how to sort a RoboHELP index:

1. **Right-click the first keyword in a section that you want to sort.**

2. **Click Sort from the pop-up menu.**

3. Click the choice you want, such as Current Level and Below.

If you sort Current Level, you sort keywords at that level but not those subkeywords at lower levels. If you sort Current Level and Below, you sort all the keywords, even those at lower levels of the hierarchy.

RoboHELP sorts the entries.

Take note that you don't get an Undo option after a sort. So, if you have some peculiar order that you want to preserve, remember that you'll have to reconstruct it by hand if you do a sort.

Figure 9-9 shows how RoboHELP nicely alphabetizes an index.

Figure 9-9:
An index sorted alphabetically.

Designing a good index

Users don't use an index the way they do a Table of Contents. Instead of moving logically from more important to less important topics as in a TOC, index users jump right into the middle of things, then associate from there.

Here are a few pointers for creating a good index:

✔ Brainstorm and put in lots of synonyms and alternative ways to get to the same topic. You can put in things like "cotton," "gin," "cotton gin," "cotton machine," and other references to direct people to "Whitney, Eli."

✔ Include "See Also" topics to help point people from one topic to other useful topics.

✔ Build a nice hierarchy of topics within topics, so people don't have to labor through one long, undifferentiated list.

✔ Sort logically, usually alphabetically.

Polishing Your Index

Like a TOC or a Topic List, an Index tends to grow out of control. Certainly it can be helpful to have many alternative ways for a reader to find things. But you don't want to overwhelm your readers, either. You'll find many occasions to delete or otherwise rearrange your entries.

Deleting from the Index Designer

You delete from the Index Designer using pretty standard techniques. Here's how to delete a keyword:

1. **Click the Index Designer tab to open the Index Designer.**

2. **Click to select the keyword you want to delete.**

3. **Click the Delete button (that ominous red X).**

    The keyword vanishes. (If you change your mind and want to restore the keyword, choose Edit⇨Undo Delete Keyword.)

Deleting a keyword from your index doesn't delete the word from the topic itself but just from the index. You can also work directly with a topic and the Topic Properties dialog box to delete a keyword.

Deleting a keyword from a topic

You can also delete keywords by looking at the list of keywords for a topic and deleting any that you disapprove of for some reason. These are the steps:

1. **Click the Topics tab to display the Topic List.**

2. **Click to select the topic that you want to work with.**

3. **Click the Properties button.**

    The Topic Properties dialog box comes up showing the list of keywords, as shown in Figure 9-10.

4. **Click a keyword you want to delete.**

5. **Click the Delete button.**

    The former keyword is toast. Gone.

6. **Click OK to complete the operation and close the Topic Properties dialog box.**

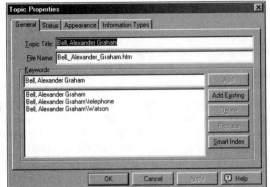

If you delete a keyword, RoboHELP religiously eliminates the connections to all topics associated with the keyword, including See Also cross-references.

Canceling the connection to a topic

Maybe you set up a connection between a topic and a keyword and don't want to keep the connection. You do, however, still need the topic and the keyword is good. But you just don't want to connect the keyword and the topic. Follow these steps to cancel the connection:

1. **Click the Index Designer tab to open the Index Designer.**

2. **Click to select the keyword whose connection that you want to cancel.**

3. **In the Topics For pane, click to select the topic that you no longer want connected to the keyword.**

4. **Click the Delete button.**

   RoboHELP ends the relationship between topic and keyword.

If a keyword has no topics associated with it, the keyword appears in bold in the Index Designer. The bold more or less poses the question, "Are you sure you still want me? I'm not fulfilling much of a purpose here."

Renaming keywords

You may decide that a keyword isn't getting the job done as it is, and you want to change its name. You can use standard procedures, like the right-click menu.

1. **Right-click the keyword you want to rename.**

2. **Click the Rename button in the pop-up menu.**

   The keyword appears in a rename box; and you can type the new name.

3. **Click outside the rename box.**

You can call up the Properties box for any keyword and change its properties. Using the General tab, you can, for example, eliminate a See Also reference. Using the Advanced tab, you can specify a custom window or a frame for the keyword when it displays. To change the properties, just select the keyword, then click the Properties button on the Project Toolbar.

Chapter 10

Indexing the Smart Way

. . . .

. . . .

*Y*ou can search for index keywords yourself. If you want to work that way, I tell you how in Chapter 9. Sometimes there is a smarter and faster way than doing something yourself, though, and Smart Indexing is just such a capability for indexing RoboHELP.

RoboHELP's Smart Index Wizard is a powerhouse of a capability. You can scan through your topics, and the wizard will suggest keywords you might want to include. You can add, rename, and remove keywords. I mean, the Smart Wizard is just a great way for pondering over your index entries for each topic, and getting them right.

The Wizard aims to please, too. You can set it up to search the way you want it to, such as searching for both new and existing keywords or finding weird terms that you use a lot but nobody else would use. (Computer programs often have special sets of terms. Even MS-DOS was once such an unusual term.)

In this chapter, you find out how to set up the Smart Index Wizard to suit your purposes and how to use it to speed up and improve all your indexing.

Both RoboHELP HTML and RoboHELP Classic offer Smart Indexing, and it's the same in both products. (To find the Smart Index Wizard in Classic, look on the left side — in RoboHELP Explorer — not in Word on the right.)

Smart Searching Your Whole Project

Indexing is all about finding the words to put into the index. Smart Indexing is an automatic capability for looking over anything in your topics that might qualify as a keyword so that you can decide whether to include the word in your index.

Starting the Smart Indexer

To start your smart search, you open the project you want to work with and use the menus to start Smart Indexing. Fire up the Smart Indexer by doing the following:

1. **Start RoboHELP HTML and open a project.**

2. **From the Tools menu choose Smart Index Wizard.**

   The Smart Index Wizard comes up, as shown in Figure 10-1. You can now work in it.

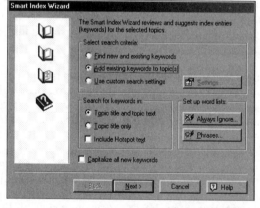

Figure 10-1: Here's your smart indexing assistant. Very smart.

You can Smart Index individual topics by starting Smart Wizard from the Topic Properties dialog box. With the Topic Properties dialog box, open a topic and click the Smart Index button.

Searching new and existing keywords

If you've done some indexing already in your project, you can decide to build an index that uses keywords you already created, while at the same time allowing you to add new ones.

To do it, you select the option to do so in the Wizard.

1. **From the Tools menu, choose Smart Index Wizard.**

2. **In the box labeled Select Search Criteria, click Find New and Existing Keywords (if it's not selected already).**

3. **Click the Next button.**

   (If you're curious about the other possibilities on the first page of the Smart Index Wizard, you can read about them later in this chapter.)

   You see a screen (shown in Figure 10-2) where you can confirm the keywords you add. Also, you can filter to limit your search.

Figure 10-2:
Use the
Wizard to
add key
words to
your index.

4. **Make your choices about adding keywords and limiting the search. Then click Next.**

   I recommend that you elect to confirm your entries (the default). (Strange index entries may come up otherwise.) Initially, also accept the suggested choice for the filter — all authors, all folders, and any status.

   The Status box is a nice opportunity to regulate your index as you get later in the cycle of managing a project. If you use the Status tab in the Topic Properties dialog box for your topics, you can choose to review only certain topics. Perhaps you're an expert indexer, and you want to review only topics that are Ready for Review. You can find out about the Topic Status stuff in Chapter 12.

   The Wizard shows suggested keywords for one of your topics, as shown in Figure 10-3.

   You do your own thinking in the dialog box that displays suggested keywords for a topic. You decide whether to accept a selection, and you have the choice to make the word a subkeyword instead or to do a number of other things.

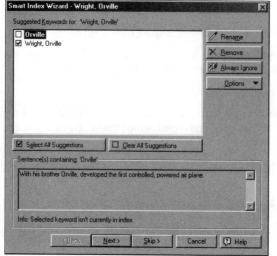

Figure 10-3:
Make your
hard
choices
right here.

5. **Click to select any keywords that you want to include. Leave any others blank. Then click Next.**

   Continue to work with your individual entries by selecting the keywords that you want to include and de-selecting any others. At the end, you see a dialog box titled Smart Index Finished that summarizes your activity. Figure 10-4 shows the Smart Index Finished box.

Figure 10-4:
A summary
tells you
how many
topics
you've
updated.

Sorting the index

An index doesn't reach its full potential until you sort it. Luckily, the Smart Indexer makes sure that you remember to sort your index. When you finish Smart Indexing a project, a dialog box appears that asks, `Would you like to fully sort the Index?` Click Yes to sort the index.

Smart Indexing a Topic

Often you'll create an in-depth Help topic. Then, to make sure that people get the most out of it, you Smart Index that individual topic. In this section, you see how to index an individual topic and work in-depth with its index entries.

1. **Click the Topics tab at the lower-right to display your Topic List.**

2. **Right-click the topic that you want to index.**

3. **Click Smart Index Topic.**

   The Smart Index Wizard comes up.

4. **Click Finish.**

   You see a box displaying suggested keywords and subkeywords for the topic, as shown in Figure 10-5.

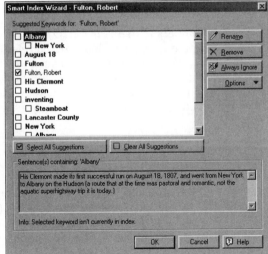

Figure 10-5:
You can work in depth with your topic.

5. **To select a suggested keyword, click the box next to it.**

6. **To rename an entry, select it and then click the Rename button. You can then type in the new name.**

7. **To remove an item, select it and click the Remove button. A message box asks if you're sure that you want to delete it. Click Yes.**

   The Wizard removes the entry.

8. **To indicate a term that you want the Indexer to ignore when indexing the whole project, select the term and click Always Ignore. Then click Yes to the message box asking if you're sure that you want to add the term to the Always Ignore list.**

Note that you don't have to guess about the context of any word in your topic. When you highlight a word, you can read about it in the Sentence(s) Containing box.

9. **If you want to put in a new keyword, add an existing keyword to this topic, view the topic, or work with the topic in a number of other ways, click the Options button and just go at it.**

10. **When you finish your work on the topic, click OK to implement your changes.**

You see a dialog box summarizing your work. Click **Close** to close the summary.

Customizing Your Searches

You may have definite ideas in mind for the keyword search you plan to conduct, whether working with a topic or your whole project. You can set up the keyword search to work the way you want it to work. You can indicate whether to select words with numbers in them (like H2O). If you're doing a chemistry paper, you may want to be sure to include such terms. You can instruct the search so that it always ignores certain nuisance words that keep popping into the Smart Index Wizard's suggestions. Also, you can make sure the search always locates certain words that you want to index wherever they appear (such as your own company name).

Establishing search settings

You can choose to customize the search and set up your criteria right at the beginning. Suppose you wanted to customize a search through a complete project:

1. **Open the project and choose Tools⇨Smart Index Wizard.**

The Smart Index Wizard opens.

2. **In the Select Search Criteria box, click Use Custom Search Settings.**

Note that the Settings box becomes available (isn't grayed out any more).

3. **Click the Settings button.**

You see the complete Smart Index Settings dialog box, with an Options tab displayed, as shown in Figure 10-6.

4. **Make your changes and click OK. (Or click Cancel to make no changes.)**

You then return to the first page of the Smart Index Wizard.

Thinking strategy in indexing

You'll probably want to evolve an indexing strategy over time. At first, if you're like me, you'll just want to get an index done and not really think about strategy. After you see the finished product, though, you'll probably realize you could make it better if you had a plan. Here are some things to consider as you index.

✔ Do you want to have a multilevel index, or just one level? If you want multilevel, you have to plan to include subkeywords in your search.

✔ Do you want to have all keywords capitalized? If you do, you get standardized. If you don't capitalize all keywords, you have to be vigilant about following some consistent pattern, such as capitalizing just proper nouns.

✔ Do you have a lot of nonstandard words to watch out for? Maybe your index goes with a music program that has terms like "rap" that are really quite important. You want to be sure to include them.

✔ Do you have a lot of "noise words?" If the Smart Wizard is presenting you with scads of useless words you don't want, be sure to click the Always Ignore button, and list them as words to ignore.

The Smart Index Wizard is more than a way to work with the particulars of your project. It's a way to work strategically with the whole thing.

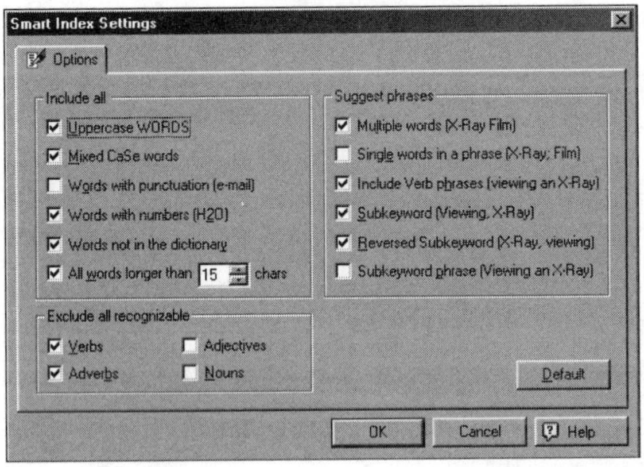

Figure 10-6: Setting the specs for the search.

You have all kinds of choices to work with, and some just may be critical to you as you're working. For example, if you want to be sure to include the term *IBM* in your search, be sure to select Uppercase WORDS. Maybe you're working with keywords that aren't normally in a standard dictionary, such as *Hotspot*. Click the option Words not in the dictionary to include the words.

You can also choose to exclude certain things, such as verbs. (They're handy for subkeywords, but you may want to just add those on your own.)

Also, you can have the Wizard suggest (or not suggest) phrases. If you want subkeyword phrases like *testing the lightbulb,* you select Subkeyword phrase.

If you change your options and then change your mind, you can get a fresh start and just use the "best guess" settings of the experts who built the Wizard. Just click the Default button, then click Yes to confirm to reset the original default options.

Often, you don't realize you need one or another of these settings until you're in the middle of indexing your project in a serious way. Then you just may find certain phrases cropping up in an annoying way or not coming up when you want them. Feel free to go in and change your settings at any time. (Be sure to read through your whole index to be sure that you maintain consistency after changing settings.)

Setting up words to ignore

How is the Wizard supposed to know what to ignore? Sure, for a program, it's pretty smart. Smart people have built it to know what to do. But, still, those builders are just guessing about what to ignore. They don't know your project. They don't know your Help users. Worst of all, they don't have the benefit of running the project and seeing what words come up over and over again that just muddy the waters for you and waste your precious indexing time.

You know what you want to ignore, and you can make sure that the Wizard ignores the right things. You may not know initially, but you will notice certain unwanted words coming up again and again. To prevent that from happening, go in at any time and set the option to ignore them. Here's how to set it up:

1. **Open the project that you want to work with, and choose Tools⇨Smart Index Wizard to open the Smart Index Wizard.**

2. **In the box labeled Set Up Word Lists, click the Always Ignore button.**

   The Smart Index Settings dialog box displays.

3. **Click the "Always Ignore" Words tab, as shown in Figure 10-7.**

   You can read through the list of terms that experience has shown are more trouble than they're worth for indexers. You can find "and," "din," "thing," "nothing" — words that, if you included them all, would make your index so overcrowded with "noise" that it would be just about worthless.

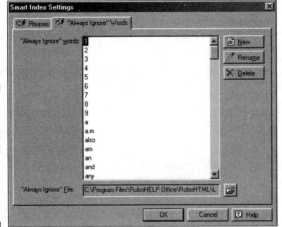

4. **Click the New button and type in the word that you want to add. Then click outside the word or press Enter and the Wizard places it where it belongs in the alphabetical list.**

   You can add as many new words as you want. You can also highlight a word and click Rename to rename a word, or you can select a word and click the Delete button to delete it.

5. **Click OK to close the dialog box and return to the opening screen of the Wizard.**

Setting up words to be sure to find

You may discover some key terms that you definitely want to index for your readers. To make certain that the Smart Index Wizard does what you want and includes those words or phrases, you can add them to the list the Wizard uses when it searches. Here's how:

1. **Open your project and choose Tools⇨Smart Index Wizard to open the Smart Index Wizard.**

2. **In the Set Up Word Lists box, click the Phrases button.**

3. **Click the New button and type in the phrase that you want to add. Then click outside the box to add the new term.**

   The button says phrases, but you can also add single words.

I find it a little confusing to have the Phrases tab in the same dialog box with the "Always Ignore" Words list. You might tend to think that the tab is for "always ignore" phrases, but it's actually for "never ignore" phrases.

4. **If you want, test your result by closing the Wizard, saving the project, and then running Smart Index on a topic containing your new phrase.**

   Figure 10-8 shows that a "never ignore" phrase *AT&T* successfully appears in the dialog box.

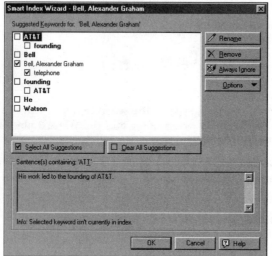

Figure 10-8:
The designated phrase (AT&T) always gets suggested as a keyword.

Making Other Useful Choices

You also have a good bit of say in where the Smart Wizard searches for its possible index entries. You can decide whether to search titles only, or both titles and topic. You can decide whether to put in links. You can also control capitalization. You find out all those things in this section.

Deciding where to search

Most of the time, you're probably going to want to search for your index terms in both the topic titles and in the text of the topics. If you want, though, you can set up the index search to take place in just the topic titles by following these steps:

1. **Click the Topic Title Only radio button.**

   You can also decide whether to include text you have used as links (referred to here as *Hotspots*). It's a good idea to include the links, because Hotspot text tends to be important text.

2. **To include Hotspot text, select the Include Hotspot Text check box.**

3. **When you're satisfied with your choices, click Next to continue with the Smart Index Wizard. (Or just click Cancel if you don't want to make changes.)**

Controlling capitalization

Capitalization can be a serious bugaboo for an indexer. I mean it. The innocuous little capitalization box in the Smart Index Wizard is way, way more important than its humble appearance would suggest. If your index comes out with willy-nilly capitalization, you have to go through a word at a time and standardize. You can have the Smart Wizard control capitalization instead. Here's what to do:

1. **Open your project and choose Tools⇨Smart Index Wizard to open the Smart Index Wizard.**

2. **Select the box for Capitalize All New Keywords (if it's not already checked).**

3. **When you're satisfied with your choices, click Next to continue with the Smart Index Wizard. (Or just click Cancel if you don't want to make changes.)**

Working with synonyms and antonyms

One of the funnest capabilities ("funnest" is my own word) to work with is synonyms and antonyms. The Smart Index Wizard comes with a built-in reference list for synonyms and antonyms. To use it, here's what to do:

1. **Choose Tools⇨Smart Index Wizard and click Next until you display your topic.**

2. **Click the Options button, then click Synonyms.** The Synonyms dialog box comes up, as shown in Figure 10-9.

3. **Select a word to look up. If you don't see your word, type it into the Word box.**

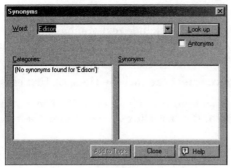

Figure 10-9:
Play with
synonyms
and
antonyms
in here.

4. **Click the Look Up button to see synonyms for your word. If you see words that you want to list, select them and click the Add to Topic button.**

5. **To look through antonyms, too, click the Antonyms check box and then click Look up.**

   The antonyms appear on the left. You can highlight one, then choose additional antonyms (which appear as synonyms to the antonym) and add them to the topic if you want.

   Most of the time, you probably want to include in your index just words that really appear in your topics. I don't know, though, I just think it's fun to think that you can put in synonyms and antonyms if you wish. Also, sometimes you may really find it helpful to do so. People don't always know the exact name of a term, but they know something close to it, and they appreciate finding the approximation in the index.

6. **When you're done playing with synonyms and antonyms, click the Close button to close the Synonyms dialog box.**

   You return to the Smart Index Wizard, where you can continue going through keywords for your topics by clicking **Next**.

Setting Permanent Smart Options

In the Smart Index Wizard itself, you can control the settings for a search on the project you're working with at the moment. Maybe you really like your settings, though, and you want to work with the same ones in whatever project you might index in the future. You can take the bull firmly by the horns and set permanent Smart Index options. You use the Smart Index tab on the Options dialog box to make choices just like the ones you make when doing an individual search. Once you set them up in the Options box, though, those options are the first ones you see whenever you start Smart Indexing.

Here's how to set them up:

1. **Choose Tools⇨Options, then click the Smart Index tab.**

   Figure 10-10 shows the Options dialog box with the Smart Index tab selected.

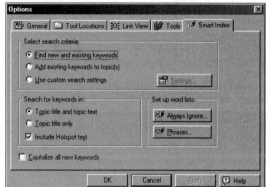

Figure 10-10:
Set up
permanent
options
here.

The choices are all the ones I talk about in this chapter. The Options dialog box doesn't offer you new capabilities for working with Smart Index Wizard. The dialog box does offer you the ability to set things up the way you always work (or the way that your company style sheet tells you to work).

2. **Just make your selections and click OK.**

   For example, you might want to select `Capitalize All New Keywords` as a default setting in your Smart Index Wizard.

For some of the choices, you can restore the defaults that the smart company designers have built in. Click `Use custom search settings` and then click `Settings`. Now click the `Default button` and then click `OK`.

Chapter 11

Working with Links

- -

In This Chapter

▶ Putting in your basic, everyday link (or "jump" in Classic)

▶ Linking so that cool Web pages are just a click away

▶ Scanning through all kinds of mostly nonsense stuff about birds

▶ Poring over pop-ups (great for definitions!)

▶ Seeing what's neat about bookmarks and how to link to them

- -

*L*inks are the lifelines of Help, whether HTML Help or WinHelp. (In WinHelp, links are called jumps.) Other aids you give the reader will no doubt be welcome. Readers crave a good index. They also love a nicely contoured Table of Contents. For a harried reader, though, nothing quite beats the satisfaction of clicking on a word to find out more about it — in other words, clicking a link to additional information. As a Help author, the more you know about linking, the more you can make life easy for your Help users.

In this chapter, you first go over your usual kinds of links — links between topics in HTML Help and WinHelp. The steps to creating a link are pretty basic. You can pretty much use your imagination about what to link to what, though. You can link text to a topic, a topic to a sound (multimedia, for example), text to an image, and — probably most fun of all — text to Web pages. Here you find out about all those links and more, and you find out about the handy capability of bookmarking.

Setting Standard Links

Links, or jumps as they're called in WinHelp, are the key to making life easy for readers of your Help file. By clicking links, readers can connect to pertinent information from all kinds of sources without having to turn a single printed page, walk to a library, or get on the phone. Links literally put the world at readers' fingertips. In this section, you find out about the most useful of the links you can use in RoboHELP.

Linking to another topic

When you link topics in RoboHELP HTML, you are actually linking a file to a file. The destination file has an address called a URL, so you are linking one topic (which has a URL) to another topic (which also has a URL).

URL stands for "uniform resource locator." For the life of me, I want to call it a "universal resource locator," but it isn't. The URL is, really, an address. The address, as you probably know, comes in the form `www.pagename.com`. Many people have wondered why the addresses have to be so complicated and why the name for the address can't just be `web address`. The answer is that they don't have to be so complicated, and the name for them could just be `Web address`. The unwieldy naming conventions arose because the techno-geeks took control of the Internet long before you and I ever came along.

Here's how to link to a topic in RoboHELP HTML:

1. **Open the project and the topic that you want to work with.**

2. **Position the cursor where you want to insert a link.**

3. **Click the Insert hyperlink button (a picture of a globe with chain links in front of it).**

   The Hyperlink dialog box comes up, where you do all your damage as you put in links. Figure 11-1 shows the Hyperlink dialog box.

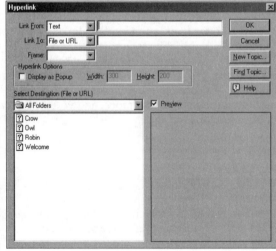

Figure 11-1:
Work here
to link to
and from all
kinds of
places.

4. **In the Link From box, select Text. In the text box, type in the text that you want for your link.**

For example, type **The Furtive, Fearsome Owl** to create a link to a topic called *Owl*. This text becomes the colored link text inside your topic.

5. **In the Select Destination (File or URL) box, click the destination to link to.**

6. **Click OK.**

   RoboHELP links the text to the designated topic and displays the link on the page in blue.

7. **To test the link, click the View button.**

   The link displays in the Preview window, shown in Figure 11-2. You can click the link to make sure it is working properly.

Figure 11-2:
Test your
link in the
Preview
window.

You can also link to existing text. In an open topic select the text that you want to link to, click the Insert hyperlink button, and follow Steps 5 and 6 in the preceding list.

Linking RoboHELP Classic topics

To link topics in RoboHELP Classic, you use a WinHelp jump, which you establish by creating a new jump and explaining what should connect to what. Here's how to do it:

1. **Open the Project and File that you want to work with.**

2. **Place the cursor where you want to put the hyperlink.**

3. **Click the button for New Jump.**

   The Insert Help Hotspot dialog box comes up, as shown in Figure 11-3.

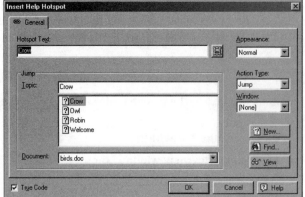

Figure 11-3:
Work on
your
WinHelp
links here.

4. **In the Hotspot Text dialog box, either accept the text that appears or type in your own text.**

5. **In the Jump box, click the topic to link to the Hotspot Text.**

6. **Click OK.**

   The text appears as a link.

Linking to Cool Stuff — Multimedia and Images

Everybody loves a song or a movie or any of the possibilities that come under that magnificent name "multimedia." Images are fun, too. The only hard part about multimedia or images might be having a powerful enough computer to run the things properly. Most recent computers do that quite well. As for putting links to images and multimedia into your topics, you set up the link pretty much the same way you link text to text. You just use the Hyperlink dialog box and tell RoboHELP HTML where to find each of the linked items. (You can't link to multimedia in RoboHELP Classic.)

Linking to multimedia

To link to multimedia, you use the Hyperlink dialog box and put "Multimedia" into the Link To box. You also specify which multimedia item you want to use. Follow these steps to try it:

1. **Open the topic in the WYSIWYG Editor and click where you want the multimedia object.**

2. **Click the Insert Hyperlink button.**

3. **In the Link From box, select Text. In the text box, type in the text that you want for your link.**

   Figure 11-4 shows the dialog box with the text Popular Songs in the text box.

4. **In the Link To box, click the down arrow and select Multimedia.**

   A Select button appears, which you use to designate your linked multimedia clip. Figure 11-4 shows the dialog box with the Select button.

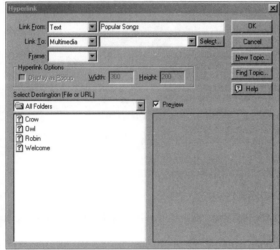

Figure 11-4:
A Select button comes up for you to choose your multimedia clip.

5. **Click the Select button and select your multimedia file. Click OK to close the Multimedia box.**

   See Chapter 6 for information on copying images and multimedia into your current project.

6. **Click OK to close the Hyperlink box.**

   You can try out your linked multimedia with a Preview. When you click the link, the multimedia plays.

Linking to images

Linking from images is nearly identical to linking from text. In the Link From box, you identify the image where the link begins. Then you choose a destination for the link, and you've got it. Here are the steps:

1. **Open the file that you want to work with and put the cursor where you want the image that contains a link.**

2. Click the Insert Hyperlink button.

The Hyperlink dialog box comes up.

3. Click the arrow at the right of the Link From list box and choose Image. A Select button appears at the right, as shown in Figure 11-5.

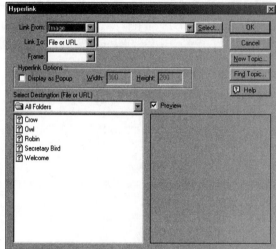

Figure 11-5:
Select your image in the Hyperlink dialog box.

4. In the Image dialog box, select the image that you plan to use and click OK.

See Chapter 6 for details on finding images and placing them in the current project.

5. Be sure that the Link To box displays "File or URL."

6. In the Select Destination (File or URL) box, click the topic that you want to link to and click OK.

The clickable image appears in your topic.

7. Click OK to accept your choices.

You can click Preview to test the link. Figure 11-6 shows the sample image in a preview window.

To see how to put multiple Hotspots on an image, see Chapter 6.

Figure 11-6:
The topic
now has a
clickable
image.

Popping in Pop-up Links

Pop-ups are instant gratification — help right on the spot without ever going to another topic. I know that when I use Help, I really appreciate being able to click text and get a definition on some hard word that everybody else might already know. Right there in private, without anybody else even seeing, you click, read, and go on about your business as if you always knew the meaning of the suspect term. In this section, you see how to put pop-ups in RoboHELP HTML and in Classic Help.

Putting in pop-up hyperlinks

You may want to put in links that simply displays a pop-up window on the spot. Such links are particularly helpful for definitions. To put them in, you use the button for pop-up hyperlinks and you link to a topic.

1. **Put the cursor where you want to display the pop-up.**

2. **Click the Insert Pop-up Hyperlink button.**

   The Hyperlink dialog box appears with the selected words in the Link From text box.

3. **Click the topic that you want to have as a pop-up and click OK.**

   The selected words appear in blue in the topic, indicating the hyperlink.

4. **Click the Preview button and then click the link to display the pop-up.**

   Figure 11-7 shows a sample pop-up window for the term *Bald Eagle*.

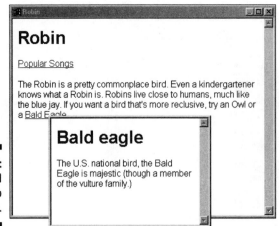

Figure 11-7:
You can add
neat pop-up
windows.

In RoboHELP HTML, pop-up links only display in Internet Explorer 4.0 or later. If your users will be using earlier versions of the browser, you'll probably want to pass on using pop-up windows. If you create WebHelp, your pop-up links will display on either IE 4.0 or Netscape Navigator (4.0 or later). I talk about creating WebHelp in Chapter 13.

Inserting Classic pop-ups

WinHelp has excellent support for pop-up windows. To put them in, you click the appropriate button, then actually type the pop-up text into the dialog box. You have the freedom to create pop-up text without even linking to a topic. Here's how:

1. **Open the file that you want to work with and display the topic where you want to place the pop-up.**

2. **Select the text to contain the pop-up link.**

3. **Click the New Pop-up button.**

   The Insert Pop-up dialog box displays, as shown in Figure 11-8.

4. **In the New Pop-up box, select the text that says** `type pop-up caption here` **and type your new caption to replace it.**

5. **Select the text that says** `type pop-up definition here`, **type in your new definition, and click OK.**

   WinHelp adds the pop-up to your topic.

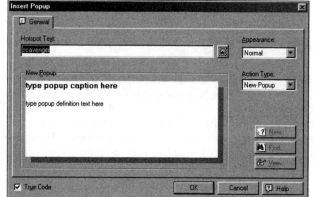

Figure 11-8:
Classic
makes it
easy to put
in pop-ups.

6. **To test your pop-up, compile and run the topic and then click the pop-up link.**

   Figure 11-9 shows the classic pop-up.

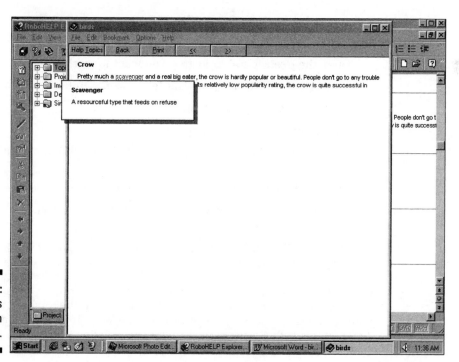

Figure 11-9:
Pop-ups
look good in
WinHelp.

Linking to Web Sites and Other Remote Spots

Say what we will, "linking," in the minds of most people today, means linking to Web sites. Everyday usage has done that — people now routinely link to Web sites. If your links don't include occasional links to Web sites, people may even be mildly disappointed. Linking to Web sites is natural in HTML Help, where your links between topics are links between HTML files to begin with. Linking to Web sites in Classic Help is also a matter of telling RoboHELP the Web address you want to use.

Linking to a Web site with HTML Help

Linking within your help project is definitely fun and useful. By linking to Web sites, though, you can connect your Help user to the almost limitless world of information on the World Wide Web.

To link to a Web site, you follow almost the same steps you follow to link to a topic. Here's what to do:

1. **Open the project and topic that you want to work with.**

2. **Highlight the text that you want to use as the link in your topic.**

3. **Click the Insert hyperlink button.**

   The Hyperlink dialog box appears.

4. **In the text box for the Link To box, type in the URL for your Web site and click OK.**

   RoboHELP then provides the link to the Web page.

5. **To test the link, be sure you're connected to the Internet, click Preview, and then click the link.**

   Figure 11-10 shows the sample Web page www.birdwatching.com displayed in RoboHELP.

RoboHELP likes to give you a nice reminder when your topic includes a URL. When you display your topic list, the URL appears in the topic list with a globe icon next to it. To try it yourself, just click the Topics tab. Figure 11-11 shows a topic list with the globe icon for the Web link.

Figure 11-10:
You can link
directly to a
Web page.

Figure 11-11:
Web
addresses
display in
the topic list
with a globe
icon.

Linking to a Web site in Classic

To link to a Web site using RoboHELP Classic, type the URL into the appropriate box, just as you would in RoboHELP Classic. Here's how to do it:

1. **Open the Help project and topic you want to work with.**

2. **Select the text that you want to make into a link.**

3. **Pick up the phone on an impulse, call your investor, and sink a huge chunk into Internet stocks. (Just kidding. Wondered if you were paying attention.)**

4. **Click the New Jump button.**

5. **In the Insert Help Hotspot dialog box, with your selected text showing in the Hotspot Text box, click the arrow next to Action Type and select HTML Jump.**

The box at the left of the screen changes from Jump to HTML Jump, as shown in Figure 11-12.

Figure 11-12:
To connect to a Web page, put in the URL.

6. **In the URL or File box, type in your Web address and click OK.**

With those few steps, you set up a link to the Internet. To test it out, compile and run your Classic file and then click the link.

Linking to remote topics and other possibilities

Linking to a News site, an FTP site ("File Transfer Protocol," simply a remote computer), or an e-mail address is much the same as linking to a Web page. In the Hyperlink dialog box, make your choice (such as E-mail) in the Link To box, then type your destination into the text box at the right.

Likewise, to connect to a file or a remote topic (a topic not within your current project), open the Hyperlink dialog box and put in the name. Try, for instance, connecting to a remote topic:

1. **Open the project and topic that you want to work with.**

2. **Select the text that you want to use as a link and then click the Insert Hyperlink button.**

3. **In the Link To box, select Remote Topic.**

4. **Click the Select button to the right of the Link To box. A Remote Topic dialog box comes up, as shown in Figure 11-13.**

Figure 11-13:
Put in the
name of
your remote
topic here.

5. **Navigate to the remote file that you want to use.**

6. **In the Topic box, select the remote topic that you want to connect to and click OK.**

7. **Click OK to the dialog box that comes up and then click OK to close the Hyperlink dialog box.**

   You have established your link to a remote topic.

Linking to bookmarks

Sometimes, let's face it, you want to link not just to another topic but to a particular place within the topic. Though most of the sample topics in this book are short, your topics in the real world will probably show a striking tendency to grow and grow. Often it's logical to link to a subhead within a topic instead of just to the topic as a whole.

You can use bookmarks to mark a particular location in a topic, and you can then link to that location. (A bookmark, then, is like that torn piece of paper you slide into your novel — something to mark a spot in the text.) In this section, you see how to put bookmarks into Help files, then how to link to them.

Inserting bookmarks

To put in a bookmark, you place the cursor where you want to have the bookmark, then insert the handy little marker. Often, for instance, you'll want to bookmark a section within a larger topic. To try it:

1. **Open the project and topic that you want to work with.**

2. **Put the cursor where you want to place the bookmark and choose Insert⇨Bookmark.**

   The Insert/Edit Bookmark dialog box comes up, as shown in Figure 11-14.

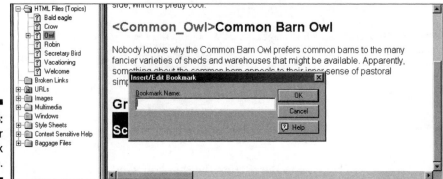

3. **Type a name for the bookmark and click OK.**

You can't use spaces in bookmarks. That's not your fault. It's just the way the program works.

RoboHELP displays the bookmark in olive inside brackets. (You can only see the bookmark in the WYSIWYG Editor.)

You put in a Classic bookmark the same way. Put the cursor where you want to have the bookmark, choose Insert⇨Bookmark, name the bookmark, and click OK.

Linking to the bookmarks

To link to a bookmark:

1. **Open the project and topic that you want to work with.**

2. **Select the text that you want to link from and then click Insert Hyperlink.**

3. **In the Hyperlink dialog box, click the bookmark that you want to use and click OK.**

   Figure 11-15 shows the dialog box with the bookmark `Owl#Common_Owl` highlighted. If you want, use Preview to test out the link.

   Bookmarks appear with a bookmark tag instead of a topic icon.

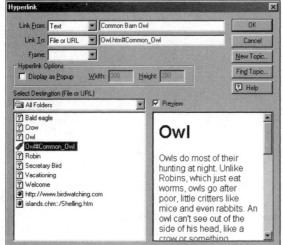

Figure 11-15:
Click on the
bookmark to
which you
want to link.

Part IV
Being a Project Manager

The 5th Wave — By Rich Tennant

"This new Help program has really helped me get organized. I keep my project reports under the PC, budgets under my laptop and memos under my pager."

In this part . . .

Sometimes you have to take a step back and take stock of what you're doing overall. You can't just have your topics running willy nilly all over the place. You have to manage them. Here you get intimately acquainted with your Project Manager (that set of handy controls on the other, or left, side of the page). You discover how to transform entire Help formats into and out of other Help formats. And then you can plunge headfirst into the inner workings of compiling an overall project.

Chapter 12

Managing with Project Manager

· ·

In This Chapter

▶ Seeing how Project Manager organizes your files into folders

▶ Noting that a Baggage file contains files that don't fit into other folders

▶ Expanding and collapsing folders

▶ Manipulating folders and topics

▶ Discovering Build Tag, Single Source, and other Classic idiosyncrasies

· ·

*O*ften in RoboHELP, you spend your time working within Topics while anxiously researching, writing, and communicating. If you aren't organized, you may spend too much time working on the wrong topics. The Project Manger is a good way for you to get your topics organized. RoboHELP also uses it to organize itself by, for instance, keeping your images in one folder and your style sheets in another folder.

People often use programming tools similar to the RoboHELP Project Manager without knowing how they work. With Project Manager, you don't have to know how it works in advance. In fact, much of the organizing happens automatically as RoboHELP stores files, such as images, bookmarks, and Web pages, in the appropriate folders.

If you decide to take a leisurely stroll through this chapter, you're certain to turn up a few shortcuts and useful approaches that can help save you time. In this chapter I discuss how to manipulate RoboHELP folders and topics by expanding, collapsing, adding, deleting, moving around, and generally bending files to your will. Also, I explain the purpose of key folders in both RoboHELP HTML and RoboHELP Classic.

Starting Project Manager

You don't have to do much of anything to start RoboHELP Project Manager; it is there at your beck and call every time you start RoboHELP. Follow these steps to start the Project Manager:

1. **Click the RoboHELP icon on the Desktop to start RoboHELP HTML and open a project.**

2. **Click the Project Manager tab (a folder) on the left pane, as shown in Figure 12-1. (Unless you have clicked one of the other tabs, the Project Manager is already open.)**

   The Project Manager appears.

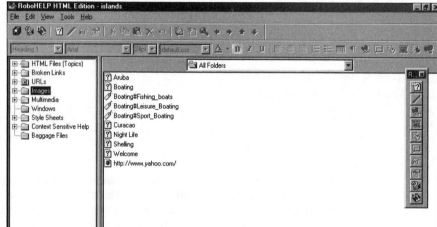

Figure 12-1: Click its tab any time to display Project Manager.

Checking Out Key Folders

Project Manager tries to get people organized, and comes with folders already established for various things for which, as organized people, you or I really ought to have separate folders — such as images, URLs, Broken Links. Left on our own, however, especially when we're new to RoboHELP, we certainly wouldn't think of something like a Baggage folder or, come to think about it, just about any of the other folders Project Manager provides.

You can't always create new folders within Project Manager where you want them. For example, you can't create a subfolder for the URLs folder or the Windows folder. If you want to know whether you can create a new folder for a Project Manager folder, right-click the folder to see if "New Folder" appears as a menu choice.

Table 12-1 summarizes the folders that come with RoboHELP HTML and what goes into each. Files get stuffed into these default folders automatically, so mostly you don't have to put it there yourself. (When you add an image to your project, for example, RoboHELP automatically puts it into the Image folder.)

Table 12-1	The Project Manager Folders
Folder	*What's in It*
HTML Files (Topics)	This folder has all your topics in it. Double-click a topic to edit it. You can also add, delete, and rename topics here. Right-click a topic to get started. If a topic has a plus sign next to it, the topic has bookmarks in it, in which case you can click the plus sign to see the bookmark underneath the topic. You can also double-click the plus sign to see the bookmark underneath the topic. You can put your own additional folders in here.
Broken Links	Here you can find the names of all files that you have deleted, thereby causing broken links. You can right-click to restore any file that you want, thereby fixing a broken link.
URLs	This folder contains references to Web pages, FTP sites, newsgroups, e-mail addresses, or remote topics that you have included in your topics.
Images	RoboHELP stores all your images here (.GIF and .JPG files). You can also see image maps and Hotspots. Here, as for HTML Files, you can add custom folders to help you get organized.
Multimedia	If you've put sound or video files into the project (.AVI, .AU, .MID, .RMI, or .WAV files, for example), you'll find them in the Multimedia folder.
Windows	You can create custom windows that display in your compiled project, instead of the pre-defined ones that come with your project. RoboHELP stores such windows here.
Style Sheets	The default style sheet for the project appears here. If you create others style sheets (.CSS files), they appear here as well.
Context-Sensitive Help	If you create Context-Sensitive Help, all of the related files go here. A special form of Context-Sensitive Help is text-only topics (topics with no formatting), and such files go into a Map Files sub-folder of Context-Sensitive Help. Map files, used in context-sensitive help to contain topic IDs and map numbers, also have a separate folder (the Map Files sub-folder). Another sub-folder (Aliases) contains Aliases (alternate topic IDs, used to match file names in a map file with those in the HTML Help project).

(continued)

Table 12-1 *(continued)*

Folder	What's in It
Baggage Files	This is a funny name for a folder. The name suggests something, uh, extra, and that is exactly what the file contains — files that are part of the project but don't have another storage file, such as bitmaps (.BMP files — imported Windows bitmaps) used for special effects and icons (.ICO files).

You're not going to remember what each of these Project folders does until you've worked with them for awhile. If you're wondering what you can do with a Project Manager folder, right-click the folder. You'll see from the available choices how to proceed. For instance, right-click the Windows folder and then click New. The Window Properties dialog box opens for creating a new Help window.

Expanding and Collapsing Folders

If you're familiar with the Windows Explorer, you know how to use the Project Manager.

Just because the Project Manager looks like Windows Explorer, don't make the mistake of actually using Windows Explorer to do things you can do within Project Manager. Changes you make within Project Manager, such as moving files from one folder to another, show up automatically in all the right places. If you make the same changes using Windows Explorer, you may get a broken link (a link to a topic that RoboHELP can't locate) or some other undesirable result (such as an image that RoboHELP can't locate).

To expand or collapse a Project Manager folder:

1. **Click the plus sign next to the HTML Files (Topics) folder to expand it.**

2. **Click the plus sign next to a topic that contains bookmarks to see its bookmarks.**

3. **To collapse a folder or topic, click the minus sign next to it.**

Figure 12-2 shows an example of an HTML Files (Topics) folder after you click both the plus sign next to the folder and the sign next to a topic.

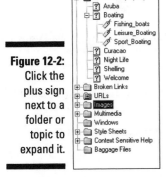

Figure 12-2:
Click the
plus sign
next to a
folder or
topic to
expand it.

Filenames and topic titles are often the same or similar. They don't have to be, though, if you don't make them that way. If you have a reason to view files by filename instead of topic name (or vice versa), you can do so using the View menu (shown in Figure 12-3). Just click to select the choice you want — By Topic Title or By Filename. (You have to choose one or the other, not both.)

Figure 12-3:
You can
view by
filename or
topic title.

If you like, you may choose not to view empty folders. Click the View menu and deselect Empty Folders.

Working with Project Manager Folders

The great thing about folders is their accessibility. Grab a new folder and throw whatever items into it you want, and if you change your mind later you can rename the folder and move it to a new location with all the files intact. In the following sections on creating, renaming, and moving folders, you discover how to manipulate Project Manager.

Creating a new folder

As you get on a roll, creating topics like mad, you may want to create folders within your initial folders to help you keep track of what you have. Here's how to create a new folder:

1. **Open the project that you want to work with and then open Project Manager.**

2. **Right-click the folder in which you want to create a new folder.**

   A Context menu appears.

3. **Select New Folder from the Context window.**

   A folder appears with the name New Folder.

4. **Type in the new name for the folder and press Enter (or click outside the text box).**

Renaming a folder

You can readily rename a folder to make it descriptive as your needs for it evolve. To rename a folder, follow these steps:

1. **Open a project that you want to work with and open the Project Manager.**

2. **Right-click the folder you want to rename.**

   A Context menu appears.

3. **Select Rename from the Context menu.**

   The text appears selected inside a text box.

4. **Type in the new name for the folder and press Enter (or click outside the text box).**

Moving folders

You can use drag and drop functionality to move folders. When you move a folder inside Project Manager, RoboHELP automatically updates all references to it. To move a folder, simply click the folder you wish to move (hold the mouse button down), drag it to its new location, and then release the mouse button.

If you try to drag a folder to someplace where RoboHELP doesn't allow it, you see a circle with a bar across it. If you try to drop the folder, nothing happens (which may make you feel powerless or frustrated).

Working with Topics

Folders can contain other things, but with RoboHELP most of the time your concern will be with the topics inside folders. You can manipulate your topics in Project Manager the same way you do with folders — adding them, moving them around, and deleting them. This section talks about some of the special considerations to keep in mind.

Adding topics to custom folders

When you create a topic, RoboHELP places it in your HTML Files folder. If you have a custom folder you want to use, though, you can have RoboHELP save it there. Here's how:

1. **Start RoboHELP and open the project that you want to work with.**

2. **Click the Project tab to open Project Manager.**

3. **Click the plus sign next to the HTML Files folder to open the folder.**

4. **Right-click the folder in which you want to place the topic.**

   A Context menu appears.

5. **Select <u>N</u>ew Topic from the Context menu.**

   The Create Topic Wizard appears, as shown in Figure 12-4.

Figure 12-4:
If you use
the Wizard
from a
custom
folder, you'll
put the topic
there.

6. **Type the name for the new topic in the <u>T</u>opic Title box.**

7. **Click OK.**

   RoboHELP creates the topic in your custom folder.

You can also drag and drop topics from either the topic list on the right or from the folders on the left into your custom folders, and vice versa.

Sometimes you may want to track down a project file you've used recently and doing so can be harder than it sounds. "Where did I put that file?" you find yourself asking. These are project files (complete help projects, with the .MPJ extension), not topic files.

To hunt down those elusive recent files, choose Tools⇨Options. The MRU box on the General tab (the default tab), shown in Figure 12-5, shows the 100 files you've used most recently. MRU stands for Mozambique Rugby Union, by the way. You see, a Mozambican rugby player was an early RoboHELP designer, and . . . oh, I'm joking, of course — MRU stands for "Most Recently Used."

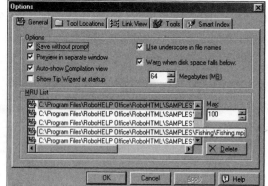

Figure 12-5:
A list of your recently used files.

Moving topics into folders

Drag and drop is an unbeatable way to move your topics around within your folders. Just click, drag, and drop. See the discussion in this chapter in the section Moving Folders.

Deleting topics from folders

You can use the Topic List on the right to delete ordinary topics. To delete text-only topic files, map files, and baggage files, you have to work with Project Manager. To delete one of those specified files using Project Manager, select a file and click the Delete button.

If you delete a file that has links to other files, RoboHELP cautions that references to your file will no longer work and asks if you want to delete the references. RoboHELP is thoughtful to save you future trouble, so, usually, you probably ought to click Yes. (You might want to keep the references for some reason — perhaps to remind you that you want to create a replacement topic for the one you've deleted.)

Looking Over RoboHELP Classic's Project Manager

Classic's Project Manager is similar to the one in RoboHELP HTML (described earlier in this chapter), but the RoboHELP Classics Project Manager is different in some ways. Whereas in RoboHELP HTML, you can create additional folders in Project Manager; in RoboHELP Classic, you can't create additional folders most of the time (the Image Folders folder is the one place I know of where you can create new folders.); mostly you just have to work with the folders that are already there.

Most of the time you don't have to worry about putting things into folders. RoboHELP puts topics, images, Web pages, and other items into those folders for you. However, understanding the Project Manager is helpful in finding and working with these files.

Much of the logic of the folders and subfolders in Project Manager may not be instantly obvious to you. That's because in many cases the organization isn't so much to help you put together your topics as it is to set up files in patterns expected by the Windows compiler as it prepares your actual Help file (which helps the compiler complete its work faster).

To find out about topics that appear in both RoboHELP Classic and RoboHELP HTML, such as the Multimedia folder, see Table 12-1 earlier in this chapter. Table 12-2 summarizes key folders that appear in RoboHELP Classic.

Table 12-2	RoboHELP Classic Project Manager Folders
Folder	*What's in It*
Topics	Here you see all your topics, broken links, and external topics.

(continued)

Table 12-2 *(continued)*

Folder	*What's in It*
Project	Here you find other key parts of your Help project. The Windows, Map IDs, and Aliases folders are the same as for RoboHELP HTML. Startup macros are programs that execute when RoboHELP starts. The Baggage folder holds multimedia or image files. (This folder is where the WinHelp Compiler looks for its files.) Build Tags are specialized. (Advanced Help authors or programmers use Build Tags to exclude certain topics when building a version.)
Images and Multimedia	Here you organize all your images and multimedia in eight folders: • Images • Standard Images • Hotspot Images • Multimedia • Graphical Buttons • Authorable Buttons • Embedded Windows • Image Folders (BMROOT)
Dependencies	When you ship a WinHelp file, you also have to include certain dependent files — DLLs (dynamically linked libraries), External Help files, and HTML files (such as Web pages).
Single Source	In this folder, you see all the options for types of Help files that you can create — WinHelp 4, Windows CE, Netscape NetHelp2, and more. You can actually generate that output starting from the Single Source file in your Project Manager.

Chapter 13

Importing, Exporting, and Converting Help Files

● ●

In This Chapter

▶ Shaping up WinHelp files as honest-to-goodness HTML Help files

▶ Getting really confused with the terms "WinHelp," "WebHELP," and "HTML Help"

▶ A pair of my bedroom slippers. (I can't find them and think I left them in the chapter.)

▶ Backfitting HTML Help into WinHelp

▶ Coolly importing single files

● ●

*I*f you're like me, most of the time when you need something you'd rather just make a new version of what you need than "retrofit" something else. Suppose you need a new pedal for your bicycle. You might have a nice, 20-year-old Schwin pedal that might work. But it might not, either. If you "had your druthers," you'd just buy a nice, new pedal that you were sure would fit.

So it is with importing and exporting in the world of RoboHELP. Given the choice, you'd probably just as soon make a new topic or Help file and not have to worry about bringing in some existing topic or Help file from some other, possibly-aging format.

At times, though, the temptation to import is just too great. In fact, the desire to import would grow exponentially with the size of the file and, thus, the amount of work involved in recreating it. Initially, at least, the concept of importing or exporting promises to save all the work of retyping and redesigning something done before.

In this chapter, you find out how to import and export two ways — from RoboHELP HTML Help to WinHelp and from WinHelp to RoboHELP HTML Help. You also find out a few other clever, occasionally useful forms of importing, too — like importing Word documents as topics in your HTML Help.

Transforming WinHelp to HTML Help Files

Chances are if you've been using RoboHELP for awhile, then you have archives of Help files — Windows Help files — made with RoboHELP Classic or some other program. Now you'd like to bring the aging Help projects into HTML Help, where you can apply the dynamic, dazzling possibilities of RoboHELP HTML to them. In this section, you see how to bring those classics into your upscale HTML projects.

Importing WinHelp into RoboHELP HTML

To import the WinHelp file into RoboHELP HTML, you have to start by creating a new project in RoboHELP HTML.

Maybe I'm being picky here, but I wonder why you can't import a WinHelp file by choosing File⇨Import. Instead, you have to go through the rigmarole of creating a new file. I could see some honest, hardworking Help authors overlooking this slightly circuitous route to importing a Help file — having to create a new Help file to do it.

To import a WinHelp file into RoboHELP HTML, follow these steps:

1. **Start RoboHELP HTML.**

2. **Choose File⇨ New⇨Project.**

   The New Project dialog box opens.

3. **Click the Import tab.**

   Figure 13-1 shows the New Project dialog box after you click the Import tab.

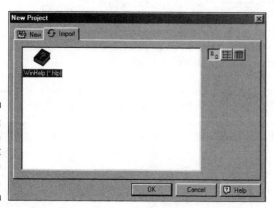

Figure 13-1:
Start here to
import
WinHelp
files.

4. **Click OK to start the Help-to-HTML Wizard, as shown in Figure 13-2.**

Figure 13-2:
The Wizard
guides you
in the
import.

5. **Choose the file to import in the Select Help File box.**

   You can click the folder icon to the right of the Select Help File box to help you locate your file.

   Before taking the major step of importing a big file, you might want to make sure you have the file you want by clicking the View button in the Help-to-HTML Wizard to preview the file you're importing. If you do, be sure to exit the Help window before continuing.

6. **Select a folder for your HTML files.**

   The wizard asks you to select the folder for your HTML files and one for any GIF files you may have.

7. **Click Next.**

   The wizard asks you to choose a style sheet.

   You can attach style sheets later if you want, so you don't have to worry about the style sheet during import. Style sheets aren't important to content so much as to your personal preference for appearance. I talk about style sheets in Chapter 16.

8. **Leave the defaults as they are and click Next.**

   The Microsoft HTML Help Options screen appears, as shown in Figure 13-3. Here you choose some options about how the HTML file will display. You are safe using the defaults; to do so, just click Next without changing anything.

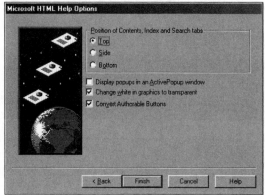

Figure 13-3:
Accept the
default sug-
gestions for
the look of
the new file.

9. **Click Finish to complete the conversion.**

   RoboHELP converts your WinHelp project into a working RoboHELP
   HTML project. You can then go in and do your worst by applying all your
   Dynamic HTML techniques to the file. Figure 13-4 shows the Table of
   Contents of the imported file.

Figure 13-4:
The TOC of
the neatly
imported
WinHelp
file.

Saving a Classic Project as an HTML Project

You can import a WinHelp project into RoboHELP HTML. (I explain how to do
this in the preceding section.) Another way to transfer a WinHelp project into
HTML format is from within RoboHELP Classic. Here are the steps to follow:

1. **Start RoboHELP Classic and open the file that you want to convert into an HTML Help project.**

2. **Click the Project tab.**

3. **Click the plus sign next to Single Source to show the options.**

   Figure 13-5 shows the options in the Single Source Folder.

   With RoboHELP Classic's Single Source capability, you create Help files in a variety of formats in addition to Microsoft HTML Help. I talk about Single Source in Chapter 19.

4. **Double-click Microsoft HTML Help (Win 98).**

   The Creating Html Help Wizard comes up, as shown in Figure 13-6.

5. **Specify the folder where you want to place your HTML files as well as one for any GIF files you have.**

6. **Click Next.**

   RoboHELP asks you to select a style sheet.

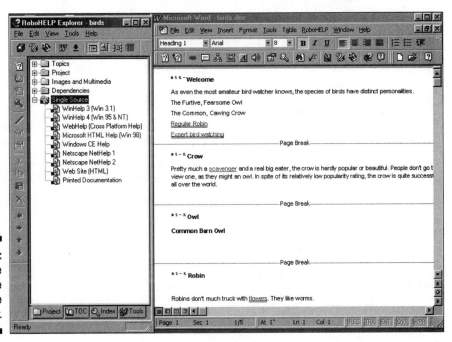

Figure 13-5:
Open the
Single
Source
folder.

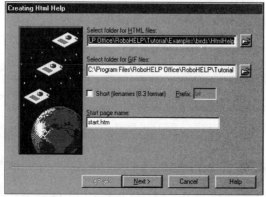

7. Click Next to accept the suggested choices — <No Stylesheet> — and other defaults.

You have the option of selecting a Stylesheet if you want, but that can be like opening a whole can of worms that you may not need now. If you choose a Stylesheet and then don't like it, you have to either change the Stylesheet or do the conversion over again. I'd accept the default if I were you.

Figure 13-6:
Use the Creating HTML Help Wizard to convert your file.

8. Click the Finish button.

This final screen sets you up with the standard placement in Windows 98 Help for your Contents, Index, and Search tabs and makes some other changes to the expected appearance in Windows 98.

A dialog box showing that RoboHELP is compiling appears and then a Results message box (shown in Figure 13-7) shows the results of your completed conversion.

Figure 13-7:
This box shows you the results of the conversion.

9. Click OK to close the Results dialog box.

Your converted file displays as an HTML Help file in its own HTML Help Window.

Converting HTML Help to WebHelp

Blue Sky Software (the makers of RoboHELP) integrates within RoboHELP HTML a product called WebHelp that displays on more browsers than HTML Help, such as Macintosh, Sun Solaris, Linux, and additional UNIX platforms. Whereas HTML Help includes certain elements like ActiveX controls that display only on Internet Explorer 4.0 or later, WebHelp is browser independent. (WebHelp uses Java applets — self-contained little programs that don't require IE — instead of ActiveX controls.) Follow these steps to create WebHelp from HTML Help files:

1. **Start RoboHELP HTML and open the file that you want to convert.**

2. **Choose File⇨Single Source Output⇨ WebHelp.**

   RoboHELP converts the file and shows a message saying the WebHelp files were written successfully.

3. **Click Yes to view the WebHelp system.**

   RoboHELP opens up your default browser and displays your newly-created WebHelp file.

Metamorphosing HTML Help into WinHelp

You may find yourself preparing Help for an audience using Windows 95 and Windows NT (which can't automatically read HTML Help). Or maybe you're working in WinHelp already and want to bring in some material from an HTML Help project. The good news is that you can indeed convert HTML Help files to WinHelp format — the bad news is that the process is not exactly a simple one.

There are two major processes involved in converting your HTML Help file to WinHelp format (the second major process — converting from the Word document to the WinHelp file — is discussed in the numbered list that follows this one).

You lose any links you have in the HTML Help when converting to WinHelp — you'll have to re-enter them in the WinHelp document.

Follow these steps to convert an HTML Help file to a Word document:

1. **Start RoboHELP HTML and open the project you want to convert.**

   If possible, select a file that has some links and images (which can get interesting during the conversion, because you lose links when converting).

2. **Choose File⇨Single Source Output⇨Printed Documentation.**

   The Document Wizard appears, as shown in Figure 13-8. (You don't really convert to print. You convert to a Word document.)

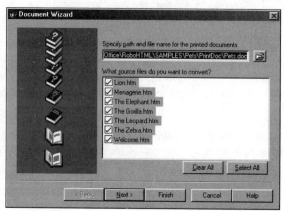

Figure 13-8:
To convert
HTML Help
to WinHelp,
first use the
Wizard to
convert to a
printed
document.

3. **To accept the default formatting options (a darn good idea, unless you're a computer nerd), click Next.**

4. **In the TOC and Index dialog box (shown in Figure 13-9), be sure there is a check mark in the Create index check box (it's checked by default), because RoboHELP uses the Word index in the conversion process.**

5. **Click Next.**

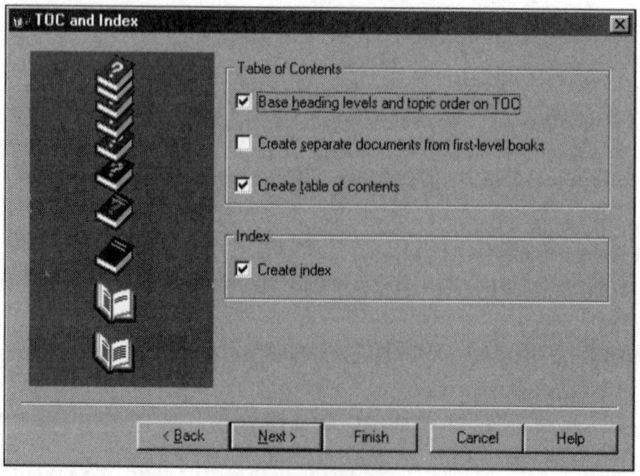

Figure 13-9:
The TOC
and Index
window —
be sure the
Create index
check box is
checked.

6. **In the Text Color and Images dialog box, be sure you have selected the choice that says "Link external images to documents." (This choice is selected by default.)**

   This option puts your JPG and GIF images into the Word document the wizard creates. (RoboHELP uses these images in the conversion to WinHelp.)

7. **Click Next.**

8. **Click Finish.**

   RoboHELP converts your HTML document to a Word document. A message box says `Conversion complete!` You can preview your printed document if you like by selecting the View Result button in the dialog box. Once you have the printed document, you're ready to finish the conversion to WinHelp.

After you have converted your HTML Help file to a Word document, you're ready to finish the conversion to a WinHelp file. Follow these steps to convert the printed Word document to WinHelp format.

1. **Start RoboHELP Classic and create a new project.**

   If you prefer, you can import the Word document into an existing project. You might find the additional file confusing in your existing project, though. If you're new to importing, I'd import into a new project to minimize possible hassles.

2. **In RoboHELP Explorer (on the left) choose File⇨Import⇨Document.**

   The Import Document dialog box appears, as shown in Figure 13-10.

Figure 13-10:
State which
document to
import.

3. **In the File box on the Import Document dialog, type in the name of the Word document that you want to import. (You might prefer to use the folder icon to navigate to the file that you need.)**

   The Import Options dialog box appears, as shown in Figure 13-11. In this dialog box you need to make sure the following options are selected (that is, make sure there is a check mark in the corresponding check boxes):

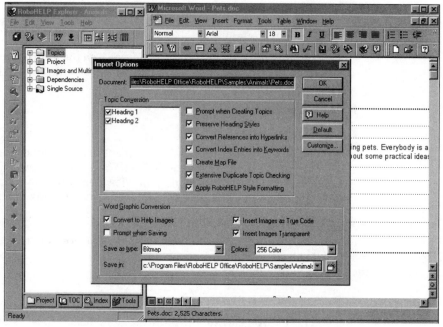

Figure 13-11:
Choose
options for
converting
your Word
document to
a WinHelp
file.

- Convert References into Hyperlinks.

- Convert Index Entries into Keywords (selected by default).

- Convert to Help Images (selected by default).

Unless you want to delve into advanced subjects, you would do well to keep the default settings.

4. Click OK.

RoboHELP converts the file. Figure 13-12 shows my converted file with the topics displayed in the Project Manager.

RoboHELP doesn't convert the Table of Contents, so you'll have to go into RoboHELP Classic and create a new one. I think making a Table of Contents is fun anyway, unless the Help file is really, really big with lots of topics.

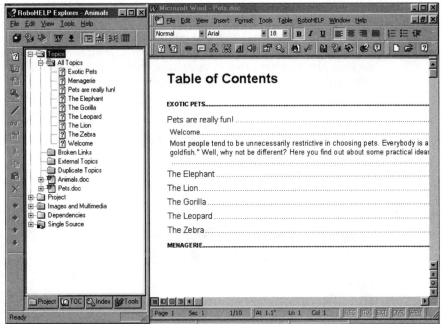

Figure 13-12:
Your con-
verted file
shows up in
the Project
Manager.

Bringing in Single Files

Often you can find yourself having to convert complete Help files from
WinHelp to HTML Help or the other way around. (I talk about such ambitious
undertakings in the preceding sections of this chapter.) Life doesn't always
operate on such a grand scale, however. Sometimes you want to import
something small — an individual HTML File, for example, or a Word document. Perhaps you have a neat Web document on your computer, and you'd
like to use the HTML file in your project.

In this section I discuss how to do some of those small, seemingly unimpor-
tant things that can sometimes make life go a little bit smoother.

Importing an HTML file

Now that the Web has come of age, people find themselves creating all kinds
of great documents in HTML format. Or you may have downloaded something from the Web in HTML format. You can import such HTML files into
your Help projects.

RoboHELP Classic doesn't have a menu choice for importing an HTML file. To copy the content of an HTML file into RoboHELP Classic, you can open the HTML file, copy the text to the Windows Clipboard, open the Classic Topic where you want to insert the text, and then paste it in. Primitive this method may be, and you have to add your links, tables, and images all over again, but you can do it.

To import an HTML file into RoboHELP HTML, follow these steps:

1. **Start RoboHELP HTML and open the project that you want to work with.**

2. **Choose File⇨Import⇨HTML File.**

   The Open dialog box appears, as shown in Figure 13-13.

Figure 13-13: Locate the file you want to import.

3. **Locate the file that you want to import.**

   You can select multiple files to import — just press and hold down the Ctrl key as you select files (from within the same directory).

4. **Click Open.**

   A dialog box appears and asks if you want to copy the file to the selected folder.

5. **Click Yes to All.**

   RoboHELP deftly adds the file to the project folder for your current project. Figure 13-14 shows an imported file in its new location.

Importing a Word document

Microsoft Word has become almost a de facto standard now for word processing. A wealth of material resides on Word documents. You can import those documents into RoboHELP HTML.

To import a Word document into RoboHELP HTML, follow these steps:

1. **Start RoboHELP HTML and open the document in which you want to import the Word document.**

2. **Choose File➪Import➪Word Document.**

   The Open dialog box appears.

3. **Locate the file that you want to import.**

4. **Click Open.**

   RoboHELP adroitly converts the Word document into an HTML file. You can see the document as a topic in your WYSIWYG Editor (as shown in Figure 13-15). To import a Word document into RoboHELP Classic, see the "Metamorphosing HTML Help into WinHelp" section earlier in this chapter.

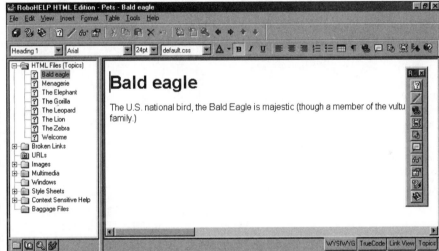

Figure 13-14: The new file appears as a topic in your HTML Files (Topics) folder.

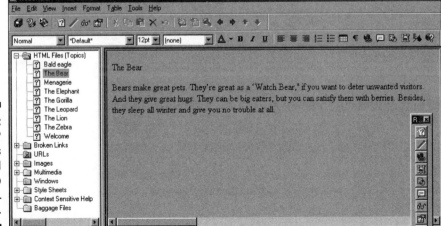

Figure 13-15: RoboHELP converts your Word document to an HTML topic.

Chapter 14

Compiling, Compressing, and Not Complaining

. . . .

In This Chapter

▶ Squeezing all your HTML topics into an actual Help file

▶ Seeing niggling reminders (reports) about what you forgot

▶ Tinkering with your compile settings

▶ Scrunching Classic topics into a Help project

▶ Taking a proud, worried look at a final ship list

. . . .

*Y*ou can have fun day after day creating topics, whipping in images, blending in lots of bookmarks, playing with your index, and just generally having a festival of Help authoring. The time comes, though, when you have to face the music for what you've done — that is, you have to compile your Help file and see if it works.

In RoboHELP HTML, when you compile you "put together" all your project files — your topic files, image files, and multimedia files. RoboHELP puts them all together in a compressed help file (a .CHM file, which people call a "Chum" file). In RoboHELP Classic, you create a .HLP file.

In this chapter you see how to compile in RoboHELP HTML as well as in Classic, how to set parameters for the compile in either type of help, and how to view reports that help you avoid errors or find out what to fix.

Compiling Your HTML Help

The word "compile" comes from the technogeek world of programming, which gives the word a certain cold, scary feel. (I admit, I can't shake that feeling even now.) To the ordinary person, compiling means "putting together." The same definition is pretty much true when you compile a Help file. The compile is the moment of truth; when you find out if your program works or if something is wrong . . . even seriously wrong.

The good news is that a compile is pretty automatic for the most part. If you compile often as you go along, you probably don't face any insurmountable problems even during a final compile.

Compiling final HTML Help files (.CHM files)

I don't know about you, but I tend to be of the "cross your fingers" school when it comes to things like compiling. Try something out. If it works, you don't have to worry about all the things that might not have worked. Even if one or two things don't work, you just fix those and then don't worry about any of the other things that might have gone wrong.

Here's how to compile an HTML Help file:

1. **Start RoboHELP HTML and open the file that you want to compile.**

2. **Once you've added or changed at least one topic, click the Save All button.**

3. **Click the Compile button.**

   RoboHELP compiles your project, and you can see the results in the Compilation pane at the bottom (shown in Figure 14-1).

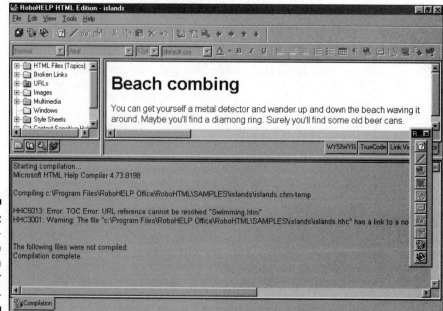

Figure 14-1: The compilation pane reports on your compile.

You can click and drag the top of the pane to resize it. You can also use the scroll bars at the side and bottom to navigate the Compilation pane.

Checking reports before compiling

Reports can tell you the state of your project and help you correct potential errors before you compile. Here's how to start one useful report — the Project Status report:

1. **Start RoboHELP and open the project that you want to work with.**

2. **Choose Tools⇨Reports⇨Project Status.**

   RoboHELP prepares the Project Status report for the current project, as shown in Figure 14-2.

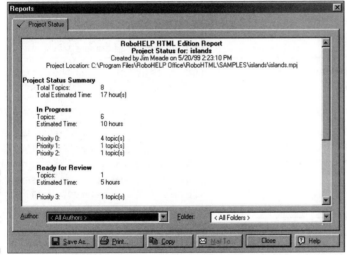

Figure 14-2:
Check your project status here.

In the Project Status report, you can find out how many topics are In Progress, how many are Ready for Review, and so on. You see the priority of topics in each category (for instance, Priority 1 topics that are in progress).

For the Project Status report to show meaningful information, you have to have been inputting that information to the Topic Properties dialog box for each topic. You can really help yourself in managing your project if you enter useful information into these non-required fields.

Table 14-1 summarizes the reports that you might want to use to help you find and fix things as you compile. I list them in the order they appear on the Reports menu.

Table 14-1	Useful Reports as You Compile
Report	*What It's Good For*
Table of Contents *(TOC)*	Shows the books and pages in your TOC so you can analyze the look.
Index	Great for proofreading an index. You should check your spelling, grammar, and consistency.
Topic Properties	If you have a lot of topics, this report helps you get a handle on all kinds of things — status, TOC, index, and more. You can read through a summary on each of your topics.
Topic References	Check out links to topics and other places topics get used. Can help you decide topics to remove as you "downsize" at the end.
Unreferenced Topics	Find topics that people can't get to. You can add links or put them into the TOC or Index.
Topics by Priority	A manager can see a quick summary of what needs to be done.
Used Files	Your .CHM file compresses all the files that go into your final Help file. With this report you can do housekeeping, make sure you've used all the files you mean to include, and decide on files to delete before compressing.
Unused Files	These files are dropouts; they aren't doing anything. Maybe they are images or other files you thought you might use but never did. You can delete them before compiling.
Style Sheets	You and possible coauthors may have used multiple style sheets. At compiling time, you may want to decide on just one.
Images	You may have duplicate versions of an image. Here you can find that out and then eliminate all but one.
Broken Links	Broken links happen pretty easily, and they bring error messages as you compile. Here you can identify them so you can go back and fix them.

Report	What It's Good For
External Topic References	If you've linked to Web pages and other external files, you can see the list here. You may want to test the links and be sure they are up to date.
Unused Index Entries	If Index Entries aren't referring to keywords, they aren't doing anything useful. You can delete them.

In Chapter 19, I show you how to use some handy tools for cleaning up in a project. For instance, you see how to use the Multi-File Find and Replace tool to find and replace text in multiple topics.

Changing compile settings

You can change the settings that affect your compilation results, including such things as the name of the .CHM file that you create when you compile. Follow these steps to change your compile:

1. **Start RoboHELP and open the project whose settings you want to work with.**

2. **Choose File⇨Project Settings.**

   The Project Settings dialog box appears, as shown in Figure 14-3.

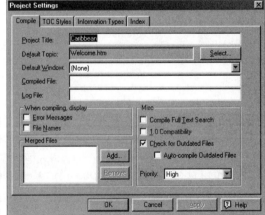

Figure 14-3: Change settings that affect your compilation.

3. **Make any desired changes to your settings.**

   Table 14-2 summarizes some of the things you can do in the Project Settings dialog box.

Table 14-2	Some of the Project Settings You Can Change
Setting	*What It Does*
Project Title	This title shows in the HTML Help window when people view the file. You can change that name here.
Default Topic	This topic appears in the Help window when someone launches the Help file. You can be sure that the first topic they see is the one you want.
Compiled File	If you don't specify a name, RoboHELP uses the name of the project and adds .CHM. You can substitute a different name, though.
Log File	If you want to be able to read a log file in Windows Notepad, put in the name of a log file here. RoboHELP will create the file when it compiles.

You can make a number of other choices in the Project Settings tab, and maybe you'll want to experiment with some of them. For instance, you can have all the file names display in the Compilation pane as you compile.

Compiling Your WinHelp

RoboHELP Classic has all kinds of cool capabilities to help you as you compile. If you like playing with diagnostics and reports and all, you can really go to town in RoboHELP Classic.

When you compile in RoboHELP Classic, you combine all your topic files, image files, and other source files into one .HLP file — a file actually used by those who use the help.

Compiling Classic files

You can work in either RoboHELP Explorer or Word to compile your Classic files. Follow this long, arduous list of steps to compile a WinHelp file:

1. **Open RoboHELP Classic and open a project.**

2. **Click the Compile button.**

   RoboHELP compiles the project and shows you the Result dialog box, shown in Figure 14-4.

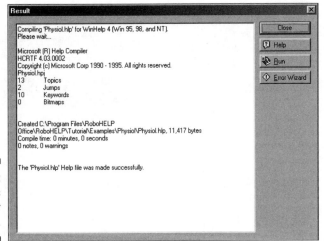

Compiling 'Physiol.hlp' for WinHelp 4 (Win 95, 98, and NT).
Please wait...

Microsoft (R) Help Compiler
HCRTF 4.03.0002
Copyright (c) Microsoft Corp 1990 - 1995. All rights reserved.
Physiol.hpj
13   Topics
2   Jumps
10   Keywords
0   Bitmaps

Created C:\Program Files\RoboHELP
Office\RoboHELP\Tutorial\Examples\Physiol\Physiol.hlp, 11,417 bytes
Compile time: 0 minutes, 0 seconds
0 notes, 0 warnings

The 'Physiol.hlp' Help file was made successfully.

Figure 14-4:
You see this report after you compile.

Fixing errors

Compiling, of course, is a cinch when you don't encounter any errors. When you do, though, as likely you will, you may have to take some action. The RoboHELP Error Wizard can help when you encounter the disturbing reality of an error in your compile. Follow these steps to use the wizard:

1. **Open RoboHELP Classic.**

2. **Open a file that contains an error and compile the file.**

   You can create a broken link by deleting a topic linked to another topic.

   When you compile in Classic, the Result dialog box appears.

3. **In the Result dialog box, click the Error Wizard button.**

   The Error Wizard appears and displays a warning, as shown in Figure 14-5.

4. **Click your particular error, then click the Locate button to go to the topic associated with the error.**

   If you have multiple errors, you have to click the particular error and then click the Locate button.

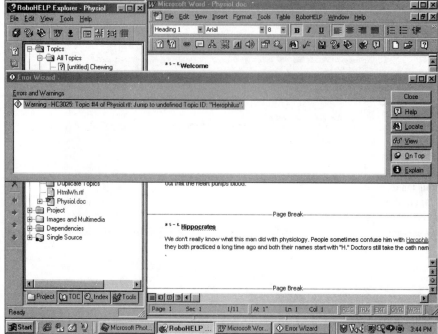

Figure 14-5:
The Error
Wizard
helps you fix
errors and
warnings.

Types of WinHelp errors

You can encounter three types of errors when you compile in WinHELP, and not all of them require any action on your part. The three types of errors are as follows:

✔ **Notes:** These are just kind of for your information. Notes point out conditions that you might want to know about but that won't seriously mess up the final help file. You can decide whether or not to do anything about them.

✔ **Warnings:** Warnings are more serious than Notes. For instance, if you reference an image

that's missing, WinHELP warns you but continues to compile. When you have missing images, the final Help file displays a "missing graphic" image in the final Help file. You probably want to fix up the file and not have such an obvious mistake display to your viewing public.

✔ **Errors:** An error stops the compiling process dead in its tracks. If you encounter an error, you have to fix it before you can finish the compile.

Checking diagnostics

You can prevent compiling problems before they arise by using certain help-ful reports. The Diagnostics Report tells you about possible errors in the project. Follow these steps to check it out:

1. **Start RoboHELP Classic and open the project you want to diagnose.**

2. **In the RoboHELP Explorer window, choose Tools⇨Reports⇨ Diagnostics.**

   The diagnostics report comes up (as shown in Figure 14-6) and warns of potential errors in your project.

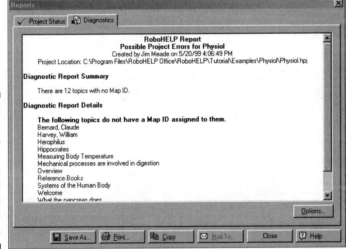

Figure 14-6:
The Reports window — you can check potential mistakes here before you compile.

Click the Project Status tab in the Reports dialog box to see your Project status. The report is the same as the one discussed in this chapter for RoboHELP HTML.

RoboHELP Classic has a complete list of other reports you may want to review at compile time by choosing Tools⇨Reports. (You review them to avoid possible errors that would come up, or to help resolve those that have come up during compiling.) See Table 14-3 for a summary of these other reports in RoboHELP HTML, where the reports are similar to those in RoboHELP Classic. The Classic list does include reports you no longer need in RoboHELP HTML, such as those pertaining to Map IDs (a link to context-sensitive Help topics not used in RoboHELP HTML).

Setting options

You have control over the settings that affect the compile. You can use the Project Settings dialog box to control such things as the type of compression and the on-screen display during a compile.

Here's how to set your compile options in RoboHELP Classic:

1. **Start RoboHELP Classic and open the project that you want to work with.**

2. **Choose File⇨Project Settings.**

    You see Classic's Project Settings dialog box.

3. **Click the Compile tab.**

    Figure 14-7 shows the Compile tab at the top of the Project Settings dialog box.

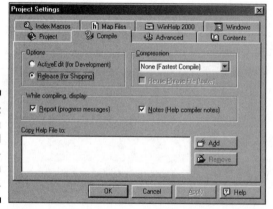

Figure 14-7:
Here you
can control
what hap-
pens as you
compile.

Table 14-3 summarizes some of the choices you might want to make with the Compile tab in the Project Settings dialog box.

Table 14-3	Some Key Classic Project Settings
Setting	**What It Does**
Options: ActiveEdit (for Development)	Puts the ActiveEdit button on the button bar of the compiled file, so you can click and go to a selected topic.
Options: Release for Shipping	Prepares a final Help file (no ActiveEdit button).

Setting	What It Does
Compression	Choose a style of compression — "None" for the fastest compile, "Maximum" for the shipping version (a version you plan to release to your end users).
While compiling, display Report	Shows the progress message during the compile (especially nice if you're using Maximum compression, which is slow).
Copy Help File to:	You can select a folder to which to copy the Help file. (For instance, you might copy to a shared folder so your programmers could get to the Help file.)
While compiling, display Notes	Notes don't necessarily require attention, but they're nice to know about.

Reviewing the Ship List

As you prepare your Help file, you may invest months and months into meeting with programmers, developing topics, doing research, and compiling and testing. All your attention is for naught, though, if you ship out a file to the user . . . and the file doesn't work. For the file to work, you have to include *everything* the file needs — not just the .HLP file but also the CNT file (Table of Contents), any .DLL files (Dynamic Link Library) used by Windows along with your application, and perhaps more.

To help you remember everything, follow these steps:

1. **Start RoboHELP Classic and open the project on which you want to report.**

2. **Choose Tools⇨Reports⇨Ship List (the choice appropriately at the bottom of the file, since the last thing you do with a Help file is ship it).**

   RoboHELP displays the list of items to include when you ship, as I show in Figure 14-8. You probably want to share the list with programmers and everybody on your team.

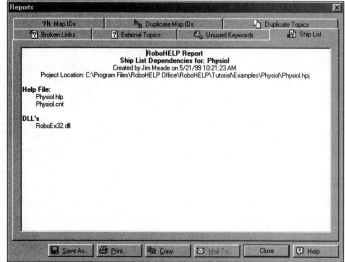

Figure 14-8:
Make sure
you don't
leave out
anything
important.

Part V
Doing Sexy Web Stuff

"What do you mean you're updating our Webpage?"

In this part . . .

If you're going to have fun, why not get downright sexy and outlandish with HTML. HTML, in particular, lets you have words and images flying around, popping up, dropping down, fading in and out, or just dazzling. You discover how to do this and more in Part V. You may also observe those behind-the-scenes guardians of Web page looks — style sheets — before plunging boldly into the world of almost programming with Dynamic HTML scripts. It's a rich diet. Take a deep breath before starting.

Chapter 15

Getting Dynamic on the Web

· ·

In This Chapter

▶ Playing with fun effects like "fly in" text

▶ Eating tacos, hamburgers, and hot dogs

▶ Adding expanding Hotspots and drop-down Hotspots

▶ Solving the problem of unwanted Hotspots

▶ Splashing a screen before your unsuspecting viewer

· ·

Sometimes you just have to have some fun in life. Just knock off on a summer day and go swimming. Go to a movie and forget about everything. Now, fun also has its practical applications, too. As the old saying goes, people learn more if you make the learning fun, but somehow, saying that "fun is practical" takes all the fun out of it. Fun is supposed to be fun; that's the main thing.

RoboHELP has some fun effects that, yes, can be really practical, too. In this chapter you basically get to play around with fun stuff. You see how to have your text fly in from one side; you get acquainted with expanding and drop-down text; and then, in one final dramatic moment, you see how to create a splash screen.

I hate to contradict myself about these effects being mainly fun, but, nevertheless, I hasten to add that expanding Hotspots are great for definitions. Drop-down text is great for showing processes.

These effects look so fancy that they might easily scare people off. "Oh, I could never do that," you might think, "I'm no programmer." While the coding to create these near effects *is* fancy, RoboHELP does this coding for you behind the scenes. Adding these dynamic effects to your Help files is actually just a matter of choosing from menus; the process is actually as easy as anything in this book and easier than most — trust me.

Creating Special Effects in RoboHELP HTML

The term "special effects" can suggest a lot of things. For movies, the term seems to get all tied together with stunts, visual effects that look like stunts, and other mysterious things. In RoboHELP, though, special effects are visual effects.

RoboHELP HTML offers these six special effects:

- **Drop Shadow:** A silhouette for the object, offset a bit
- **Fade In:** Your object appears slowly, as if fading in
- **Fly In:** The object comes flying onto your page
- **Font Formatting:** Causes font to change on an object when someone passes the mouse over it
- **Glow:** Causes an object to look radiant when someone passes the mouse over it
- **Transitions:** Lets you reveal an object by using effects like "Wipe Left" and "Vertical Blinds"

You apply all these cool effects the same way; follow these steps to try one for yourself:

1. **Start RoboHELP HTML and open (or create) the file that you want to work with.**

2. **Open (or create) the topic where you want to add the effect.**

3. **Click to put the cursor in the line where you want to use the effect.**

4. **Choose Format➪Special Effects.**

   The Special Effects (Dynamic HTML) dialog box comes up, as shown in Figure 15-1.

   You can insert images as well as text when you use RoboHELP's special effects, like the cornucopia (shown in Figure 15-2) that I downloaded from Microsoft's clip art library at `http://msdn.microsoft.com/downloads/`.

5. **Select the desired special effect or effects.**

   You can just accept the suggested settings or make special choices for the effect, such as changing the direction from which the text or image flies in with the Fly In effect.

   (In some cases, you can use more than one effect at a time. You can experiment and try things out.)

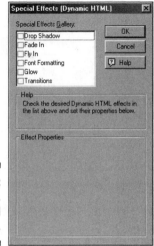

Figure 15-1:
Get hip.
Use special
effects.

When you click to select an effect, you see a description of that effect in the Effect Properties field of the Special Effects (Dynamic HTML) dialog box. For instance, the description for the Fly In effect is "Causes the visual objects (text, images, and so on) to 'Fly' onto the page from any direction."

6. **Click OK.**

   RoboHELP adds the effect into the topic.

7. **Right-click the topic and choose Preview Topic to preview your effect.**

   The image comes flying in from the right, as I've tried to show in Figure 15-2 (and failed rather miserably, unfortunately — the figure is a stationary picture, after all).

8. **Click X in the upper right of the preview window to close it.**

I should warn you (knowing full well that almost nobody can heed such a warning): These special effects are insidious, and are known time consumers. I don't want to call them outright "time wasters," but you can invest a lot of time toying with the various possibilities, such as, "Shall it fly in from the bottom-right or from the top-left?"

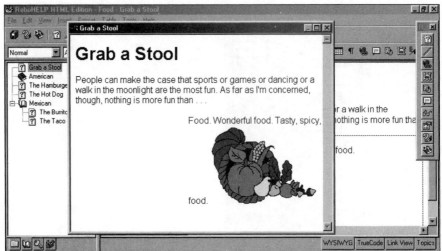

Figure 15-2:
Watch out
for flying
food.

Playing with Dynamic Hotspots

I could pretend to be businesslike here and say something like "Using Dynamic Hotspots is helpful in business," but these things are toys, no matter how serious your overall purpose. (A *Hotspot* is any area in a topic that does something when you click it, such as jump to another topic, run a script, or even play a video.) There are two kinds of dynamic Hotspots — expanding Hotspots and drop-down Hotspots, which I describe in the following sections.

Hotspots are a great way to insert links and multiple links. You can try cool things like allowing people to click a Hotspot of a window in a house to see the room behind the window. See Chapter 7 for additional information on how to use Hotspots and multiple Hotspot links.

Putting in expanding Hotspots

Expanding Hotspots (text areas that expand to show more text when you click them) are much like pop-up windows; they're great for definitions and quick, short information. Follow these steps to create an expanding Hotspot:

1. **Start RoboHELP and open the project that you want to work with.**

2. **Create or open the topic that you wish to add an expanding Hotspot to.**

3. **Select the text that you want to have as the Hotspot (that is, as the text that you click).**

   In the present version of RoboHELP HTML, you can't use images for expanding Hotspots . . . just text. But you can have an image in the material that appears when someone clicks.

4. **Choose Insert⇨Expanding Hotspot.**

   The selected text turns green, indicating that it's now clickable text (that is, something happens to the text when you click it).

5. **Select the text that you want to make into expanding text (the text that appears when people click).**

6. **Choose Insert⇨Expanding Text.**

   The text appears in red.

7. **Try out the effect by right-clicking the topic and selecting Preview Topic.**

   Figure 15-3 shows the preview before clicking a topic that expands into a Hotspot; Figure 15-4 shows the preview after you click the topic.

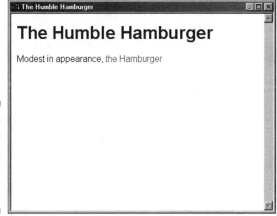

Figure 15-3:
Here's an unassuming screen before I click.

8. **Click the X in the upper-right corner of the Preview window to close it.**

Be sure to put the expanding text to the right of the expanding Hotspot — RoboHELP only looks for it there. If you put the expanding text to the left of the expanding Hotspot and click the Hotspot, you'll be disappointed when nothing happens.

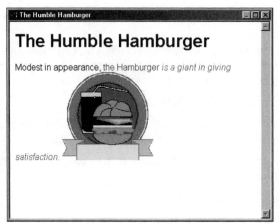

Figure 15-4:
Here's the
screen with
full-blown
expanded
text.

Using Hotspots that drop-down

Drop-down Hotspots (a Hotspot you click to show text, usually a list, that drops down) are great for describing step-by-step processes.

Creating drop-down Hotspots isn't a lot different from creating expanding Hotspots. The difference is that in this case the dynamic text drops down. The experts at Help authoring have found that such drop-down text is great for numbered steps (though you can use it for whatever you want). See for yourself by following these steps:

1. **Start RoboHELP HTML and open or create the project you want to work with.**

2. **Type in the text that will use the effect.**

3. **Select the text that will be the Hotspot.**

4. **Choose Insert⇨Drop-down Hotspot.**

   The selected text turns green and italic, indicating that it's now clickable. (That is, when you click it, it will show the drop-down text you create in the next step.)

5. **Select the text that will be the drop-down text.**

6. **Choose Insert⇨Drop-down Text.**

   RoboHELP encloses the text in a box. Figure 15-5 shows the topic as it appears on the screen with the box around it. In the final Help file, the text inside the box doesn't appear until the user clicks the Hotspot.

To have each numbered step drop-down on its own line, put each numbered item on a separate line when you create the list by pressing return at the end of each line.

Figure 15-5:
Your drop-
down text
has a box
around it.

7. **Click the View button to preview the text, and then click the Hotspot in the preview window.**

Figure 15-6 shows the topic before clicking the Hotspot; and Figure 15-7 shows it after clicking.

Figure 15-6:
Here's the
Hotspot
waiting to
be clicked.

If you don't like the formatting of your Hotspots (such as green italics for a Hotspot link), you can change it. Nothing stops you from just selecting the text and applying formatting by using the Format menu. Or, you can readily change the styles throughout your document by using style sheets. I explain how to use style sheets in Chapter 16.

It's a bird; it's a plane . . . . No! It's Dynamic HTML!

RoboHELP's Expanding and drop-down effects depend on Microsoft Dynamic HTML. If you were to click the TrueCode tab, you'd see a page with drop-down text containing a script — refer to Figure 15-5. Browsers before Microsoft Internet Explorer 4 couldn't use Dynamic HTML. That is, they had to use Java applets because they couldn't use scripts.

Dynamic HTML introduced an "object structure" into HTML, which allows you to isolate individual elements on the page (such as the

steps for eating a hot dog in Figure 15-5) and apply a script to them. It's the script that causes the "dynamism" — the appearing and disappearing of the text. People with browsers that pre-date IE 4 can still display the dynamic text. However the text won't have the dynamic effect, but rather will display flat text (which leaves the page no worse off than before Dynamic HTML came along).

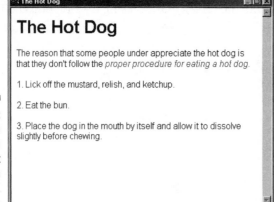

Figure 15-7:
Click the Hotspot and the text drops down below.

Getting rid of Hotspot formatting

Suppose after creating a dynamic Hotspot, you find you hate it. Getting rid of the effect isn't quite as automatic as a lot of the deleting you might do with other things. Deleting the text does exactly that, leaving you with no text at all. You can, if you choose, delete all the text that goes with the Hotspot, and delete the Hotspot along with it. To get rid of just the special formatting:

1. Select the Hotspot text whose special formatting you want to clear.

2. **Right-click the selected text and choose Clear Special Formatting from the Context menu that appears.**

   RoboHELP gets rid of the formatting without getting rid of the text. Figure 15-8 shows the topic with the box no longer present.

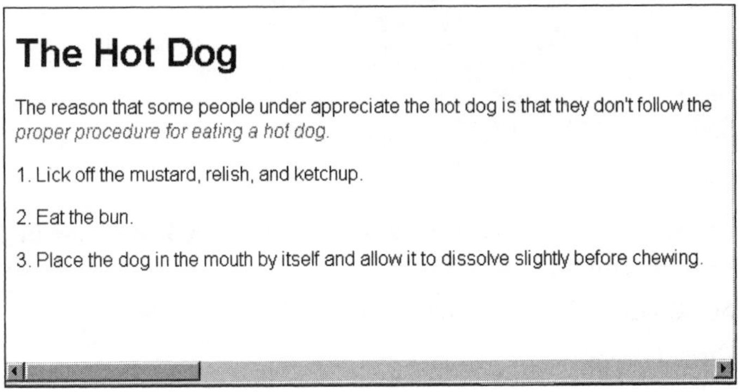

Figure 15-8:
You can
clear
special
formatting
without
deleting the
text that
goes with it.

The Hot Dog

The reason that some people under appreciate the hot dog is that they don't follow the *proper procedure for eating a hot dog.*

1. Lick off the mustard, relish, and ketchup.

2. Eat the bun.

3. Place the dog in the mouth by itself and allow it to dissolve slightly before chewing.

Tossing In Splash Screens in HTML Help

Hey, everybody likes to create a splash now and then. They aren't essential to most Help authors most of the time, but *splash screens* are too neat sounding for us to overlook altogether. People usually use splash screens right at the beginning of a file or topic. In computer terms, the splash screen is a control you can put into your Help file that causes an image to display for a time that you specify and then disappear.

Follow these steps to add a splash screen to your HTML Help file:

1. **Start RoboHELP and open the project and the topic where you want the splash screen.**

2. **Position the cursor in the document at the location where you want to have the splash screen.**

3. **Click the Insert HTML Help control button; then click Splash Screen.**

   The Splash Screen Wizard comes up, as shown in Figure 15-9.

4. **To choose an image, click the folder button to the right of the box labeled Image File for Splash.**

   The Graphics Locator appears.

Figure 15-9:
Start here to
create a
Splash
Screen.

5. **Use the Graphics Locator to locate an image file to use (a .BMP or .GIF file) for your splash screen.**

   See Chapter 6 to see how to use the Graphics Locator.

6. **Click Finish.**

   RoboHELP puts a control into your topic — a box with the word "Splash" in it. When the topic opens, the Splash Screen displays.

7. **Click Preview to display the splash.**

   The topic opens and the splash screen displays for 3 seconds and then goes away. Figure 15-10 shows the topic with the splash screen displayed.

8. **Click the X in the top right of the Preview window to close it.**

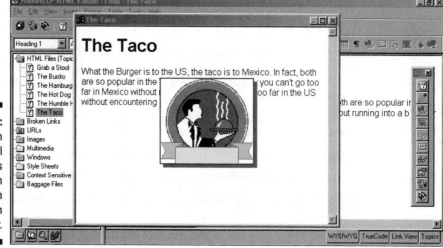

Figure 15-10:
You can
have cool
images
splash on
the screen
and then
disappear.

Chapter 16

Stepping Out with HTML Style Sheets

. . . .

. . . .

If you've worked very much with RoboHELP or even with word processing in general, you probably know what style sheets are. At least, you probably know what styles are. (Style sheets in HTML are very similar to templates in Microsoft Word.) On the *WYSIWYG* (What You See Is What You Get) HTML toolbar you get to set the look of your paragraph by choosing styles like Heading 1 style or Normal style. A style has characteristics. For instance, Heading 1 is Arial font and its size is 24 point.

A *style sheet* is a collection of all the styles you use in characters, paragraphs, and the document. That is, you can go in and define for yourself what Normal style looks like, and you can create styles of your own. You can feverishly determine the whole look of your Help file.

Using style sheets has one primary advantage over not using them — style sheets allow you to control the look throughout a project in a single stroke. For instance, by changing the look of Heading 1 on the style sheet, you change the way the Heading 1 style looks throughout the entire project, or you can change the color of the background throughout your Help file by changing it in just one place. Also, by using style sheets you get consistency. Try changing Heading 1 in all 100 places it appears and you're bound to get something messed up. (Of course, you will have gone insane long before you get to the 100th instance.)

In this chapter you see how to create your own style sheets, attach them to topics, and change them if you want to give your topics a different look. You also see how to copy and delete styles, get some sound advice on using style sheets, and find out how to use something that you probably shouldn't use very often — embedded styles.

Don't rely a whole lot on style sheets you create yourself. One of the foremost experts on style sheets, Jakob Nielsen, said that most authors mangle their style sheets terribly, and I believe that. I would suggest that if you want to work with your style sheets, be conservative and make only small changes. See how your changes look and then maybe make some other small changes. Style sheets are a powerful technology that can drastically affect the look of your HTML pages. Professional designers created the default style sheet. Unless you're professional designer, you're not likely to make a better one anyway.

Creating and Editing Your Own Style Sheet

Your topics come with a style sheet already attached — default.css. The style sheet defines character, paragraph, and document styles, and you don't have to worry about creating them yourself; you just fervently apply them to your documents. For additional information on applying styles by selecting text and making choices from the WYSIWYG toolbar, see Chapter 5.

Creating brand new style sheets

Follow these steps to create a style sheet by default:

1. **Start RoboHELP HTML and open the project that you want to work with.**

2. **Click the Project tab (on the left).**

3. **Open the HTML File (Topics) folder.**

4. **Right-click the topic that you want to work with and select Properties from the Context menu that appears.**

   The Topic Properties dialog box comes up.

5. **Click the Appearance tab.**

   On the Appearance tab (shown in Figure 16-1), you can work with the appearance of your style sheet.

Figure 16-1:
Create a
new style
sheet in this
dialog box.

6. **Click the New button.**

   The Save As dialog box comes up.

7. **Type the name of your new style sheet into the File name box.**

8. **Click the Save button.**

   The Edit Style Sheet dialog box comes up, as shown in Figure 16-2. Here you create the styles for your new style sheet.

Figure 16-2:
Here you
create
styles for
your new
style sheet.

Creating a new style from scratch

If you are adventuresome, desperate, or motivated for some other reason, you can create your own style sheets to use with your projects. Follow these steps to create a new style:

1. **Start RoboHELP HTML and open a project of your choice.**

2. **Click the plus next to the Style Sheets folder to open it.**

3. **Right-click the style sheet that you want to edit and choose Edit from the Context menu that appears.**

   The Edit Style Sheet dialog box comes up.

4. **If you want to base your style on a similar existing style (which saves a lot of work), click the style you wish to base your new style on.**

   The Normal style is the default setting.

5. **In the text box at the top of the Style box, type the name for your new style.**

6. **Click the New button.**

   RoboHELP puts the new style at the bottom of the list. Figure 16-3 shows the Edit Style Sheet dialog box with a new style added.

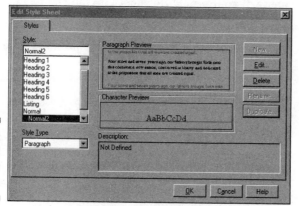

Figure 16-3:
You can add
a new style
to the list.

7. **With your new style selected, click the Edit button to open the Edit Paragraph Style dialog box.**

   Suppose you wanted to create a style similar to Normal but with some differences.

8. **Click the various tabs (Font, Paragraph, and so on) to choose the styles you want to use.**

   For example, click the Font tab and, in the Color box, choose Blue.

   You'll notice that all the choices in the Edit Paragraph Style box appear as undefined. You might think that you then have to define them all, but you don't have to do anything. Just change the settings you want to change — if any.

9. **Click OK to close the Edit Paragraph Style dialog box and then click OK again to close the Edit Style sheet dialog box.**

   You have created a new style, which you can now use as you edit.

Editing and defining style sheets

After you create a style sheet, you don't have to rest on your laurels — you can go in and tinker as much as you want. You may click any of the styles to edit and redefine its appearance. To edit a style sheet, you follow almost the same steps as for creating one. Here's what to do:

1. **In the Style Sheets folder in Project Manager, right-click a style sheet and choose Edit from the Context menu.**

2. **In the Style list box, click a style that you want to edit.**

   The Edit Paragraph Style dialog box appears, where you can work with whatever style you've chosen to edit. Figure 16-4 shows the Edit Paragraph Style dialog box editing the Heading 2 style.

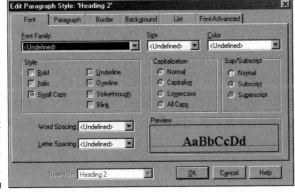

Figure 16-4: Create your new style in the Edit Paragraph Style dialog box.

3. **Make your choices in the Edit Paragraph Style box (for Font, Border, and so on).**

4. **Click OK when you're satisfied with your changes.**

   The Edit Style Sheet dialog box reappears.

5. **Click OK in the Edit Style Sheet dialog box to accept your changes.**

6. **Then click OK to close the Edit Style Sheet dialog box.**

7. **Finally, click Save All to save the project with its new style sheet.**

   RoboHELP uses the new style sheet for the present topic.

Linking and Detaching Style Sheets to Topics

Style sheets are a powerful way to change the look of a topic or even a series of topics with a single stroke. Once you choose a style sheet that you're happy with, you can simply attach it to your topics to achieve the look that you want.

Attaching a style sheet

Attaching a fresh style sheet changes the look of all the topics that use it. Follow these steps to attach a style sheet to a topic:

1. **Start RoboHELP HTML and open the topic that you want to attach the style sheet to.**

2. **Select the style sheet that you want to use from the style sheet drop-down list on the WYSIWYG toolbar.**

   The topic takes on the formatting of the new style sheet.

3. **Click the Save All button.**

Linking a style sheet to several topics

If you get a style sheet that really works for you, you may want to attach it to multiple topics, instead of one. The point of using style sheets, after all, is to save work when formatting multiple topics and even entire projects.

Follow these steps to attach a style sheet to more than one topic:

1. **Start RoboHELP and open the project containing the topics that you want to attach your style sheet to.**

2. **Click the Topics tab (on the right of the RoboHELP screen), hold down the Ctrl key, and click one at a time on the topics that you want to use the style sheet.**

3. **Click the Properties button.**

   The Topic Properties dialog box opens.

4. **Click the Appearance tab.**

5. **Choose the style sheet that you want to apply to your topics from the Style Sheet box.**

6. **Click OK.**

7. **Click Save All to save the project.**

   RoboHELP applies the style sheet to your selected topics.

Unattaching a style sheet

After you attached a style sheet, you might change your mind (being human, after all!). You might prefer the look of the previous style sheet, for example, or just want to try a new one. Here's how to unattach a style sheet:

1. **Start RoboHELP and open the project and topic that you want to remove the style sheet from.**

2. **Click the arrow next to the style sheet drop-down list in the WYSIWYG toolbar and click (none).**

   The style sheet is unattached.

 RoboHELP Classic doesn't use style sheets for the WinHelp files that it creates. If you decide to convert a RoboHelp Classic project to WebHelp, (HTML) you may choose a style sheet during the conversion process. See Chapter 13 to find out about converting to WebHelp.

Manipulating Styles

A style sheet may contain numerous styles, and you can manipulate those styles in various ways. You can, of course, apply the styles to your topics. You can also copy a style and use it as the basis for a new style. You can delete styles (which is always a fortunate capability when you're creating new styles — you want to be able to get rid of something that doesn't work). And you can get fancy by adding things like a background to a style.

Applying styles

After you create your styles, use the WYSIWYG toolbar to apply them. If you want to try using that nifty bright yellow Old English italic style you made (yuck!), follow these steps:

1. **Open the topic that you want to use the style in.**

2. **Put the cursor in a paragraph you want to change the style of.**

3. **Click the arrow next to the paragraph styles box on the WYSIWYG toolbar.**

Figure 16-5 shows my style list with the style I have added (Normal2).

Figure 16-5:
After you
add a new
style, you
can apply it.

4. **Click on the style to apply it.**

If you change the look of a style you've already applied, paragraphs with that style take on the new look automatically. If you have created styles that you haven't used, you have to go into your topics and apply them to characters, paragraphs, or the document as a whole. See Chapter 5 for additional information on applying styles.

Copying styles

You might like some things about default styles but not everything, and perhaps you don't want to go through all the work of defining every little detail of a new style. The answer — copy a style, give it a new name, and change just the characteristics that you need to.

Follow these steps to copy a style:

1. **Start RoboHELP HTML and open a project.**

2. **Open the Style Sheets folder and double-click the style sheet that you want to work with.**

   The Edit Style Sheet dialog box appears.

3. **In the Style box, click the style you want to duplicate.**

   The Normal style is the default selection.

4. **Type a new name for the style in the text box at the top of the Style box.**

5. **Click the Duplicate button on the right side of the Edit Style Sheet dialog box.**

   RoboHELP duplicates the style under the new name.

6. **Click the Edit button and make any changes you want to make.**

   Figure 16-6 shows the Paragraph tab of the Edit Paragraph Style dialog box while I'm editing the indent of the Normal style. (The figure shows the style before I make any changes.)

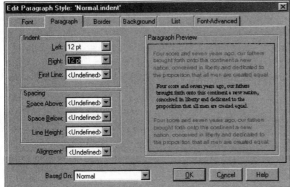

Figure 16-6:
Set up
the look
of your
duplicated
style.

7. **Click OK to close the Edit Paragraph Style dialog box.**

8. **Click OK again to close the Edit Style Sheet dialog box.**

   RoboHELP adds the style to your style sheet, and you can apply it using the WYSIWYG toolbar.

Deleting styles

Keeping your style sheets simple has great advantages. If you plan to use only certain styles, why not get rid of the others? Or, if you have gotten carried away creating new styles (explained in the preceding section), you may want to undo some of your creative work so that you can make sense of what's left. Here's how to delete a style:

1. **Start RoboHELP HTML and open a project.**

2. **Open the Style Sheets folder and double-click the style sheet you want to work with.**

   The Edit Style Sheet dialog box opens.

3. **In the Style box, click the style you want to delete.**

4. **Click the Delete button.**

   RoboHELP deletes the style.

If you've formatted a bunch of paragraphs with the style you've deleted, you might worry that the paragraphs will be confused, but this is not the case. The paragraphs just keep the formatting that they have until you reformat them or apply a different style to them.

Editing style sheets directly is not for the faint of heart (or, at least, not for those unaccustomed to working with codes). However, you can edit the styles in your style sheet directly instead of using the Edit Style Sheet dialog box. Locate the style sheet on your hard drive and then open it using the Microsoft Notepad (under your Windows Start menu in the Programs⇨ Accessories folder) and then edit the codes directly. Figure 16-7 shows the sample file colorsty.css opened in Notepad.

```
colorsty.css - Notepad
File  Edit  Search  Help

H2 { color : maroon;}
.mvd-H2 { color : maroon;}
CITE.expandspot { font-style : normal;
                  color : green;
                  cursor: hand;}
.mvd-CITE-expandspot { font-style : normal;
                       color : green;
                       cursor: hand;}
DFN.collapsed { font-style : italic;
                font-weight : normal;
                display :          'none';
                color : red;}
.mvd-DFN-collapsed { font-style : italic;
                     font-weight : normal;
                     display :          'none';
                     color : red;}
DFN.expanded { font-style : italic;
               font-weight : normal;
               color : red;}
.mvd-DFN-expanded { font-style : italic;
                    font-weight : normal;
                    color : red;}
EM.dropspot { color : green;
              cursor: hand;}
.mvd-EM-dropspot { color : green;
                   cursor: hand;}
P.Normal2 { color : blue;}
.mvd-P-Normal2 { color : blue;}
P.indent { margin-left : 12.0pt;
           margin-right : 12.0pt;}
.mvd-P-indent { margin-left : 12.0pt;
                margin-right : 12.0pt;}
P.red { color : maroon;}
```

```
Start | RoboHELP HTML Edi... | Microsoft Photo Editor... | colorsty.css - Notepad |        10:55 AM
```

Figure 16-7: You can edit style sheet codes directly, if you choose.

Changing background color

Changing background color is one of many choices you can make when working with your style sheets, and doing so is popular and useful. The background of your topics creates a "look" for the project. For instance, a blue background gives a cool feel. If you have all your topics linked to the same style sheet, you can change the background color of your whole project by changing the style sheet.

Using style sheets properly

Style sheets are powerful — *really* powerful. By *powerful* here, I mean that you can make small changes that have big effects all over your HTML Help file. Change the look of your Normal paragraph, for example, and most of your paragraphs take on the new look. When using such power, you probably ought to follow some guidelines.

Dr. Jakob Nielsen is a great guru of the Web and Web style sheets. His Alertbox column, available on the Web, talks about effective use of style sheets. Check him out at www.useit.com. Following is a summary and paraphrase of some of his excellent advice, with some thoughts of my own mixed in.

✔ Although you can use lots of style sheets in a Help file, *use only one.* Think about it — consistency is the goal, and you want to be able to change something every place by changing it in just one place (the style sheet).

✔ Use linked style sheets rather than embedded styles (which I discuss later in this chapter). You can make global changes in the linked sheets and still maintain consistency.

✔ Have experts design your style sheets — "a single, central design group" as Nielsen puts it. Style sheets call for professional knowledge of design.

✔ Don't use more than two fonts. Fonts are tricky. There are rules about them, mostly known only to designers. For example, don't mix serif and sans serif fonts within the same part of the text. Start putting in lots of fonts and you can make people seasick.

Follow these steps to change background color in your style sheet:

1. **Start RoboHELP HTML and open a project.**

2. **Click the Project tab, open the Style Sheets folder, and double-click the style sheet that you want to edit.**

   The Edit Style Sheet dialog box appears.

3. **In the Style Type box, choose Document.**

   The program automatically selects Body as the default style in the Style list box.

4. **Click the Edit button.**

   The Edit Document Style dialog box appears.

5. **Click the Background tab.**

   Figure 16-8 shows the Background tab in the Edit Document Style dialog box.

6. **Click the arrow for the Background Color list box and then choose a color.**

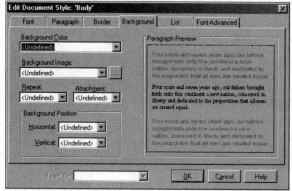

Figure 16-8:
You can
change
background
color here.

7. **Click OK to close the Edit Document Style dialog box.**

8. **Click OK again to close the Edit Style Sheet dialog box.**

All sheets linked to the style sheet now display with the new background.

Creating Embedded Styles

Embedded styles are styles based on a style sheet that you embed within a topic. That is, the styles you create in the embedded style sheet apply only to the one topic. Such narrowness of application, of course, undermines the very purpose of style sheets, which is to create uniform, consistent styles across topics. Most of you, most of the time, probably ought to just skip this section.

However, if you're experienced and have a good use for embedded styles, I can tell you how to create them. There are good uses for them, after all; for example, you might have a large Help topic that has special considerations that you don't use anywhere else, such as a lot of separate paragraphs that are italic, indented a special amount, and use a particular typeface.

Here's how to create an embedded style:

1. **Start RoboHELP HTML and open the topic that you want to create an embedded style for.**

2. **In WYSIWYG mode, right-click in the topic and choose Edit styles from the Context menu that appears.**

The Edit Style Sheet dialog box appears.

3. **In the Style Sheet box (in the lower-left of the dialog box) choose Current Document.**

Follow the steps to create a new style as explained in this chapter in the section "Creating a new style from scratch."

The style you've defined is available only in the individual topic in which it was created. Figure 16-9 shows a sample file with the embedded style applied.

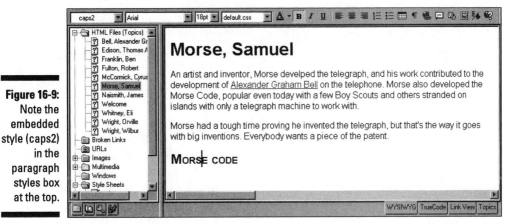

Figure 16-9: Note the embedded style (caps2) in the paragraph styles box at the top.

See Chapter 5 for additional information on *inline styles* — styles applied just to a specific area of the page, such as directly adjacent to a line of text.

If you're around HTML style sheets for very long, you may hear the term *cascading style sheets*, a term developed by the World Wide Web Consortium (also known as W3C). *Cascading* refers to how style sheets take precedence over one another. W3C has set up an elaborate specification, which you can read at www.w3.org. For the styles mentioned in this chapter, you may want to know that inline styles take precedence over embedded styles and embedded styles over the styles of the linked style sheet.

Chapter 17

Practically Programming: Forms, Scripting, and ActiveX

● ●

In This Chapter

▶ Seeing that ActiveX isn't as hard as it sounds (just hard)

▶ Playing with radio buttons (just one "station" at a time)

▶ Writing some very basic code (just one line, really)

▶ Copying more advanced Scripting code for fun

▶ Surveying the world of RoboHELP Classic macros

● ●

*I*f I may be permitted to use the "p" word, I must say that the material in this chapter deals with *programming* (or at least with *practically programming,* that is, with controls and forms that are not programming but need programming to make them work). For the most part, you may skip this chapter unless you're a programmer. But if what I hear on the street is true, you probably won't. That is, I hear that people love to try out scripts and are dying to see what they can do with them in their Help topics.

In this chapter, you see how to put in one of Microsoft's inscrutable-sounding ActiveX Controls and have fun with Forms and buttons (that look like those in real programs but can't work without a little help from your programmer). You see how to write scripts that work and how to copy scripts that might work. (Okay, they do work, but copying scripts is not for those without any experience at all.) Finally, you take a quick look at the tantalizing world of RoboHELP Classic macros.

Novices may not be ready to use stuff like ActiveX controls and scripting, but, if I can make a confession, the stuff in this chapter really "floats my boat." These programming tools are fun, and they're liberating. You find that you can do all kinds of things on your Help pages that you never dreamed of before. You can put the power of programming to work for you.

For some of the sections in this chapter (having to do with forms), you can do what the book describes. But you need to get code from a programmer to make the form do something useful. That is, you can create what you need in the Help file, but you have to work hand in hand with application developers for the element, such as a form or a form button, to have a meaningful result.

Inserting ActiveX Controls

ActiveX controls are *COM objects*. (That helps, right?) The *Component Object Model* (COM) is a Microsoft technology that allows different programs to interoperate with each other. When you add an ActiveX control to a RoboHELP topic, you're putting an existing program into the program you're working in (RoboHELP, in this case). Most of the time, you probably don't even need to know all this silly COM stuff. You add a control to your topic from a menu and if it works, it works, end of story. You don't care if what you put in is from your own program or from outside. Well, ActiveX (when it works properly) helps you add in programs from outside as if it's from inside.

You can put in ActiveX controls two different ways: the first way is without knowing what you're doing — just use the Insert HTML Help Control button within RoboHELP; the second way is by using the Insert menu to insert the ActiveX control. In the first section that follows, I discuss the former method. In the second section that follows, I discuss the latter method.

Inserting HTML Help controls

You can insert a variety of Help controls (programs) directly into a topic. Doing so allows you to have the capabilities of those programs added to your topics.

First, you can actually put a control in to see how it works. Just use the Insert HTML Help control button and then insert the control that you want. See Table 17-1 for a list of Help controls and their functions.

Here's how to insert HTML Help controls:

1. **Start RoboHELP HTML and open a project.**

2. **Select a topic from your list.**

3. **Click the place within your document where you want to insert the ActiveX control.**

   You can click, for example, on a separate line right after the words "Go ahead, add up the cost of your typical fast food meal."

4. Click the Insert HTML Help Control button on the WYSIWYG toolbar.

A drop-down menu appears.

5. Click Shortcut.

The Shortcut Wizard appears, as shown in Figure 17-1.

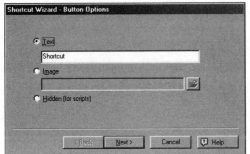

Figure 17-1:
The Wizard
helps install
your
shortcut.

6. Choose Text or Image.

For example, click the radio button for Image and then click the file-folder button at the right of the Image text box to search for an image. (Images are more fun than text.)

7. In the graphics locator, select an image and then click the Select button.

For example, select the calculat.bmp image from the clipart folder on the companion program within RoboHELP Office, RoboHELP Classic.

You return to the Shortcut Wizard.

To get the skinny on using the graphics locator, check out Chapter 6.

8. In the Shortcut Wizard, click Next.

The Shortcut Selection dialog box appears.

9. Type in your shortcut and then click Next.

In the Topic to display if Program Cannot be Found text box, put in a topic, such as Grab a Stool. For the example, I put calc.exe (the Microsoft Calculator).

For an additional program to work from within your Help file (like the calc.exe program in the preceding example), you have to copy the program file (a file with an .EXE extension) into the same folder as the help file (the .CHM file).

The Shortcut Wizard Font Options dialog box comes up.

10. **Click Finish in the dialog box to accept the recommended font settings (which determine the font settings of the control when it appears in your topic).**

11. **Compile and run the program.**

    RoboHELP adds a button to your topic with the image that you've selected on it. Figure 17-2 shows my sample topic containing the short-cut to a program.

Figure 17-2:
A shortcut to place the calculator in the Topic listing. Wow.

See Chapter 7 to put in the HTML Help Control that's most obviously useful to a Help author — the Related Topics button. Most of the other HTML Help controls have specialized uses, but the Related Topics button is almost a must. To find out about the Splash Screen (one of the controls on the Insert HTML Help Control menu), check out Chapter 15.

Table 17-1 summarizes the HTML Help controls you can put in.

Help controls are really specialized. Don't feel shy to skip this section of the book unless you're an advanced user or plan on getting some help from your programmer friends. (See Chapter 25 to discover 10 ways to bribe a programmer.)

Table 17-1	HTML Help Controls
Help Controls	*Function*
Related topics	Display text links to related topics.
WinHelp topic	Inserts a WinHelp topic into an HTML Help file.
Shortcut	Great for starting a program inside your topic. Allows you to put in a neat button.
Table of Contents	Adds an additional Table of Contents to your project. (You receive one automatically when you set up.)

Help Controls	Function
Index	Adds an additional Index to your project. (You receive one automatically when you set up RoboHELP.)
Splash screen	Splashes up an image for a short time. Exciting!
Close window	Closes an open window.
HHCTRL version	Shows the version number for an ActiveX control you have in your topic.
Keyword search	Displays a list of keywords. A user can click a word to see the list of topics connected to the keyword.

Inserting your own ActiveX controls

You don't have to limit yourself to the ActiveX controls on your Insert HTML Help control button. You can put in any ActiveX control to add fancy capabilities to an otherwise innocent-looking topic. Use the Insert menu and choose the control you want.

Here's what to do:

1. **Start RoboHELP HTML and open the project and topic that you want to work with.**

2. **Click inside the document, positioning the cursor precisely where you want to insert the control.**

3. **Choose Insert⇨ActiveX.**

   The Insert ActiveX Control dialog box comes up, as shown in Figure 17-3.

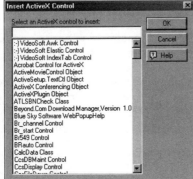

Figure 17-3: Pick an ActiveX control to insert.

When RoboHELP shows its list of ActiveX controls after you click Insert⇨ActiveX, where does this list come from? Does RoboHELP scan the entire contents of your computer? No, in Windows 98 at least, it looks in the Windows\System directory. If you add a new control and want to find it on this list, you have to copy it into the Windows\System directory. You have to register a new control for it to appear on the list, although it doesn't cost you anything. An ActiveX file has the extension .OCX. To register an ActiveX file, click the Windows Start button, choose Run, and when the Run window opens type the filename Regsvr32.ocx into the Open field and press OK (or Enter).

4. **Select the control you want and click OK.**

The ActiveX dialog box comes up (Figure 17-4 shows the dialog for the Calender Control 8.0) where you can modify the size, position, properties, and other characteristics of the control.

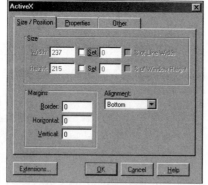

Figure 17-4: You can modify properties here.

5. **Make any desired changes in the ActiveX properties dialog box and then click OK.**

If you make no changes in your example, RoboHELP inserts the control onto the page.

6. **Click the View button to see the control in the file.**

Figure 17-5 shows an example of my sample control — kind of a fun calendar. You can modify its properties to get the look you want.

If you add ActiveX controls into your topics, you have to be sure to distribute those controls with your Help file. Otherwise, you'll just frustrate people looking for the controls. It's like saying, "Hey, take a ride in my car," but then not giving the person the car. Also, be sure your controls work with HTML Help — not all do.

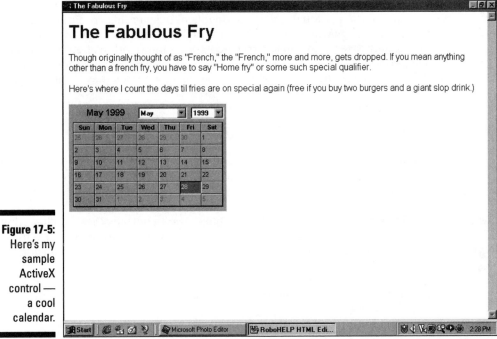

Figure 17-5:
Here's my
sample
ActiveX
control —
a cool
calendar.

Inserting Forms and Form Elements

You can put forms and buttons into your Help files, too. Now, I should tell you right at the outset that you can create the form, but you can't completely make it work. The form has to have a corresponding CGI script on the server. (See the following "Technical Stuff" icon for an explanation of CGI scripts.) You can put in cool looking buttons and stuff, though, and the right nerd can actually make them work.

CGI stands for Common Gateway Interface. Browsers use this interface (a set of programming rules) to get at programs on the server, and the programs there can send information back through the interface as well. Programs on the server are CGI scripts, written by application developers (engineers, technogeeks, and nerds to the Nth degree). The script recognizes the names and values you (or your programmer friend) put on the form and works with them to get information and send it back. Bottom line? Take your developer to lunch. Several times. Offer to walk his/her dog. Never raise your voice to such a person. Pretend you really, really like him/her, because to get your pretty buttons to do anything, the programmer has to connect those buttons to real programs. You can check out the section on scripting later in this chapter.

Forms may seem specialized at first, but you might find yourself getting attracted to them. Actually, you can do lots of businesslike, profitable, and productive things with forms. You can do surveys and collect information like names, addresses, and e-mails from people; get information about products that people want; send them order forms; or ask people where they need specialized help and then send them information on courses they should take.

Putting a form on your Help page

Really, a form is nothing in and of itself. A form is what potato chip packaging is to the chips inside or what Christmas wrapping paper is to the diamond ring. A form is the form; the form elements are the substance to the form.

To add form elements, such as check boxes, radio buttons (see the "Inserting radio buttons" section in this chapter), and so on, you must first have a form to add these elements to. See the following section for information on adding form elements.

To add a form to a topic, here's what to do:

1. **Start RoboHELP HTML and open a project and then a topic.**

2. **Click inside the form and place the cursor where you want to add the form.**

3. **Choose Insert⇨Form.**

   RoboHELP summarily puts the form onto your page — no further dialogs, no questions, no tips. Figure 17-6 shows my empty form.

4. **If you like — to make your form look more like a blank form — hit Enter four or five times to expand your form.**

Inserting radio buttons

Form elements have become standard ingredients in many mainstream programs, some of which you have probably used yourself. These form elements now have standardized uses, which are summarized in Table 17-2. To add a form element, follow these steps:

1. **Start RoboHELP HTML and open a project and a topic.**

2. **Create a form in the topic.**

   To discover how to put in a form, see the "Putting a form on your Help page" section earlier in this chapter.

Survey

Indicate your junk food preferences here:

3. **Click inside the document, placing the cursor inside the form where you want to insert the form element.**

4. **Choose Insert⇨Form Element⇨Form Element Type.**

   A properties dialog box appears.

   If you want a radio button, for example, choose Insert⇨ Form Element⇨Radio Button. In the case of the radio button the Check Box / Radio Button Properties dialog box appears, as shown in Figure 17-7.

5. **Type a name in the name field and then click OK to insert the button.**

   You won't see the name on the button — it's a name the programmer uses to connect to the button.

6. **To the right of the button, type in some text to go with it.**

   Radio buttons come in pairs or groups, never alone, so you need to add at least a second button by repeating Steps 4, 5, and 6.

7. **Click the View button to see your buttons on the page.**

   Figure 17-8 shows my sample form.

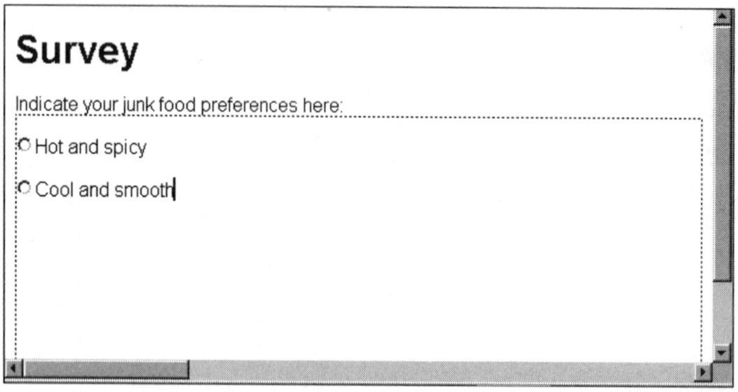

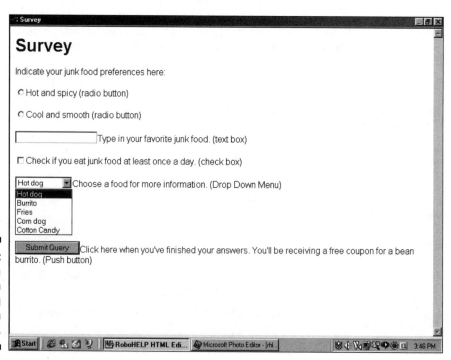

Figure 17-8:
I'll use these radio buttons in my survey.

Table 17-2 summarizes the types of form elements you can add to your forms and describes each. Because I think that you can better understand these elements by both seeing and reading about them, I've also included Figure 17-9, which shows an example of each of the types of form elements.

Figure 17-9:
Here's a sample form showing each form element.

Table 17-2	Form Element
The Element	*What to Use It For*
Text box	For the user to input text
Check box	For users to make choices
Radio button	For users to select only one option from more than one
Drop-down menu	For users to choose from a list
Push button	Submit forms, reset it, or do something else (like run a script)

Scripting HTML Code

Scripting is the brave new world of HTML coding. Before scripting came along, HTML was a relatively tame business. People essentially used HTML to format a page with text and photos.

In 1997, though, Microsoft introduced Dynamic HTML, which included the ability to do scripting. "Script" is a thinly disguised, supposedly "friendly" name for a "program." Scripts may be more modest programs than, say, full-blown Java or C++ programs. They're code, though. They're programs. To write them, you have to know how to program.

In this section, you see how to write a simple script of your own, edit a script, and copy and paste in a script from another source (a practice programmers use all the time).

Key to scripting — the object model

The real breakthrough in Microsoft Dynamic HTML, introduced in 1997, was not the scripting itself but the "object model." Scripting languages are variations on Visual Basic (in the case of VBScript) and Java (in the case of JavaScript).

The scripting (that is, programming) languages have been with us for awhile. However, before Dynamic HTML came along, scripts had no way to get at the various elements on an HTML page — the HTML "tags" (paragraphs, basically), "events" like mouse clicks or the opening of a page, images, styles, and various other "objects" on the page.

The object model "blew open the doors" to the elements of an HTML page, that is, it gave separate identities to those elements on the page so that scripts can identify them and do things with them. Scripts then go "storming through the doors" to have their way with words, pictures, and anything else on the HTML page.

Writing an original script

To insert a script of your own, follow these steps:

1. **Start RoboHELP HTML, open a project, and open the topic where you want to use a script.**

2. **Choose Insert⇨Script. (This is the easy part.)**

   The Edit Script dialog box appears, as shown in Figure 17-10.

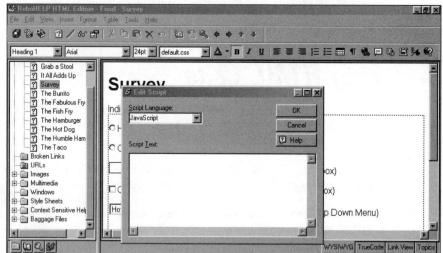

Figure 17-10:
Write your
script here.

3. **In the Script Language box, choose your scripting language — JavaScript or VBScript.**

   For this example, I'll assume you chose VBScript.

   If you're creating an original script, you choose the scripting language that you know better from the two choices. If you're copying a script in from somewhere else, be sure to match the Script Language box with the actual language of the script (or else, ouch! the script won't work).

4. **In the Script Text box, type in the script. (This is the hard part.)**

   For example, type this single line:

   ```
   Msgbox "Please complete whole survey."
   ```

Programming experts often recommend enclosing your script in comment tags `<!--` and `-->`. Recent browsers are smart enough to know that there's a script between the tags, and older browsers ignore whatever is between them. The older browsers that can't run the script just don't try to run it, and the result is that those browsers don't see a bunch of code/gobbledygook when they run the page with the script. While saying this may not be politically correct, to me the comment tags just mean one more thing that could go wrong — and so I tend to avoid them. It's every person for himself. Browsers are free, after all, so why shouldn't people use a recent one?

5. **Click OK to put the script on the page.**

   RoboHELP puts an `<S>` symbol where the script is.

6. **Click Preview to preview the script.**

   Figure 17-11 shows an example of a message box from my sample script.

7. **Click OK to close the message box.**

8. **Click the X at the top right to close the preview window.**

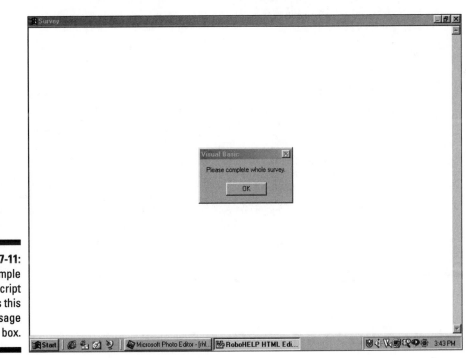

Figure 17-11:
My sample
script
creates this
message
box.

Copying and pasting in script

As programmers readily will tell you, many if not most programs are not written so much as rewritten. Why work from scratch and risk making typing mistakes when you can just modify an original program? Also, you can often find JavaScript and VBScript readily available for copying from the Internet.

Warning: You'll probably have better success copying to the TrueCode page than copying into the Edit Script dialog box (discussed earlier in this chapter). The Edit Script dialog box is strictly for editing scripting language in the pure form — that is, for you techno gurus out there, for editing material within a tag that identifies a script language. Here's an example, `<SCRIPT LANGUAGE = "JavaScript">`.

Here's how to copy a script:

1. **Start RoboHELP, open a project, and create a new topic to work in.**

2. **Display the code for the Web page (or other HTML-based page) that you want to copy and modify.**

   To display a Web page's code in Internet Explorer, click View⇨Source (View⇨Page Source in Netscape Communicator).

   If you click View⇨Source, you see the code in Microsoft's ever-useful Notepad. Figure 17-13 shows the source code for a simple Web page.

3. **Use your mouse to click and drag across the code you want to copy. Right-click your mouse and choose Copy to copy to the Windows Clipboard.**

   Your material is placed on the Windows Clipboard.

4. **In RoboHELP, click the TrueCode tab for the topic you're working on.**

5. **Choose the point at which you want to paste, right-click, and choose Paste.**

   The copied code is "pasted" onto your page.

   You have to pay attention to the tags as you paste in the new code. When pasting within the `<BODY>` portion of the HTML code, be careful to paste there and not, say, within the `<HEAD>`.

6. **If you want to work on the text as it appears in the actual topic, click WYSIWYG and edit the text to adapt it to your own uses.**

7. **Right-click your mouse and choose Preview Topic from the menu to see how your script is working.**

Figure 17-14 shows an example of Dynamic HTML on a Help page after clicking preview. Figure 17-15 shows the preview after typing something in the entry box and clicking the button.

Editing an existing script

Once you create a script, you likely need to tailor it to your own uses. To edit the script, you open the Edit Script box and make your changes.

Here's what to do:

1. **Start RoboHELP HTML and open the project and topic containing the script you wish to edit.**

2. **Double-click the <S> on your page to open the Edit Script dialog box.**

3. **Make your changes.**

    For my example, I just use the words "be sure to" so that the code now reads like this:

    ```
    Msgbox "Please be sure to complete whole survey."
    ```

4. **Click OK to close the dialog box.**

5. **Click the View button to preview your script.**

    Preview your new script.

If there was ever a time when you would find cause to use the TrueCode tab in the lower right of your RoboHELP HTML Explorer, it would probably be when working with scripts. You can edit your script in the TrueCode view instead of in the Edit Script dialog box by clicking the TrueCode tab and editing directly on the page. Figure 17-12 shows the TrueCode tab displaying the codes for my sample page. You can see the script right in the middle of the page beginning like this: `<SCRIPT LANGUAGE="VBScript">`.

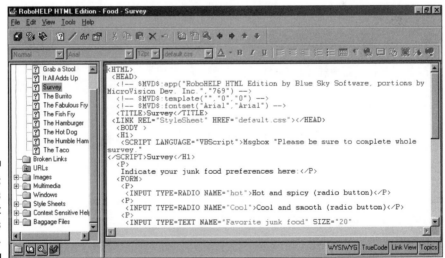

Figure 17-12: Hardy souls can edit their scripts right here.

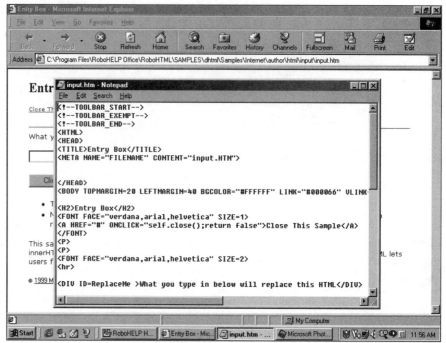

Figure 17-13:
You can
view the
source code
for any
Web page.

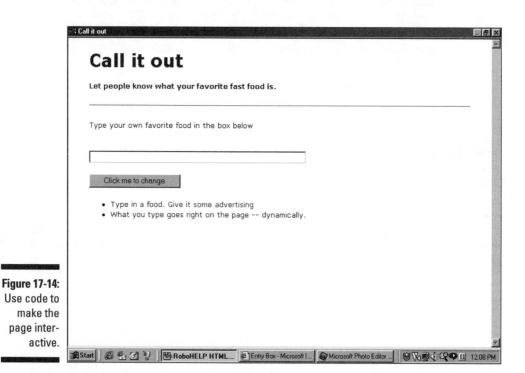

Figure 17-14:
Use code to
make the
page inter-
active.

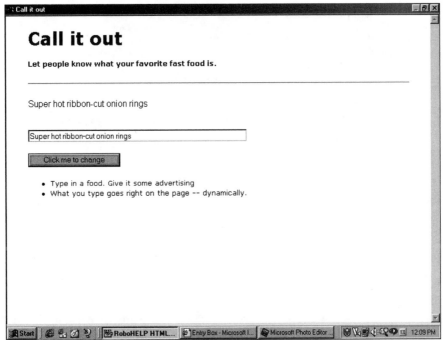

Figure 17-15:
What you
type in is
what comes
out.

Checking Out RoboHELP Classic Macros

WinHelp macros in RoboHELP Classic allow you to insert small programs inside your RoboHELP Classic Program. RoboHELP Classic offers the following macros:

- ✓ **Startup Macros:** These activate when your Help system first opens.
- ✓ **Topic Entry Macros:** These activate when the user displays a particular topic.
- ✓ **Hotspot Macros:** Linking macros that go with a Hotspot. When the user clicks the Hotspot, the macro goes off.

The macros listed above exist already. You can choose to insert them and add parameters to determine how they behave.

To create a startup macro, follow these steps:

1. **Start RoboHELP Classic and open the project you want to work with.**

2. **In RoboHELP Explorer, click File⇨New⇨Startup Macro.**

   The New Startup Macro dialog box appears, as shown in Figure 17-16.

Figure 17-16:
Start here to
build a
macro.

3. **Click the button at the right of the <u>M</u>acro text box.**

The Macro Editor comes up, as shown in Figure 17-17.

Figure 17-17:
Select a
macro for
editing.

4. **Click the <u>W</u>izard button to open the Macro Wizard (shown in Figure 17-18).**

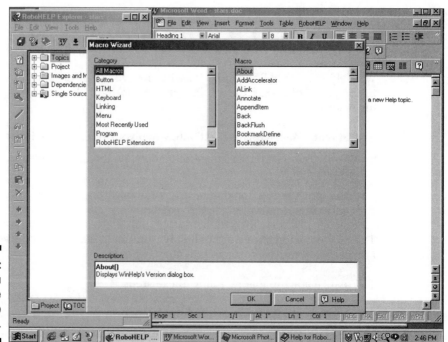

Figure 17-18:
Here you
choose the
macro to
work with.

5. **Select a category from the Category list box or simply accept the default "All Macros" selection. Select a macro from the Macro list box.**

6. **Click OK to close the Macro Wizard dialog box.**

7. **Click OK again to close the Macro Editor.**

8. **Click OK once more to add the New Startup Macro.**

   The new macro appears in the Project/Startup Macros folder in your Project Manager.

Unlike RoboHELP HTML scripts, which employ the widely used VBScript and JavaScript, RoboHELP Classic macros are a language of their own. In other words, RoboHELP Classic macros are a specialized endeavor. Unless you're a programmer already, you probably don't want to invest the time you would need to become effective with them. You may enjoy knowing that the macros are available. You may wish to turn to a programmer buddy to help you accomplish something you have in mind. (See Chapter 25 for the top ten ways to bribe a programmer.) Most of the time, though, you should probably "simply pass by" when you get the urge to get involved with RoboHELP Classic macros, because the complexity may not be worth the trouble for a language that works only with itself.

Part VI

Tidying Up at the End

The 5th Wave   By Rich Tennant

"I tell him many times – get lighter tool kit. But him think he know better. Him have big ego. Him say, 'Me Tarzan! You not!' That's why him vine break."

In this part . . .

The course of true Help authoring rarely runs smoothly. Links get broken or misplaced. References get overdone or forgotten. In a few words, "things go wrong." Even misplaced, unintended, or lost items aren't catastrophic, though, when you have tools to rearrange, fix, or find them. Here you take a long look at tools — most of which you won't use often at the beginning, but many you truly appreciate at the end of a topic or a project.

Chapter 18

Tidying Up Links and References

*Y*ou may discover that using tools from the menu can be very helpful as you go along creating your Help files. You may look occasionally to make sure that you have no broken links, for instance. But as you create a topic, check to make sure its links connect where you want them to connect. If you're working in RoboHELP Classic, make sure that you check periodically on your browse sequence.

In the heat of the battle (or the Help file creation), it's easy to get sidetracked and forget to check and recheck such things. As you finish, you'll probably want to go over your whole project carefully to make sure that your links and references go the way you want them to and that readers won't be getting lost or frustrated.

In this chapter, you see how to check on your links and references and how to fix them up if they are remiss in some way. Also, you discover how to check your topic links and references with the RoboHELP Tools menu.

The term *tools* is so useful that a software programmer can be tempted to use it in many different ways. See Chapter 4 for information on RoboHELP Toolbars. Also, see Chapter 19 to discover RoboHELP Office tools and the Tools tab. The Tools tab allows you to collect programs you use often.

For several of the steps and figures in this chapter, see the sample Help files physiol.hpj and pets.mpj on the accompanying CD-ROM.

Checking HTML Links and References

RoboHELP tools appear as collections of useful icons on a menu. You can use the Tools menu to apply the tools you use most frequently in working with your topics. To use a tool, click the Tools menu and then click the topic that you want. You can use tools to check your links to and from topics or to check all the references to a topic.

Troubleshooting your links

Links give life and meaning to your Help topics. Thanks to links, help users can navigate effortlessly from key topic to key topic to key topic. However, as a Help author, you want to assure that your links take your readers exactly where the links are supposed to take them (and not to someplace silly or irrelevant). You may use the Tools menu to check that your links go where you want them to go and to fix broken links.

Touring your chain of links

You can check your topic links by using the Tools menu and navigating freely among your links to make sure that your topics connect the way you'd like them to.

Here's what to do to check your links:

1. **Start RoboHELP HTML and open a project.**

2. **In Project Manager, click the topic that you want to work with to select it.**

3. **Choose Tools⇨Show Topic Links.**

   RoboHELP opens in Link View, as shown in Figure 18-1. The current topic appears in the middle with connecting topics on the left and linking topics on the right.

In Link View, double-click any topic to display the links coming into and going out from the topic. For instance, Figure 18-2 shows what happens if I click the icon for The Elephant from Figure 18-1.

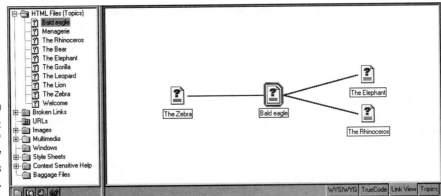

Figure 18-1: RoboHELP will display a topic's links.

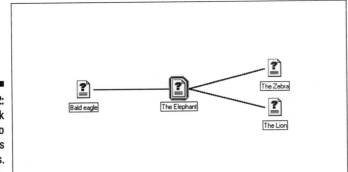

Figure 18-2: Double-click any topic to show its links.

From Link View, you can check the links for any topic. Just drag the topic from Project Manager onto Link View.

Repairing broken links

Links are awesome, but broken links are a disaster. For a Help user, clicking a broken link brings an error message, which is much more disconcerting than finding, say, a simple spelling error.

Broken links happen, generally, when you delete a topic that has links to it. To check for broken links, you can use the Tools menu. Try it.

1. **Start RoboHELP HTML and open a project and a topic.**

2. **Choose Tools⇨Resolve Broken Links.**

   The Resolve Broken Links dialog box appears, as shown in Figure 18-3.

Figure 18-3:
Fix your
broken
links here.

On the left, you see the topic that has a missing reference. The missing topic is on the right.

3. **To fix the broken link, click the Restore button.**

   A dialog box comes up. If the missing file exists, you can restore it — (right-click it in the Broken Links folder and then click Restore). If it doesn't exist, you can create it. (Click the New Topic button, and create the topic.)

4. **Click Close to close the Resolve Broken Links dialog box.**

Just a thought here — I think there ought to be a "fix broken links" utility for modern families. Just click, and a missing member of the family gets back in touch. Click, click, click, and the entire family is complete and harmonious. That would be cool.

You can get reports on many of the possible error conditions by going to the Tools menu and choosing Reports. See Chapter 23 for additional information on the broken links report.

Inspecting all references (not just links)

Links aren't the only references to a topic in your project. (A *reference* is any citation of a topic anywhere in your project.) You also have references in the TOC and the Index. (If you find that you don't have any of the references, you should probably put them in before finishing your Help project altogether.) To check all your references at once, go to the Tools menu and choose Show Topic References.

Verifying references for a specific topic

To check references for a particular topic, select the topic from the Topic List and then choose Tools⇨Show Topic References. Try it:

1. **Start RoboHELP and open a project.**

2. **In Project Manager, select your topic from the HTML Files (Topics) folder.**

3. **Choose Tools➪Show Topic References.**

   The Topic References dialog box shows all references to the topic — links, TOC entries, and Index entries. Figure 18-4 shows the Topic References dialog box for a sample topic.

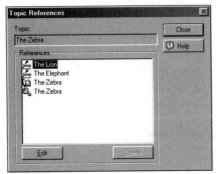

Figure 18-4:
You can
check all
references
to your topic
in one
place.

4. **If you want to close the dialog box, click the Close button.**

You can edit your topic references directly from the Topic References dialog box if you want. (See the following section.)

Editing topic references

To edit topic references for a particular topic, here's what to do:

1. **Start RoboHELP HTML and open a project and then a topic.**

2. **Choose Tools➪Show Topic References.**

   The Topic References dialog box comes up.

3. **Select the reference that you want to work with.**

4. **Click the Edit button.**

   RoboHELP accommodatingly displays the linked topic in the WYSIWYG Editor. You can then remove the link or make whatever changes you wish to the topic.

To clear a hyperlink, right-click the link and then choose Clear Hyperlink.

You may notice the Delete button in the Topic References dialog box. You can't delete jumps or Keyword references from the Topic References dialog box, but you can delete TOC references. Click the TOC reference in the References box and then click the Delete button.

5. **Click the Close button to close the Topic References dialog box.**

Modifying external topic references

External topic references are references to topics in other Help projects. References to such topics don't show up in the Topic References dialog box for a single topic. Nevertheless, you can edit your links to those, also, from within the current topic. Here's what to do:

1. **Start RoboHELP and open a project and topic that you want to work with.**

2. **Choose Tools⇨Edit External Topic References.**

   The External Topic References dialog box comes up, as shown in Figure 18-5.

Figure 18-5: Here you edit references to topics outside your project.

3. **To edit the link to the topic, click the Edit button.**

   You see your topic in the WYSIWYG Editor, where you can remove the link to the remote topic if you want.

If all this talk about external topics makes you want to set up some of your own, turn to Chapter 11 to see how to do so.

Checking references for all HTML topics

At times, you may want to work painstakingly with the references in individual topics. At a late stage in your project, though (and perhaps earlier), you may want to work with your topic references in the entire project.

Here's how to do it:

1. **Start RoboHELP HTML and open or create a project. (Your project should have multiple topics for these steps to be useful.)**

2. **Choose Tools⇨Edit Topic References. The Topic References dialog box comes up, showing the list of All Topics on the right and references to the topic on the left.**

3. **Click any topic in the box on the right to see all references to it on the left, as shown in Figure 18-6.**

4. **Click your topics to check their references.**

5. **Click the Edit button to edit a topic and change any references.**

6. **Click the Delete button to delete a selected TOC reference.**

7. **When you're satisfied with your work, click the Close button to close the dialog box.**

Figure 18-6: Check references for a list of all your topics.

Examining Classic Links and References

Like RoboHELP HTML, RoboHELP Classic has tools for checking your links and references. Also, only in RoboHELP Classic, you can check your *browse sequence* (the sequence the reader follows by simply clicking the browse buttons). To check links and references, use the appropriate options from the Tools menu. To check the browse sequence, use the Tools menu to display the Browse Sequence Editor.

Tracing Classic links

To check the links for a Classic topic, try the following:

1. **Start RoboHELP Classic, open a project, and open a topic.**
2. **Choose Tools⇨Show Topic Links.**

   Your topic opens in Link View.

   Figure 18-7 shows my sample topic in Link View.

Links from the topic appear to the right of the topic, and links into the topic (if any) appear on the left.

You can, if you like, click the << and > buttons in Link View to navigate to the next or preceding topic in the browse sequence.

To view the links for a different topic already displayed in Link View, double-click the topic.

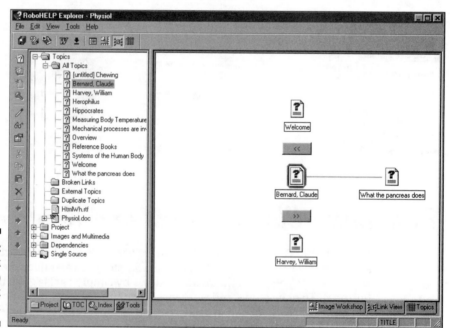

Figure 18-7:
Use Link
View to
check
your links.

Editing topic links

If you don't like something you see when using Link View (I explain how to use Link View in the preceding section), try this out:

1. **Start RoboHELP Classic and open a project and then a topic.**

2. **In Project Manager, right-click the topic and choose Show Topic Links.**

   The topic opens in Link View.

3. **To edit any of the topics in Link View, right-click the topic and then choose Edit.**

   Your cursor shows up inside the topic in Microsoft Word.

To delete a link (Hotspot) in RoboHELP Classic, click the Hotspot and then, choose Edit⇨Delete⇨Hotspot.

To check topic references in Classic, follow the same steps as for RoboHELP HTML. You use RoboHELP Explorer (not Word). You can check jumps, TOC references, Index references, and aliases. In the Topic References dialog box, you can click the Edit button to edit a topic and the Delete button to delete a keyword or alias.

Working with browse sequences

After you compile and run your file, you see the browse sequence, that is, the sequence of your topics as they appear to the reader. You can also see your browse sequence in Link View, explained in the section "Tracing Classic links" in this chapter. You may want to rework your browse sequence. Here's what to do:

1. **Start RoboHELP Classic and open or create a project.**

2. **Choose Tools⇨Browse Sequence Editor.**

   The Browse Sequence Editor dialog box opens.

3. **In the Browse Sequences box, click the plus sign next to any folder to show the topics inside.**

   Figure 18-8 shows a browse sequence in a sample project.

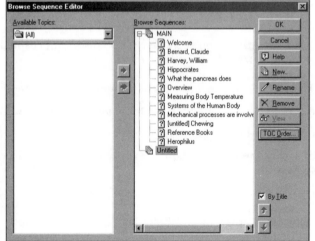

Figure 18-8:
Here you
can work
and rework
your browse
sequence.

You can use the buttons to rename, remove, or view topics. You can also create new browse sequences (using the New button) or view any topic in the Browse Sequences box (by selecting it, then clicking the View button).

4. **To rearrange the sequence, drag topics into the position you desire in the list.**

5. **When you're satisfied with the order of your topics, click OK to close the Browse Sequence Editor.**

When you have your Table of Contents arranged the way you want it, you're likely to want to base your browse sequence on the TOC. You can do so with a couple clicks. From the Browse Sequence Editor, click the TOC Order button and then click OK.

Chapter 19

Tinkering with Special Tools

· ·

In This Chapter

▶ Putting tools in and changing their looks

▶ Finding something in multiple topics and changing it

▶ Writing, directing, and starring in your own video

▶ Inspecting in a cursory way with WinHelp Inspector

▶ Quickly considering PC HelpDesk

· ·

*A*s you're building an HTML or Classic Help file, you probably have plenty to think about just in getting your topics right, putting in links, and getting the index right. You're not likely to be concerned about something like directing your own on-screen video, complete with sound.

You may come to a day, though, when you've mastered enough of the basics, and you want to enhance your skills. RoboHELP offers tools for the skilled user and puts them together in one panel — the Tools panel. (The Tools panel is the fourth tab in from the left, probably because it is in fact the least important and most specialized of the panels available.)

In this chapter, you first see how to use the Tools panel itself by dragging programs into it and setting up the look and feel of the programs. You experiment with some fun RoboHELP HTML tools like Multi-File Find and Replace or the Software Video Camera. You also briefly survey some specialized Classic tools, like WinHelp Inspector.

For several of the steps and figures in this chapter, see the sample file fishing.mpj.

Taming the Tools Tab

On the left side of the screen are a number of tabs. The Tools tab is enticing, with an icon of a red tool chest on it. The Tools tab is noteworthy not only for what it does (namely, contain useful programs) but for what it can do (collect lots of programs for you in one place). In this chapter, you see numerous examples of starting tools from within the Tools panel.

To discover more about using the tabs on the left side of the screen for creating TOCs, project managing, and indexing, see Chapters 8–11.

Opening the Tools tab

Opening the Tools tab is similar to opening any such tab. Try it if you like:

1. **Start RoboHELP HTML and open a project.**

2. **To open the Tools panel, click the Tools tab. (It sports a picture of a tool chest, and is located at the left side of the screen toward the bottom.)**

   The Tools panel opens, as shown in Figure 19-1.

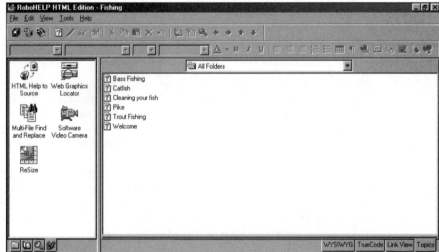

Figure 19-1:
Collect special tools here.

Using tools

The icons in the Tools panel are program icons. Double-click any of them to start a program.

Putting in a new tool

You can add your own additional icons to the Tools panel. Simply use Windows techniques to place a program icon in the panel. Here's what to do:

1. **Start RoboHELP HTML and open a project.**

2. **Click the Tools tab to open the Tools panel.**

3. **Drag a program icon from your Desktop or from Windows Explorer into the panel.**

   The icon appears in the panel, as shown in Figure 19-2.

Figure 19-2:
You can drag pro-gram icons into RoboHELP.

You may feel that you have quite enough programs to deal with already in RoboHELP without adding new ones. However, you may have some standard programs that you use along with RoboHELP, and having them right inside RoboHELP as you work is convenient. Some common programs to put in the RoboHELP toolbox are Microsoft Word, Internet Explorer, and even the icon for RoboHELP Classic.

Adjusting the look of tools

You can deploy your icons in a way that suits you. From the Tools menu, choose Options and set up your Tools icons. Try it out:

1. **Start RoboHELP HTML and open a project.**

2. **Choose Tools⇨Options.**

3. **In the Options dialog box, click on the Tools tab.**

   Figure 19-3 shows the Tools tab in the Options dialog box.

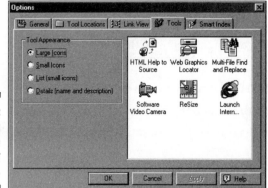

Figure 19-3:
Here you
can change
how your
tools look.

4. **Click to choose the option you want.**

You can try before you buy. When you click a choice in the Tool
Appearance box at the left, a preview of the choice appears in the
Preview box at the right.

5. **When you are satisfied with your choice, click OK to close the dialog
box and apply the choice.**

Trying Special Tools

You can add your own tools to the Tools panel. However, RoboHELP has
placed some neat, advanced tools in the Tools panel for you. You can use a
tool to find and replace multiple topics (which seems like a "must have"). You
can initiate the Web Graphics Locator, which helps you find graphics for your
Help files. You can resize graphics, record videos of your screen activities,
and more.

Performing Multi-File Find and Replace

To replace text across multiple files, use Multi-File Find and Replace. Specify
where you want to search for text and, if you want to replace the text, what
you want to replace it with.

Though you can search and replace in all kinds of files, Multi-File Find and
Replace is particularly useful in RoboHELP for finding and replacing text in
multiple topics.

Though you can search within topics using the RoboHELP Edit menu, you can't search through multiple topics. You have to use Multi-File Find and Replace to do that, which makes the tool quite useful.

Here's what to do to search and replace across multiple files. For example, search multiple topics in a Help file:

1. **Start RoboHELP and open a project.**

2. **Click the Tools tab to open the Tools panel.**

3. **Double-click Multi-File Find and Replace to start the tool.**

   Figure 19-4 shows the Multi-File Find and Replace dialog box.

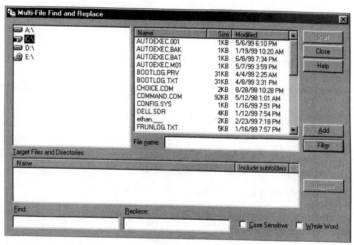

Figure 19-4:
Use the
Multi-File
Find and
Replace
dialog box
to find and
replace mul-
tiple files.

4. **In the list box on the left, navigate to the directory you want to use.**

5. **In the File name box, specify a file.**

6. **Click the Add button to add files to the Target Files and Directories box.**

7. **In the Find text box, type the text you want to search for.**

8. **Click the Start button.**

   The Search Results dialog box displays the results of the search, and a message box tells how many occurrences were found. Figure 19-5 shows the Search Results dialog box.

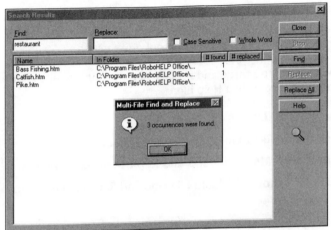

Figure 19-5:
Here you
see the
results of
the search.

9. Click OK to close the message box.

You can follow these steps to replace the text as well. Here's what to do:

1. **Use the MultiFile Find and Replace to find a word, as in the preceding steps.**

2. **With the word you want already displayed in the Find text box, type in the replacement in the Replace box.**

3. **Click Replace All.**

   The find and replace program replaces all the instances, even though they are in different topics.

4. **Click Close to close the Search Results dialog box, and click Close again to close the Multi-File Find and Replace dialog box.**

   You may want to go through and check the replacements to make sure they appear the way you would like.

Looking at Web Graphics Locator

Graphics look great on a Help page. The key to having good graphics, of course, is finding suitable graphics in the first place. You can use Web Graphics Locator to get the job done. See Chapter 6 for real-life examples of using the Web Graphics Locator.

Running ReSize

You can resize an image from within RoboHELP. You can also use a special tool — ReSize — dedicated to resizing images. Here's how to use the tool:

1. **Start RoboHELP and open a project to work with.**

2. **Click the Tools tab and double-click the ReSize icon.**

   The ReSize dialog box shown in Figure 19-6 opens.

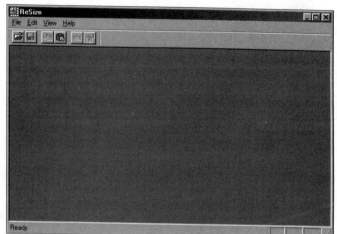

Figure 19-6:
Change the
size of an
image here.

3. **Click File⇨Open.**

   The Open dialog box comes up. Navigate an image that you want to work with.

   To see how to locate images and use the Open dialog box, see Chapter 6. You can find all kinds of clip art on the Web and in Microsoft Office as well as within RoboHELP.

4. **Select an image and click the Open button.**

   The image displays in the ReSize dialog box, as shown in Figure 19-7.

5. **To resize the image, drag the handles (two-headed arrows). Drag the corner handle to resize proportionately. Drag either side to enlarge that side.**

   You can also specify a width, a height, and the unit of measurement to use by working in the Image Properties dialog box that comes up. (Myself, I'd rather drag to a certain size.)

   As a Help author, you may find yourself often working with screen shots. ReSize is a handy tool for doing so. For instance, you can save screen shots in PCX format (PC Paintbrush). You can then open those PCX images in ReSize to work with them.

6. **When you're satisfied with the size of the image, click File⇨Save to save the image and then click File⇨Exit to exit the tool.**

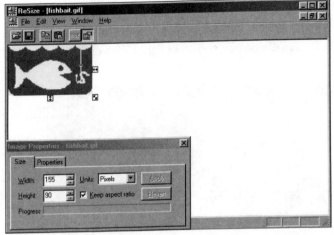

Figure 19-7:
When you
have an
image,
you're
ready to
resize it.

Shooting with Software Video Camera

You can capture not only still images but also actual videos of your activities
on the screen. That is, you can actually walk your users through the steps in
accomplishing something. You use Software Video Camera to do so.

Recording a video

To record a video you use Software Video Camera. After you name the video,
you have an on-screen video to share with Help users. Try it out:

1. **Start RoboHELP and, if you wish, open a project. Click the Tools tab.**

2. **Double-click Software Video Camera to start it. If a message box
   comes up, click OK.**

   Software Video Camera opens, as shown in Figure 19-8.

Figure 19-8:
The video
camera is at
the top left.

You have to set your Display options to 256 colors for Software Video
Camera to work. Use the Windows Control panel to do so. See Windows
Help if you need assistance.

3. **Click the Rec button to start recording.**

Go through the steps you want to capture in your video.

You can put in sound with your video, too. You have to have a sound card and a microphone on your system. Click Setup on the Software Video Camera's playbar and select Capture Audio with Video. It's cool that you can even narrate your video if you want.

4. **Click the Stop button to stop recording.**

5. **In the Save As dialog box shown in Figure 19-9 and type in a name for your video file (a file with the extension .AVI).**

   For example, type the name **start_cat**.

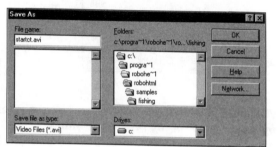

Figure 19-9: Name and save your video.

6. **Click OK to save the video. Software Video Camera creates the file and puts up a message with the results. Click OK.**

You probably ought to practice the steps in your video and write them down before "going live" with your video.

Playing a video

What fun would it be to make a video and not look at it? (Besides, you have to look at it to be sure it came out right.) To play your video:

1. **Start RoboHELP and open a project.**

2. **Click the Tools tab and double-click the Software Video Camera tool.**

3. **In Software Video Camera, click the Play button.**

4. **In the Open dialog box that appears, choose the file you want to play.**

5. **Click the Play button in the lower-right of the AVI file.**

   Figure 19-10 shows my sample video being played.

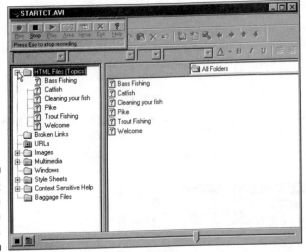

Figure 19-10:
Your video
plays on the
screen.

6. **Close your AVI file box. Then, to close Software Video Camera, click the X at the top-right corner of the program window.**

Software Video Camera doesn't give you tools for editing your video. You can find special products for editing (like Microsoft's VidEdit), but you don't just have them available within the Software Video Camera that comes with RoboHELP. If you don't like the way your video looks, do multiple takes (as they say in the film industry).

For additional information on putting multimedia — including Software Video Camera clips — into your Help pages and starting a film clip from a Hotspot, see Chapter 7.

Glimpsing Classic Tools

RoboHELP Classic has some pretty clever tools that some programming team spent quality time developing. With WinHelp Inspector, you can find out statistics about your WinHelp files. And with PC HelpDesk, you can create a customized electronic HelpDesk — a complete Help system often used to provide technical support. With What's This Help Composer, you can create context-sensitive help for applications.

For information on another tool, you can discover how to convert electronic files into print documents by using the Help-to-Word and Help-to-Source tools in Chapter 20.

These tools are pretty specialized and pretty advanced. If you happen across them, you may find them too enticing simply to pass over altogether. Unless you're an experienced Help author, a programmer, or a glutton for punishment, don't spend much time with them. Maybe scan this section to see what they are and then come back to them later (if at all).

Inspecting with WinHelp Inspector

WinHelp Inspector is sort of a quality assurance worker. You use it to check up on certain information about your Help files, such as what startup macros you're using in each one. The Inspector is useful, for instance, if you want to be sure to use the same startup macros in each of several Help files.

To start WinHelp Inspector, double-click its icon in the Tools tab of RoboHELP Classic. Here's what to do:

1. **Start RoboHELP Classic.**

2. **Click the Tools tab.**

   The Classic Tools panel appears, as shown in Figure 19-11.

Figure 19-11: Use these Tools with RoboHELP Classic.

3. Double-click the WinHelp Inspector icon.

WinHelp inspector opens, as shown in Figure 19-12.

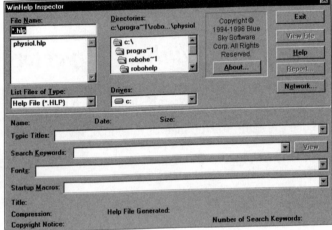

Figure 19-12:
In this one spot you can thoroughly check on your file.

4. In the File Name box, choose a file.

The Inspector shows information on your file. You can see the fonts and the startup macros used.

Press various buttons to check further on the information.

5. To close WinHelp Inspector, click the Exit button in the top-right corner.

In this section, I just give you a glimpse into WinHelp Inspector. If you're curious, motivated, or somewhat technical, go ahead and check out the possibilities on your own.

Hopping around in PC HelpDesk

PC HelpDesk isn't just a tool you may use as you're authoring with RoboHELP Classic. It's an actual authoring tool itself. You use it to present Help information in a HelpDesk format.

Try it:

1. Start RoboHELP Classic.

2. Click the Tools tab and double-click PC HelpDesk.

The PC HelpDesk dialog box opens.

Peeking at What's This Help Composer

What's This Help Composer is a way to create Context-Sensitive Help for your projects — that is, help for a program's controls that people view in a pop-up window. What's This Help Composer automatically generates the pop-up help for the controls in a program and enables you to edit the help and put in your own text.

Though powerful, What's This Help Composer is not widely used. People find it a bit unwieldy and hard to understand. To use it, double-click its icon in the RoboHELP Classic Tools panel. The figure shows the What's This Help Composer dialog box.

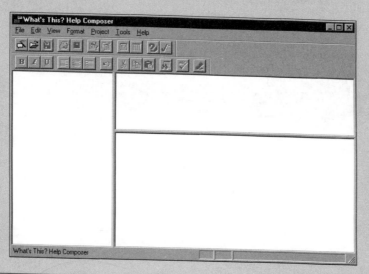

3. **From the HelpDesk File menu, choose a file to open.**

   For example, open sample.phd (a sample HelpDesk database that comes with RoboHELP).

4. **In the Display Topic list on the left side of PC HelpDesk, click the plus sign to display topics. Double-click a topic to open it.**

   Figure 19-13 shows a file open in PC HelpDesk.

5. **From PC HelpDesk, you can create a new PC HelpDesk product and work with a HelpDesk you have already created. The PC HelpDesk program can be useful for an audience that expects it, but it's specialized (and a bit dated).**

6. **To close PC HelpDesk, choose File⇨Exit.**

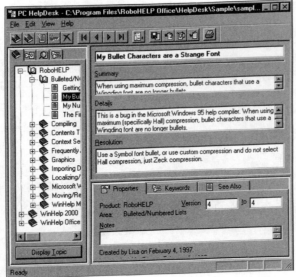

Figure 19-13:
Use PC
HelpDesk to
create your
own PC
HelpDesks.

Chapter 20

Getting Converted: Intranet, Print, Netscape NetHelp

•••

In This Chapter

▶ Going wild and woolly on your own intranet

▶ Getting into print from HTML Help

▶ Breaking into print Classic style

▶ Making Classic files into Netscape NetHelp 2 files

▶ Trying Blue Sky Software's tantalizingly named "Single-Source" technology

•••

*T*he world can be a rich and varied place. Sometimes, knowing what you want to say just isn't enough. You need to say it in a form that your audience can understand. In the world of Help authoring, for one thing, you need to address the needs of those who want to hold a printed page in their hands as they get Help. In other words, you sometimes (make that *usually*) must convert your Help files into printed documentation. You may also find yourself by necessity converting your Help files into other formats as well, such as Netscape NetHelp. Often you may even want to prepare your Help files for display on the company intranet.

In this chapter, you see how to create intranet Help on RoboHELP HTML and then face all kinds of converting tasks — to print, to print from Classic, and to Netscape NetHelp.

Creating Intranet Help

Intranets form great universes of their own — company networks in Web format. You can put information onto the intranet for everyone else in your company to see, but you don't need to worry about random Web surfers coming along to read company information. RoboHELP is a handy tool for putting information on an intranet. With RoboHELP, you're simply creating general intranet information pages that you happen to create using RoboHELP. Once you've created the intranet content, save it as WebHelp (Blue Sky Software's browser-independent Help format, which I discuss in Chapter 13). By using RoboHELP, you can easily perform tasks (like creating a handy Table of Contents) that maybe aren't so easy without it. Following are some examples of RoboHELP features that you may want to use on an intranet:

✔ Expandable, collapsible table of contents

✔ Multilevel index (with cross-references)

✔ Pop-up windows

✔ Ads for your yard sale or your kid's lemonade stand (always intranet favorites)

✔ Related topic buttons

✔ Links, image Hotspots, and fun stuff that helps people navigate

✔ Sizzling Dynamic HTML

If any employees at your company aren't using Internet Explorer 4.0 or a later version, those people can't appreciate your "sizzling Dynamic HTML" and some other features. The Dynamic HTML won't display in its dynamic form but instead as mere, flat text. Check with your company's Web/network guru to make sure that you design your intranet stuff right for your company.

Getting started — the intranet template

If you want to build a special intranet Help file, you can start by using the RoboHELP intranet template. (Of course, if you want, you can just take an existing RoboHELP Help file and put it on your intranet.)

If you start with the intranet template, you may want to import RoboHELP HTML files, RoboHELP Classic files, or other materials into your intranet Help Project. (I discuss importing in Chapter 13.)

To use the intranet template, just follow these steps:

1. **Double-click its icon on the Desktop to start RoboHELP HTML.**

2. **In the RoboHELP HTML Edition dialog box that appears, select the Create a new Help Project radio button and click OK.**

   The New Project dialog box appears.

3. **Select the Intranet icon.**

   Selecting the Intranet icon selects the intranet template for use in creating your Help Project. Figure 20-1 shows the New Project dialog box with the Intranet icon selected.

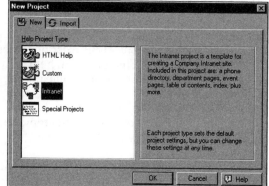

Figure 20-1:
Select the
Intranet
icon to
begin creat-
ing a Help
system for
your
intranet.

4. **Click OK to open the Create a New Project dialog box.**

5. **Type a name for the Project in the Enter the title of this Help project box, a filename in the Enter the filename for the project text box, and a title into the Enter the title of the first topic box.**

6. **Click the Finish button.**

   RoboHELP creates your intranet Project and displays its first topic (see Figure 20-2) in the RoboHELP HTML WYSIWYG Editor. You're off to a flying start in creating a nifty intranet site.

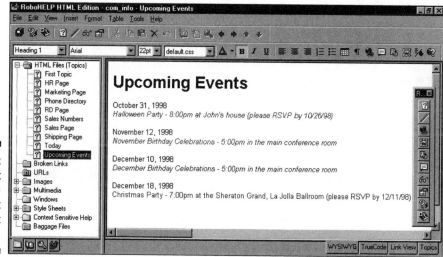

Figure 20-2:
Start right
off by creat-
ing your first
intranet
Help Topic.

Checking out the template pages

Templates are time savers. If you use RoboHELP's intranet template, you discover yourself customizing and deleting some of the existing topics and adding many of your own. The pages in the template can help get you in the mood for creating an intranet Help file, however, and some of the pages may adapt quite readily to your own uses.

To check out any template page, you just double-click the topic name in the HTML Files (Topics) list. Try it out by following these steps:

1. **Start RoboHELP and create a new Project by using the intranet template, as I describe in Steps 1 through 6 in the preceding section.**

2. **Click the plus sign next to the Project to expand the HTML Files (Topics) folder.**

3. **Double-click any topic in the expanded list that appears beneath the HTML Files (Topics) folder to see the sample text included in the intranet template.**

   For examples, see Figures 20-3, 20-4, and 20-5.

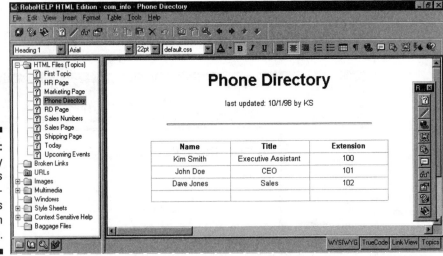

Figure 20-3: Everybody forgets phone numbers. This information can help.

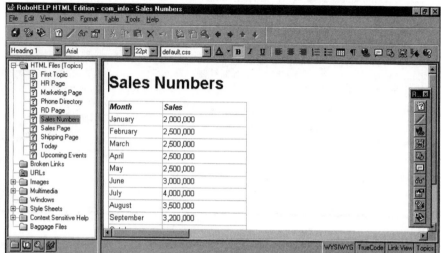

Figure 20-4:
Inspire (or depress) people with your real sales numbers.

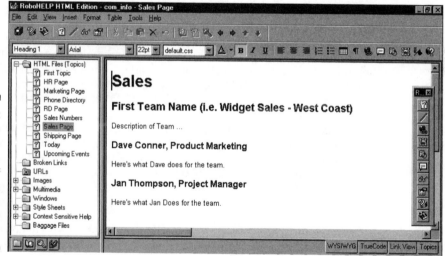

Figure 20-5:
Help people come to know the members of your sales team with this information.

Thinking about WebHelp

Check with your networking manager to determine whether you can use Microsoft HTML Help directly on your intranet.

If you know that everyone in your company uses Microsoft Internet Explorer 4.0 or later, you can simply place your files on the intranet as HTML Help.

WebHelp is a RoboHELP technology for cross-platform Help. If people are using Netscape Navigator or other browsers instead of Internet Explorer, you can accommodate everyone by saving your intranet files as WebHelp. WebHelp systems are also deployable on Unix and Macintosh computers, as well as Windows.

See Chapter 13 for all the steps that you need to create WebHelp.

Going to Print by Using HTML

Going from your electronic HTML Help pages to printed documentation can become a source of some confusion. Going to printed documents is often a source of outright denial. People tend to accept the idea that making printed documentation is automatic and effortless, and they don't find out otherwise until they're at the end of the project, the shipping date looms, and people are looking at them expectantly for the final product. RoboHELP offers a way to get from electronic HTML to print. To convert your HTML Help to printed documents, you must use RoboHELP's HTML Document Wizard.

The actual steps for converting from HTML Help to printed document are quite easy. The complete, formal process of getting it right, however, takes time. You may find that you have to spend much more time than expected to get your printed doc to look right. (You can read more about printed documents in the list of "Ten Things You Should Have Asked Yourself Before Starting," in Chapter 24.)

To convert an HTML Project to printed documentation, you need to open the Project in RoboHELP HTML and then use the HTML Document Wizard to make the conversion. Follow these steps:

1. **Start RoboHELP HTML and open the Project you wish to work with.**

2. **Choose File⇨Single Source Output⇨Printed Documentation from the RoboHELP menu bar.**

   The Document Wizard rears its helpful little head, as shown in Figure 20-6.

3. **Choose a path and a filename for your printed documentation. Click the arrow to the right of the box that says Specify path and filename for the printed documents. Or just click to accept the default suggestion.**

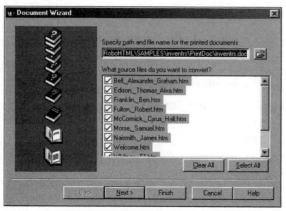

Figure 20-6:
Start in this
first dialog
box of the
Document
Wizard to
convert your
HTML Help
files to print.

4. **In the What source files do you want to convert? list box, select the files to convert and then click Next. (All the source files are already selected.) If there are some files you don't want to convert, click them to deselect them.**

The Style Sheet dialog box appears, as shown in Figure 20-7.

Deciding what style sheet to use for your printed document — or even whether to use one at all — isn't as earth shaking as it may at first appear. Whether *you* choose to use a specific style sheet or to forego one, RoboHELP goes ahead and uses the styles from your HTML Topic. But if you do choose to use a style sheet, RoboHELP creates a Word template (a DOT file) that affords all the advantages of such a template (one advantage being that you can use this style sheet for multiple documents). If you choose not to use a style sheet, RoboHELP uses your document formatting but doesn't create a Word template.

Figure 20-7:
The Style
Sheet dialog
box enables
you to
decide
which style
sheet to use
for your
printed
document.

Chapter 16 is the place to bone up on style sheets. You can find out a good bit there about HTML style sheets and a tiny, insignificant amount about Word document templates. To find out everything you ever wanted to know about Word templates, turn to the appropriate *Word For Windows For Dummies* book published by IDG Books Worldwide, Inc. (depending on the version of Word you're using, there are several).

5. **Click the appropriate radio button — either Use Style Sheet (the default) or Use Topic Formatting — and then click Next.**

   If you accept the default, you don't have to choose a special style sheet. (You can choose one, though. Click the folder icon to the right of the Use Style Sheet list box, and click the one you want.) If you choose Use Topic Formatting, you don't have to do anything more. (Your printed file uses the same formatting as your Help file.)

   The Document Wizard now displays the TOC and Index dialog box, as shown in Figure 20-8. You decide here whether to have a Table of Contents and an Index for your printed document. You're probably going to elect to add them now unless you prefer to use Word tools to create them later. If you spent a good deal of time structuring the table of contents and index in your HTML Help files, go ahead and use them for your printed document.

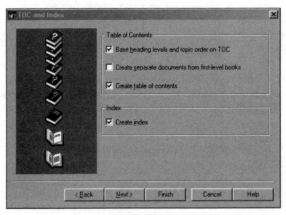

Figure 20-8:
Decide
whether you
want the
Wizard to
create a
printed TOC
and Index
for your
document.

6. **Make your selections for TOC and Index by selecting or deselecting the appropriate check boxes and click Next.**

   For example, you can accept the suggested default settings — Base heading levels and topic order on TOC, Create table of contents, and Create index — which chooses to have the printed TOC's heading levels and topic order like the electronic version, to generate a TOC and an index.

In the TOC and Index dialog box, you can choose to create separate documents from the first level books in your HTML Help Project. (Each first level book then appears in a separate .DOC Word file.) If you have long topics and quite a few of them in each book, you may want to use this option.

The Text Color and Images dialog box appears, as shown in Figure 20-9.

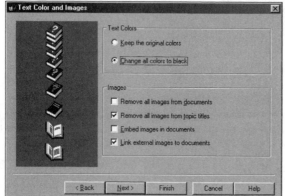

Figure 20-9:
Choosing
your text
color and
images.

7. **Make your choices in the Text Color and Images dialog box and click Next. You can keep original colors or include or remove images.**

   As for colors, if you're using a black-and-white printer, I suggest that you use the default choice of Change All Colors to Black. You may want to include images within the text but remove images from topic titles as the default settings recommend. If you link external images to your documents (also a default setting), you display the images that appear in your HTML Help files in your printed document.

   The Page dialog box now appears, as shown in Figure 20-10.

8. **In the Page dialog box, choose the options you want for your printed pages by selecting or deselecting the appropriate check boxes and then clicking Finish.**

   You can choose to add page numbers to your documents (very useful on the printed page) or insert a page break after each topic, which nicely starts each topic on a new page. (You can even choose to insert a page break after each book, but you probably get that effect anyway if you have breaks after your topics.) If you want, you can even tinker with your page size by clicking the Page Setup button (which opens the Page Setup dialog box, refer to Figure 20-10). The default setting is for standard 8½-by-11-inch office paper.

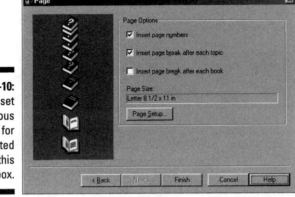

Figure 20-10:
You can set
up various
options for
your printed
pages in this
dialog box.

The Document Wizard converts your HTML file to Microsoft Word documentation. A message box appears onscreen to tell you that the Conversion is complete.

9. **Click the View Result button at the bottom of the message box to see your printed documentation.**

Figure 12-11 shows the table of contents for the sample file inventrs.doc that I created. RoboHELP opens up Word automatically so you can view the printed documentation.

Table of Contents

Figure 20-11:
The printed
sample of
your Help
file's Table
of Contents.

Going to Print in Classic

You can use a Wizard to take you from your Classic Help files to printed documentation, just as you can in RoboHELP HTML, as I describe in the preceding sections. The Wizard guides you as you make decisions about the index, Table of Contents, and images. To do so, just follow these steps:

1. **Double-click its icon to Start RoboHELP Classic, click a project and then click OK in the Open a Help Project dialog box to open the Project that you want to save as printed documentation.**

2. **Choose File⇨Generate⇨Printed Documentation from the menu bar in RoboHELP Explorer.**

   The Documentation Wizard dialog box opens, as shown in Figure 20-12.

3. **On the first page of the Documentation Wizard, select the files that you want to convert and then click Next.**

   All files are selected initially. Click to remove the check mark for any files you don't want to convert.

   The second page of the Wizard opens, where you make choices related to the TOC and index of your printed versions.

Figure 20-12:
This Documentation Wizard guides your conversion from RoboHELP Classic Help file to printed document.

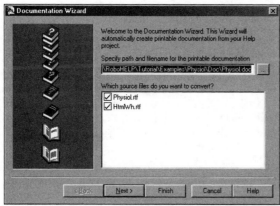

4. **On the second page of the Wizard, choose whether to base your heading levels and Topic Order on the CNT file.**

   Yes is already selected, unless you haven't created a Table of Contents and, therefore, a CNT file.

   The *CNT file* is your table of contents file. If you set up your TOC in the Help file, choosing the default selection of Yes here should serve you well. On this page, you also choose whether to create a TOC and index.

Converting to print may take, uh, some time

You can't really prepare for a shock — because it's not a shock if you're prepared. You're likely to be shocked as you face the reality of the printed documentation that you make from HTML Help. The conversion takes only two minutes; the cleanup and reconversion that you probably may face, however, may take two weeks or more. You may have to work with style sheets, add to topics or change them, or rework the index. The following list describes some of the things you need to consider:

✔ What if you don't like the look the style sheet creates after the printed documentation comes out in print? (The style sheet includes fonts, background graphics, and the like.) You must then work and rework the style sheet until it comes out right (which could take days).

✔ What if some of the topics are too short and don't look good starting on a separate page. You may want to work some more with page breaks to compensate for such problems (which could also take days).

✔ You may rely on links to create the right flow in your Help file. Links, however, don't work in printed documentation. You may end up working and reworking the table of contents to get the right flow (which could take, oh, a couple more days).

✔ *See Also* references (which are a form of link), don't work the same way in printed documentation. You need to spend some additional time getting them to work.

✔ Printed documents cry out for screen shots. You may not have screen shots at all in your HTML files, where people can often just switch windows to look back at their own screens to see what your Help file is discussing. Figure that you're going to need some more time to add additional visuals to the printed versions.

✔ Don't forget about taking lunch breaks, going to your kid's school play, scheduling some much needed mental-health downtime, and compensating for simple human error. Figure in some more lost time for such tasks.

✔ What about reworking the Word template while you're at it? Yes, the Wizard can create a Word template for you, as I explain in this chapter. But can you really resist reworking it to your own specifications? *Should* you resist? Plan on spending some more time to get hands-on with your template.

✔ As you rework your printed documentation, maybe you realize, too, that you need to do some things differently in the HTML Help files themselves. (Did I say that?) Sometimes you can feel as if you *never* finish your entire Help Project. (But you do. You do . . . eventually.)

5. **Click the Do you want to create documents from Books in the CNT File? check box to clear the check mark, deselecting the option, and then click _N_ext to access the next page of the Wizard.**

   By deselecting this option, you create just one file for your printed documentation. Otherwise, you end up with one file for every first level Book in your CNT file, which means the hassle of dealing with multiple files.

6. **Make your choices about the color and graphics to appear in your printed documentation by clicking radio buttons and check boxes, and then click _N_ext to access the next Wizard page.**

   Saving graphics inside your document file can make for an unwieldy file and can cause problems in the printed documents. You're probably better off accepting the default and not saving graphics inside the Word documents.

7. **Make your choices about page numbers and page size on this page of the Wizard by selecting the appropriate check boxes.**

   For the example, I accept the defaults — insert page numbers and use standard 8½-by-11-inch paper.

8. **Click the Finish button.**

   RoboHELP converts your Help file to a Word document. A message box appears to tell you that the conversion is complete (see Figure 20-13).

Figure 20-13:
This message box tells you your Help file's ready to print.

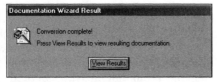

9. **Click the _V_iew Results button at the bottom of the message box.**

   RoboHELP opens up another copy of Word to display the printed documentation it created, as shown in Figure 20-14.

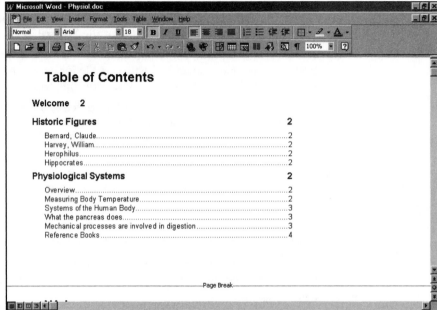

Figure 20-14:
RoboHELP
creates nice
Word docu-
mentation
for you.

"Single Sourcing" Some Netscape Help

Most Help authors are likely to create printed documentation. In various situations, however, you may need to create other kinds of output as well. RoboHELP addresses the need for creating varying kinds of output with its *Single-Source* solution. By using Single Source, you use the one source that you create automatically — your Help file. From that file, you can then create other kinds of output if needed (such as Windows CE Help or Netscape NetHelp).

By using RoboHELP HTML, the Single Source feature enables you to create either WebHelp files or printed documentation. (In Chapter 13, I discuss creating WebHelp and in the section "Going to Print by Using HTML," earlier in this chapter, I show you how to create printed documentation from RoboHELP HTML.) By using RoboHELP Classic, you can use this feature to create WinHelp 3, WebHelp, Microsoft HTML Help, Netscape Help, and a few other forms of Help. (In Chapter 13, I discuss creating HTML Help from Classic Help, and in the preceding section of this chapter, I show you how to create printed documentation from Classic Help.)

To create your alternative form of Help from a Classic Help file, you simply choose File➪Generate from the RoboHELP Explorer menu bar and then choose the form of output you want from the Generate submenu. To generate Netscape Help from Classic Help, for example, follow these steps:

1. **Click its icon to start RoboHELP Classic and, in the Open a Help Project dialog box during startup, click to open a project that you want to save as a Netscape file. Click OK.**

2. **In RoboHELP Explorer, choose File⇨Generate⇨Netscape NetHelp 2 from the RoboHELP Explorer menu bar.**

   The Creating NetHelp 2.0 dialog box appears, as shown in Figure 20-15. You can choose a style sheet in this dialog box by clicking its name if you want or just accept the default settings. Unless you deselect the two choices at the bottom of the list, RoboHELP will convert bulleted lists and numbered lists to HTML style bulleted and numbered lists.

3. **Choose a style sheet and then click Next or just click Next to accept the default settings.**

   The HTML Conversion Options dialog box appears. You can change your Help file options in this dialog box if you want, such as adding a Browse button to the Help file that enables users to follow a *browse sequence* that you set up. (The best place to read about browse sequences in this book is in Chapter 18.) If you choose to have the Browse buttons, you can indicate where to put them. If you accept the suggested setting for changing white in graphics to transparent, the white areas in the graphics will appear in the color of the paper you print on. For the example, I just accept the suggested settings.

Figure 20-15: Start here to generate Netscape Help.

3. **Click Finish.**

   Single Source creates the Netscape Help file. A Results dialog box appears telling you what files you created, as shown in Figure 20-16.

Figure 20-16:
This Results
dialog box
tells you
how the
Netscape
conversion
went.

4. Click the OK button to view your results.

Netscape NetHelp starts and displays the Help file. Figure 20-17 shows
my sample file in NetHelp.

The need for a special form of output may come up unexpectedly. A new
client may be using an older browser, or a client may want to display Help
files on a palmtop computer that uses Windows CE. Have no worries:
RoboHELP does all the converting for you; you simply need to follow some
simple steps in the Wizard. In RoboHELP Classic's RoboHELP Explorer, click
the Single Source folder in Project Manager and choose a form of output.

Figure 20-17:
You can
view your
converted
file in
Netscape
NetHelp.

Part VII
The Part of Tens

The 5th Wave   By Rich Tennant

"Well heck, all the boy did was launch a search in RoboHELP and up comes Tracy's retainer, your car keys, and my bowling trophy here on a listing in Seattle!"

In this part . . .

*L*ists — how can anybody be organized without them? Without lists, you forget key things. Here you can indulge in a phantasmagoria of lists. You can see neat things to add to a Help project (one or two of which you might otherwise have neglected). You can contemplate scintillating Web techniques. You can reflect rather seriously on what you should do in a Help file and what you should have done. Above all, you see a carefully researched, psychologically sound catalogue of tips on influencing technogeeks.

Chapter 21

My Ten Favorite Things to Add to a Help Project

*T*he items in this ten-favorite list are just "ticklers" for you. Check them over as you make decisions about your RoboHELP project and see whether you find any items that look particularly important to your project or fun for you. I talk about these favorites in the order that I consider most important for creating a useful Help system, so try using the list to set priorities for your own systems.

Topics

I suppose that this first entry in my favorites list is of the "duh" variety. You can't build a Help project without topics. Still, I love to click the New Topic button and create a topic on the spot. Creating a good selection of topics is the heart of every good Help system. Check out Chapter 3 for the whole story on topics.

Table of Contents

The TOC doesn't just happen. You have to make it happen. To be honest, I like that feature of RoboHELP. Lovingly constructing the TOC gives me (and you!) a chance to get organized and gives the Help system a logical outline. While building your TOC, you can plan the books and subbooks and put the Help topics where they belong. Don't you just love it that you can drag and drop TOC items?

Text Links

When you're creating a Help system, do you find yourself thinking, "What goes with what?" or "How can I get my reader where he or she wants to go?" I find it really fun to allow users to click the mouse and find themselves in a completely different topic — as if they've just clicked their heels together and been transported. Adding text links to your Help system lets you achieve this magic for your users. Chapter 11 tells you how to add and maintain text links in your Help system.

Index

The index isn't that much fun early in the project. It's okay, and I like thinking about the best way to index each topic. But I love going in at the end of the project to set up all kinds of index signposts so that almost anybody can find almost anything. You can be particularly cool if you set up Always Ignore lists and, especially, synonyms. For example, imagine rescuing a Help system user who can't remember the word *mastodon* but can find the topic by clicking *prehistoric elephant*.

Styles

Don't you like adding boldface, italics, large point sizes, indentations, numbered lists, centered text, colored text, and so much more? Using a variety of text styles adds visual appeal and entices the Help system user. Special styles can call attention to this content, mute the importance of that content, and play a symphony on the unsuspecting emotions of the reader. Styles are good.

Style Sheets

The problem with styles is that you can lose your Help system's uniform look by using too many styles, changing the style on parallel elements, and (if you use multiple style sheets) having the same style look different in different topics. Often, if I really like a style — such as a point size or a font — I'll immediately go to the style sheet to make that nice-looking style into a standard throughout my project. Also, style sheets are helpful at the end of a project when you want to play with the appearance of elements throughout the whole Help system. Check out Chapters 5 and 16 for the rundown on using styles and style sheets.

A Frog

I hate to ship a Help system without putting a frog in the box. Kidding.

Links to Web Pages

Links, links, links. I think that people are lazy — like me. They don't particularly like even having to reference the index or table of contents. They are reading "right here, right now," and that's where they want to stay. Clicking on a link, though, feels like staying "right here." And that's why I include Web page links among my ten favorite Help system elements. You can let your users be lazy and still give them the help they need. A link to a Web page can take your users to distant information that many would never bother to track down on their own. Also, I encourage using pop-up links, because people really don't have to leave the current page (and risk getting lost in the maze of links) to find out some juicy bit of information like a definition.

Author confession: I had to squeeze the information on popup links in with my discussion of Web page links because I used up one of the ten precious slots with my "frog" entry.

Bookmarks

I don't especially like bookmarks in themselves. You can use bookmarks in word processing programs, and I don't think I ever find the occasion to do so. In Help systems, though, bookmarks are another story. Often you want to have headings and subheadings within a single topic. Bookmarks allow your users to click a link and jump directly to those subheadings. That's good (and efficient for your users, too). The longer the topic, the more useful bookmarks become.

Links from Images

I don't have any problem listing links from images as number ten in importance. Your Help project can live if you don't ever make your images "clickable." Most people would admit, though, that it's fun to click an image and go to explanatory information about it. Chapter 7 gives you more information about using graphics and links to benefit the Help system user.

Chapter 22

Ten Favorite, Fun Web Techniques

● ●

In This Chapter

▶ Reviewing glitzy stuff that looks neat but isn't hard to do (usually)

▶ Reflecting on why you may (and may not) use scripts

▶ Checking out the power of ActiveX

▶ Getting colorful and pictorial

▶ Seeing why you may (and may not) use marquees

● ●

*T*he Web techniques that I present in this chapter are mostly for fun. Deadline-conscious Help authors often don't have time to play with and enjoy them. That's okay. Your Help project can usually live (and function just fine) without adding special elements. However, you can get creative with these things and brighten the sometimes humdrum lives of your Help system viewers. For example, you can liven up the Help experience with sound and video, or offer that next tidbit of information via a clickable image. Sometimes the techniques open up whole new worlds of possibilities, such as gathering information from your Help users via scripts. (Although these are Web techniques, many of them apply to RoboHELP Classic, too.)

Scripts

The term *script* is a polite, modest way of saying *program*. Scripting languages may not have all the power of full programming languages, but they are programming languages nonetheless. The bad part of that story is that, unless you're a programmer yourself, you probably can't do much with scripts. The good part is that, if you are a programmer or know one who can help, you can put applications right on your Help pages. For example, you can collect the user's name and job preference to place in a database, by adding the appropriate script to your Help system. Chapter 17 talks about other applications that you can use scripts for. (Macros are the RoboHELP Classic counterpart to Scripts. I talk about them briefly in Chapter 17.)

ActiveX Controls

ActiveX controls, like scripts, are a lot of power in a small space. They're programs; but in the case of ActiveX controls, they're prepackaged programs. You don't, thank goodness, have to code them. You can put ActiveX controls into your Help topics to include calendars, calculators, and all kinds of neat things for your Help system users. The only catch is that you do have to install the ActiveX controls on your system before you can use them. See Chapter 17 for information on installing and using ActiveX controls.

Multihotspot Images

The best way to show the versatility of multihotspot images is to give you an example. So, here goes. Suppose that — as an element of your Help system— you have a picture of the human brain with various Hotspots marked. The Help system user can click one spot to go to a topic about the thalamus, another spot to go to a topic about the cerebellum, and a third spot to go to a topic about the cerebral cortex. That's neat, and it's also an intuitive way to lead your users to helpful information.

Images

Pictures are great. Talking about a whale is one thing. Talking about it with a picture of a whale to refer to is quite something more. Talking about the topography of Asia can get rather confusing. Talking about it with a map on hand isn't confusing at all. So what does this discussion of images mean to you as you create your RoboHELP Help system? Chapter 6 tells you how to include pictures in RoboHELP HTML or Classic, how to put in cool things like borders and backgrounds, and how to resize or even crop an image.

Backgrounds

Nobody says all paragraphs and pages have to have white backgrounds. Perhaps your company image calls for a gentle teal, shocking red, or even plaid. You can often add class to a Help page by adding a background. Use the formatting and style sheet features in RoboHELP (see Chapters 5 and 16) to bring this ornamental spice to your Help systems.

Multimedia

Sound. Video. Sound and video together. These items are hard to beat for bringing entertainment and an alternative presentation style to your RoboHELP Help systems. Just as adding images to a Help topic may increase a user's understanding, multimedia may provide that extra tidbit that really gives your topic life. But use multimedia carefully: Your computer equipment (or your reader's browser) may not support these elements. If the equipment is right, though, the effect is just great.

Dynamic Hotspots (Expanding)

Things get fun when you start to get dynamic. Expanding Hotspots in RoboHELP HTML Edition work much like popups in RoboHELP Classic. Users click these Hotspots to get additional information, like definitions, in the form of text that appears when the user clicks the Hotspot. You can find information on adding dynamic Hotspots to your Help system in Chapter 15.

Dynamic Hotspots 2 (Drop-Down)

Drop-down Hotspots are good for showing lists. For example, when a Help system user clicks a phrase like *tree house*, the drop-down Hotspot might show the steps for building one:

1. **Find the wood your Dad has set aside for the new addition.**
2. **Use this wood to try to build the tree house yourself.**
3. **Get your Dad to build it.**
4. **Grow up really fast and never use it any more.**

Special Effects

Drop shadows look cool. Text that flies into the page before taking its place will probably elicit a smile. Text that fades in can make the Help system users feel that they're in a movie theater. You can have your text glow when people mouse over it. The term *special effects* hardly means what it does in *Star Wars* or anything, but using Web-type special effects can be fun. See Chapter 15 for ideas on including special effects in your Web pages. With a little thought, you can use them to bring out the meaning of your Help system text.

Marquee

A *marquee* is text that scrolls across your Web page again and again. Marquees are fun at first but can tend to grow old because of their constant repetition. Try one for amusement, or when you really need to reinforce an idea presented by your Help system text, but don't get hooked.

Chapter 23

Ten Things to Check Before Finishing Help Files

*B*eing at the end of a project is satisfying, even though often you have to work intensively for days on end before you really finish. At a certain point, though, you know you will finish, and you go through your Help project, "cleaning up" and putting things in order.

Finishing up can take longer than the project itself, or so it may seem. The old rule says, "80 percent of the work gets done in 20 percent of the time." Then you spend that last 80 percent of the time doing what looks like 20 percent of the work. What you do in that last phase, though, makes the difference between a lackluster project and a "*have-luster*" project.

RoboHELP gives you great clues on what to do at the end. For example, just choose Tools⇔Reports. (In Classic, use RoboHELP Explorer — on the left of the screen — to make the same choices.) The submenu (shown for RoboHELP HTML in Figure 23-1) lists all the things you ought to review at the end of your project and provides reports on them besides.

In this list, you get a handy reminder of what elements to check at the end of the RoboHELP project — everything from your TOC and Index to broken links. You'd probably remember most of them anyway, and they're all important. So, refer to the Reports submenu for a reminder on checking out your links or reviewing the index.

For the steps in this chapter, see the sample file pets.mpj.

Is the Overall Look Right?

First, just compile and run your project; then stand back and look at it. Be innocent. Have an open mind. Play with the Help system a little, the way a user would. Open some topics, and click some links. For example, Figure 23-2 shows my file Islands.mpj when I compile and run it.

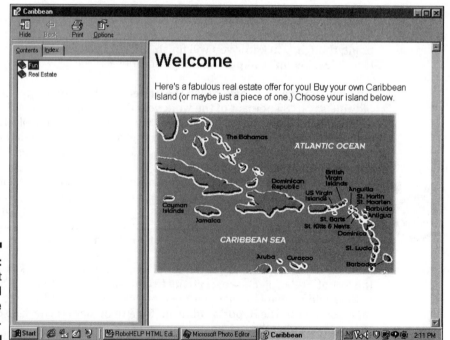

Figure 23-2:
Check out
the overall
look of the
Help file.

Chances are, you'll get lots of ideas for enhancing the Help system as you look over it. Maybe you'll want to change the images that you use. Maybe you'll think of topics to add or delete. Maybe you'll want to adjust the style sheet. Help authors spend lots of time tinkering with the look of their Help files.

Is the Topic Content Good?

A Help author is, in the final analysis, a Topic author. In the topics is where you put real information. The topics is where users plunge in to get real answers. Also, the experts you work with will be rather touchy about what you put into the topics; they'll want the content to be accurate. Read through the topic content to get it right.

Be sure to check spelling in your topic content. Readers love to pounce on spelling mistakes as evidence of carelessness. Here's how to check your spelling:

1. **Start RoboHELP HTML, open a project, and double-click a topic in the Topic List to open the topic in WYSIWYG view.**

2. **Choose Tools⇨Spelling.**

   The Spell Check dialog box appears.

3. **When spell checking at the end of your project, as in this case, be sure to click the Whole document option.**

   Figure 23-3 shows the Spell Check dialog box with Whole document selected.

Figure 23-3:
Spell check
your whole
document.

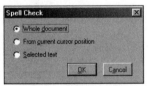

To check spelling in Classic, open a topic, then click Tools in the Word menu (right side). Choose Spelling and Grammar, then use the Word spell checker.

And the Topic References? Good?

You refer to your topics several ways — namely, with links, in the table of contents and in the index. As you're creating the topics, you have a lot more to think about than whether or not the references are the way you want them. At the end of your Help project, as you're seeing the big picture, you can check out your references (in either RoboHELP Classic or RoboHELP HTML). Here's how:

Choose Tools➪Reports➪Topic References.

(You can open the Tools menu regardless of what tab you're working in on the left side — the TOC, Index, or whatever.)

Even more important than topic references, though, could be the lack thereof. After all, the point of electronic Help is for people to be able to find things just about any way they try to do so (Table of Contents, links, index, or whatever they come up with). Here's how to check unreferenced topics:

Choose Tools➪Reports➪Unreferenced Topics.

Figure 23-4, for example, shows the report for my Help file inventrs.mpj. The file was in an early state of development when I captured the figure, so I had lots of topics still unreferenced by links or the Table of Contents. Such a condition is not good, and I should correct the deficiency.

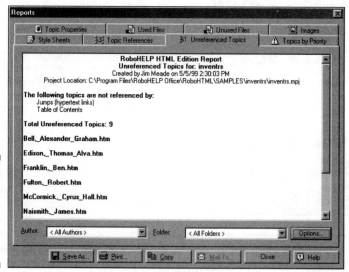

Figure 23-4:
You can find neglected little topics that need references.

Do My Images Fit the Image?

Lots of quirky things can happen to an image you've included in your Help system. Your image may be too big or too small. The colors may look bad.

Images can be out of place or missing altogether. Suppose, for example, that you found a topic like the one shown in Figure 23-5. I've mistakenly placed a picture of bee-eaters in my topic labeled "The Gorilla." This is not good.

Figure 23-5:
If you want a picture of a gorilla, make sure you don't show a bee-eater instead.

Also, you almost certainly want to check the Hotspots on your images. Here's how to check Hotspots:

1. **In the Project panel (left side), click to open the Images folder (Image Workshop).**

2. **Make sure that you see a plus sign next to any image that should have a Hotspot.**

3. **Click the plus sign and then double-click the topic.**

   The Image Map Properties dialog box appears, as shown in Figure 23-6. Use this dialog box to verify that the Hotspot connects to the topic you want it to.

Do I Like My Style Sheet's Style?

If you're working in RoboHELP HTML, you use HTML style sheets. If you're working in RoboHELP Classic, you use Microsoft Word style sheets. Each type of style sheet has its own considerations, but the overall concept is the same. You set up styles in the style sheet that control the look throughout a Help file.

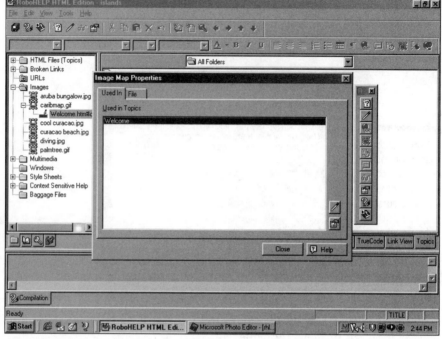

Figure 23-6:
Make sure
your
Hotspots
link to the
topics you
want.

Using a style sheet means that you can change the appearance of your text, headings, background, and so on, throughout your Help file by making the change in one place (in the style sheet, that is). As I mentioned in the first section of this chapter, Help authors spend a lot of time perfecting the overall look of the presentation. Style sheets facilitate the activity of fiddling with overall look. (See Chapter 15 for an extensive coverage of style sheets.)

Are My Links Linking Nicely?

As you work with your topics, you develop a firm idea of what interconnects with what. You're probably going to want to make certain that you've made those obvious connections through your Help system's links.

Here's how to test the links for a given topic:

1. **Open the topic in the WYSIWYG Editor.**

2. **Click the Link View tab at the lower-right.**

   On the Link View tab, you see all the links coming into and out of the topic, as I show in Figure 23-7.

When viewing the links, you can see the overall information flow and determine whether you made the connections you really wanted (and not made others you didn't want).

Test your Hotspots, too. They will show up in Link View. I talk about Hotspots in this chapter in the section, "Do My Images Fit the Image?"

In RoboHELP Classic, you have an additional tool besides Link View. In a compiled file, you can navigate using the Browse buttons in the Help file. And you can edit the browse sequence by choosing Tools⇨Browse Sequence Editor.

What About Reprobate (Broken) Links?

Broken links are a black eye on your Help file. To the observant Help-file viewer, broken links are a bigger faux pas than spelling mistakes. You really don't want to have them in your file.

In the hubbub of creating and revising your Help files, of course, you're probably going to end up causing some broken links.

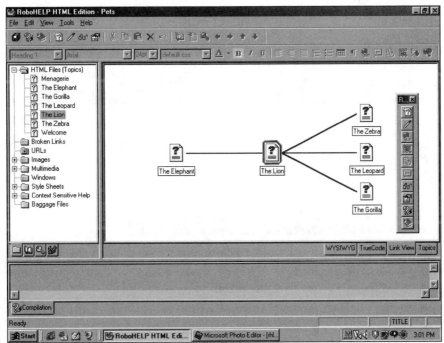

Figure 23-7: Check out the associates (links) of your topics.

You can use these methods to locate your broken links:

- ✔ In the Project pane, on the left side, look in the Broken Links folder to see the broken links.
- ✔ From the main menu, choose Tools➪Reports➪Broken Links for a report on broken links.

The report shows you any broken links and the topics to which they connect. Figure 23-8 reports that I have a broken link to a missing file called Duck_Billed_Platypus.htm.

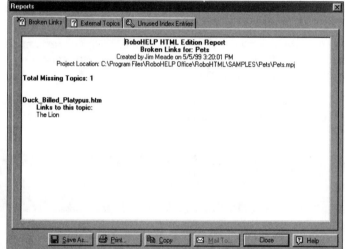

Figure 23-8: You can get a report on broken links.

You can readily restore a missing topic to fix the broken link. Right-click the topic and then choose Restore from the pop-up menu. You can do the same thing in Classic's RoboHELP Explorer.

How Smart Is My Index?

Sure, people love links. And they'll use a Table of Contents, sometimes browsing through the TOC at their leisure. Mostly, though, people look up stuff in your Help file by using the index.

Here are some things about your index to check:

✔ Make sure that all your topics appear in the index at least once.

- **Click Topic View on the right side of your RoboHELP screen and the Index tab on the left side (which is RoboHELP Explorer in Classic).**

- **Take note of topics without an index entry; these appear with a white icon next to them. (All topics with index entries have blue icons.)**

✔ Look for index entries that you haven't used at all (that is, index entries not linked to a topic).

Unused index entries appear in bold type in the Index Designer (left side).

✔ Make sure that you've remembered to sort at the end, putting the index in alphabetical order.

You probably want to check lots of other things about your index, too. Is the capitalization the way you want it? Do you have subkeywords, and do they come in where you want them? Are you making good use of synonyms and antonyms? Do you have good *See Also* references?

Be sure to use the Smart Index Wizard (Chapter 10) to put in keywords from your topics, put in new keywords, and screen out "noise" keywords.

Is My TOC Cool?

The index may be the way for readers to zoom right to a particular topic. But sometimes Help users want to move "from outside in" to find out information about a topic. That is, they may want to look first at the main books, then at books within the books, then at topics.

For such people proceeding in a linear fashion, the TOC is the tool of choice. Click your TOC tab (left side), and make sure that your TOC has a nice, logical flow. Make sure that your books are what you'd like and that they contain enough, but not too many, topics. Compare your topic titles with the TOC entries to make sure that they match.

You can see a report on your TOC. From the main menu, choose Tools⇨Reports⇨Table of Contents.

Figure 23-9 shows a sample Table of Contents report.

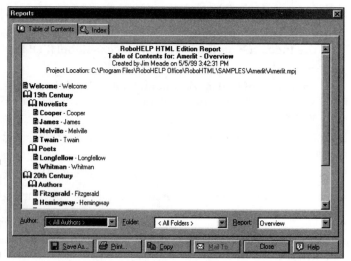

Figure 23-9:
Use the
report to
check on
your TOC.

You can get the same report in Classic's RoboHELP Explorer.

Where Do I Bail Out of This Joint?

You can look over lots of other things at the end of your project, too. Compile your project and look for bugs (which you have to fix if you find them). Go to the Reports menu and get a report on Unused Files. In that report, you're hauntingly reminded of the images, style sheets, and topics that you once meant to use but never did. Clean out those miscreant (or, at least, unused) items, which can be a little bit like cleaning out the attic. (You mean to get to it, but something else keeps getting in the way.)

You can find more things to put on the "To Do" list. But enough is enough. As a self-respecting Help author, you have to ask yourself the question, "Where's the nearest exit?" You can take only so many broken links, missing files, spelling mistakes, style sheets that don't look right, lousy browse sequences, and whatnot. Suppose that it's Friday afternoon or four o'clock on another day. Find the exit. Look around to make sure nobody is watching. Then bolt. You deserve it. You can finish cleaning up tomorrow.

Chapter 24

Ten Things You Should Have Asked Yourself Before You Started

In This Chapter

▶ Psychologically profiling your programmer

▶ Setting priorities in the beginning so you can manage them in the end

▶ Considering compiling very, very, very often

▶ Facing hard realities about making printed docs from Help files

▶ Thinking truthfully about the way Help authors are misunderstood

*W*hy am I putting, at the end of my book, this chapter on what to think about before you start? Because that's where I think people are most likely to read it. Be realistic about human nature. Almost nobody wants to sit down and think about all the things they're supposed to think about before they begin. The list is too long. The whole thing is overwhelming. And they don't have anything to relate it to.

"If you're going to kick a football," I always say, "then go out and kick it a whole bunch of times." If you find that the ball always squibs along the ground or that you swing and miss a lot and end up in precarious positions, you may be receptive to some suggestions on "how to kick a football."

I certainly hope that people find this list at the back of the book and read it before making the mistakes this list cautions against. After all, isn't that human nature, too — to begin at the end? People love *...For Dummies* books' "Part of Tens," and we put really important stuff in its chapters. But most of the points in this list are things that people learn the hard way — by not doing them in the first place.

In this chapter, I point out how to set and use priorities in your projects, how to prepare for a particular audience, how to cut up your work into salvage-able pieces, and how to deal with being misunderstood.

Here's a particular thought to keep in mind. What should be foremost in your mind as you develop a Help system is that users use the Help system to get fast answers and move on. If that doesn't happen, then the Help system isn't doing the job.

Where Can I Learn Enough About RoboHELP to be a Help Author?

If someone prepared you systematically to write RoboHELP Help, then understand that you are a very fortunate exception. Usually, it just doesn't happen that way. People prepare their programmers systematically, not their Help authors.

Usually, the Help author has to teach herself, most of the time with deadline pressure already looming — as in, "Oh, my gosh. This program is actually starting to work, and we don't have any Help. We're gonna ship. We're gonna ship. . . ."

Keep these emergency aids in mind as you jump into the mission, totally unprepared, and begin to prepare RoboHELP files for a program:

- ✔ **Use this book.** I'm really serious. Forgive the self-promotion, but if you want to get off to a flying start (from a cold initial position), a ...*For Dummies* book is going to be your best friend. Take the very list you're reading, for example. These are things you need to know that nobody ever tells you.

- ✔ **Use RoboHELP Help files, including the tutorials.** What's the old saying — "the cobbler's children go barefoot?" Help authors, on the one hand, love to admire their own handiwork at making other people's Help files look so nice. On the other hand, they have a decided propensity to forget to turn to Help files for help. Break out of that mold. Use excellent RoboHELP Help files.

  I find it especially helpful to click the Help button within any RoboHELP dialog box. That way, you get in-depth help on the very area you're working with.

- ✔ **Ask your boss for some training.** Look, it's worth putting in the request. Blue Sky Software (maker of RoboHELP) provides training or can direct you to it. The point is, training is systematic preparation that pays for itself just about immediately in the time you save and in the quality of your work. Hey, the training is just a thought; if you're lucky, it may happen for you.

- ✔ **Use the RoboHELP documentation.** People would rather ask somebody or just "wing it," but the documentation can help you out.

What Does My Programmer Like to Eat?

Study your programmers' eating habits. Maybe they've changed from the Twinkies and coffee that my programmer associates ate in the '80s. Bottled water might be big now. Maybe health bars or veggie burgers. But you have to work hand-in-hand with your programmer as you develop Help for that program. Who would know better than the program's developer how the program works and why it works that way. Programmers are also essential when you look for bugs at the end (which may come from you or from him/her) or when you want to add a script.

The point is, get to know every foible and idiosyncrasy of your programmers, and cater to those traits shamelessly. (I mean, almost shamelessly. Use some sanity here.)

You have to work with the programmers. You have to share information so that you're certain the Help system you write presents the program in the way it's best used. Now and then a programmer is a people person, but it's more *then* than *now*. Usually, the Help author is the people person — the communicator, the compromiser. So, treat your programmers the way you would a visiting dignitary (or your cherished pet cat). You need to work well with these programmers throughout the project, and chances are, you have to be the one to make the relationship work.

What Other Eating Habits Should I Study?

The programmers aren't the only ones you may have to talk with. Suppose, for example, you're doing a Help file for a Human Resources package that helps manage performance reviews. Your programmers know how the program works. But you may have to talk with a couple of Ph.D.s in social science to find out the subject-matter side of things. At the project outset, think about whom might know the subject matter you need to brush up on and don't be embarrassed to ask. You don't have to act as if you know everything already. After all, the very existence of Help files means that lots of people, lots of the time, don't know everything already.

What Does My Manager Eat?

I'm not saying that your manager is going to be as time-consuming a challenge for you as your programmers. Like everyone else, though, you have to manage your boss.

That supervisor is going to want to know difficult, very difficult things such as, "How long do you need for this project?" "When will it be done?" Estimating time is very difficult for Help authors, and (I have heard on good authority), most Help authors "don't have a clue how to do it."

You can use RoboHELP (HTML or Classic) to assist you if you actually put the Topic Properties dialog box to good use. Take a look at this dialog box:

1. **Select any topic in the Topic List window of your Help project and then click the Properties button.**

   The Topic Properties dialog box appears.

2. **Click the Status tab.**

   You see the nice organizational tools on the Status tab, as shown in Figure 24-1.

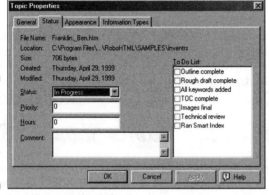

Figure 24-1:
Here are some nice tools to help plan your project.

If you really do put meaningful information — like a priority ranking and time commitment — where prompted by the dialog box, you can track your topics later using the Project Status report.

Put some thought into estimating hours for a topic. Consider, for example, that you need longer if you have to talk with a programmer than if you can work on your own.

By the way, note the To Do List at the right of the Topic Properties dialog box. This helpful guide will do you a lot more good if you know about it — and start using it for organization and tracking — at the beginning of your Help project.

Who Is My Audience?

First, you ought to get some basics out of the way right at the outset of your Help project.

You must know the operating environment that your readers will be using, because, after all, that information determines whether you use RoboHELP Classic or RoboHELP HTML. See Chapter 1 for a discussion of operating environments and the two RoboHELP authoring environments.

If you're creating a RoboHELP HTML Help system, find out about the browsers your audience will be using. Dynamic HTML doesn't work for browsers earlier than Microsoft Explorer 4.0, for example. If you have to create Help that works in most browsers, you may want to limit yourself mainly to text topics.

What Does My Audience Eat?

Getting the right help format and the right browser is the easy part of determining specifications for your Help project. You really need to understand the inner workings of these creatures you have to satisfy, that is, your Help system users. What don't they know? What do they know already? What do they really need to know? What do they want to know (which often isn't the same thing as what they need to know).

For example, a human resources audience may want to know some cool tips for getting meaningful performance reviews. What they really need to know, though, may be how to get their program to produce meaningful reports.

You have to come up with the right topics to meet the needs of your audience. You may have to feed them some of the topics they want to know just to get them warmed up for the ones they need to know.

Will I Remember to Compile Often?

Throughout the development of your Help system, compile a lot. Perhaps the procrastination arises because compiling seems like something you do at the end, like assembling the parts of a car in the factory. (That is, first you have to build the parts.)

Actually, though, you can compile your Help project anytime and get a good look at how things are going. In case you're reading this before reading the chapters on compiling, here's how to compile: With your project open, click the Compile button.

When you compile, you get error messages — something like "Warning: The file [name of file] has a link to a non-existent file" — if anything is wrong. If you compile often, including a small number of topics each time, you can probably solve the problem quickly. If you've built up a mountain of topics without compiling, as people often do, you'll be going crazy trying to find the source of the problem.

How Can I Modularize My Project?

Compiling your Help system often, as described in the preceding section, can be one form of modularizing your project. But you should look for others. Divide up your work into manageable pieces. Perhaps you'll be working on the project with other Help authors. In RoboHELP Classic, you can each prepare a series of .hlp files instead of working on one humongous file. Even if you're working by yourself, break up your project into parts.

What Will I Do About Printed Docs?

Printed documentation is a big one. I probably should have listed this higher than ninth in this chapter's list, but all the cautions in this list are quite important.

You can quite easily get a false sense of security from reading, in RoboHELP Help files, that the Document Wizard "automatically creates your printed documentation."

Follow these steps to take a look at the Document Wizard.

1. **Open the Help project you plan to print.**

2. **Choose File⇨Single Source Output⇨Printed Documentation.**

   The Document Wizard opens to help you out, as I show in Figure 24-2.

   (In RoboHELP Classic, click the plus sign next to the Single Source folder in Project Manager, then click Printed Documentation.)

Consider a few differences between Help files and printed docs:

✔ Help files use links; printed pages don't.

✔ Printed books need illustrations, but the images from your Help files may be tricky to work with. (Figure you're going to have to put in screen shots for your printed docs.)

> ✔ *See Also* references work in electronic Help, but on the printed page, people can't just click them any more. Do you convert them to text or delete them?

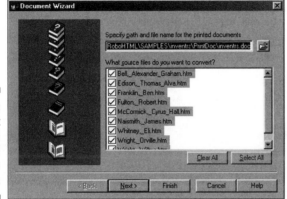

Figure 24-2: Don't expect more from this Wizard than it can deliver.

Many of us naturally tend to go into denial about things that are going to make more work for us. So when developing a Help system, you may find a natural tendency to think, "Oh, at the end, I'll just automatically print out nice documentation. RoboHELP does it for me."

The hard reality is something else. As one RoboHELP former insider told me, "It took us a minimum of 40 hours over three weeks to do a manual from our help files."

Why Doesn't Anybody Understand Me?

"I think of Help authors as the redheaded stepchildren," one friend told me. "People don't understand what we're doing and how we do it. They think we're glorified word processors."

You're a writer, but you're not writing printed text. You're working with electronic materials, but you're not a programmer. You're essential to the project, but maybe you're not thought of as essential.

You're probably going to be misunderstood, under appreciated, neglected, ignored. The truth of the matter, of course, is quite the opposite. Without good Help authors, any programming project is just about useless.

Remember, then, you — the Help author — are indispensable, skilled, and invaluable. You just may have to live with the reality that, at times, you're the only one who seems to remember that.

Chapter 25

Top Ten Ways to Bribe a Programmer

*I*t's easy for me to be glib here and talk about bribing a programmer as if such a thing is easy to do. Believe me, I know that influencing a programmer can be really, really tough. Not to generalize or anything, but these hardworking geeks can be skeptical, cynical, leery, suspicious, sometimes unapproachable, occasionally unreceptive, generally busy, and so on. They can certainly be one tough audience.

But boy, as a Help author, you need them! If you get into ActiveX at all, you want them around. If you want to put in some nice forms and buttons, you absolutely have to have your programmers to make them work. Want to do something with a Classic macro? Good luck doing it on your own, but macros are small potatoes to people who program daily.

In Chapter 17, I talk about ActiveX and lots of other things where you really need the help of your programmers.

Besides all the specialized cases where you might need your programmers, you're most likely providing help for a program. Who knows better what the program does, or should do, than the programmers who are building it?

Others may be free simply to dismiss your programmers as "a bunch of nerds." The Help author has no such luxury. The Help author generally must court, cater to, cajole, wheedle, and otherwise ingratiate himself or herself with the programmers. The Help author has to get along with them at least minimally.

Here, for what they're worth, are a few ideas you can use to bribe your programmers inconspicuously.

Cash In on Caffeine

Drop off a cup of coffee now and then at the programmer's desk. Take a coffee break together, and you pick up the tab. As you're leaving at night and the coder is preparing to work until morning, drop off a Red Bull. Some Up Time. An Irish Cream Mocha Frappuccino from Starbucks. Even some M&Ms. Caffeine is pure nerd fuel and softens the nerd heart.

You may want to determine the type of caffeine your programmers like first, otherwise if you give that much-needed person something he or she doesn't care for, the programmer won't like you.

Talk a Little Star Trek

Hardcore programmers have an irresistible affinity for Star Trek — TV episodes, movies, anything. Try watching a Star Trek movie one evening and then bringing it up casually the next morning. Try something like this. "Hey, I've always liked that *Star Trek 2, The Wrath of Khan*. I think it's the best one, don't you?"

Discuss DVD

Non-technogeeks don't really care whether they're using a CD-ROM or a DVD. Nor do they know the difference. Technophiles both know the difference and care. A lot. Stop by an electronics store, browse the Internet a little, and bone up on DVD, a source of endless fascination for techno folks.

DVD, by the way, stands for "Digital Video Disc, Digital Versatile Disc, or nothing," according to one source I contacted. It's bigger and faster than a CD and can hold video (besides the usual audio and computer data). It's a cornerstone of home entertainment, which opens a giant Pandora's box.

Do a little time management here. Don't bring up DVD unless you can spare a good bit of time to talk about it. If you bring it up, then end the discussion prematurely, or you'll do more harm than good.

Praise a Pocket Protector

The best thing is to come in wearing a pocket protector yourself, but such a gesture may smack of insincerity. Most genuine nerds have heard the flap over pocket protectors, but many remain ambivalent about them. On the one hand, wearing one tends to typecast them. On the other hand, they have lots of pens and pencils, and pocket protectors protect their pockets. Showing a little appreciation for their perspective (all the shirt stains they avoid) is a possible, though risky, tactic.

Pause over a Palmtop

Though often heralded as the next coming of the telephone — that is, as a universal device with practical applications — the handheld computer remains a fascination of the nerd. (Nerds, in fact, carry palmtops in their breast pockets, sometimes inside a pocket protector.)

Show some interest. Perhaps share a palmtop program. Ask for street directions when walking with a geek, allowing said specialist to find a location using a handheld device. Ask whether the person liked the now-defunct Apple Newton.

You may also want to ask them about Windows CE (the operating system for handheld computers). If the programmer doesn't like it, you may want to mention the derogatory name for Windows CE — "Wince."

On the question of directions, see the brief discussion of GPS at the end of this chapter.

Linger over Linux

In case you missed the news somewhere, Linux is a free alternative to UNIX. Imagine someone — unhappy with current operating systems (UNIX, Windows, or whatever) — who just decides to develop his own OS and offer it free. That happened. The person who developed Linux is Linus Torvalds.

Your perfect opportunity to make an impression might come up if you see your supergeek using his/her palmtop. Simply ask, "Hey, I hope you're using Linux on there." You'll be making a running start toward setting up a real friendship.

Get Fascinated with "Wireless"

You probably can't score points with your neighborhood nerd just by talking wireless phones any more. (The window of opportunity for that has closed, though it once existed.) Now, talk "wireless modem" or, even better, talk "wireless combo phones/modems."

Dispose of Unwanted Opera Tickets

Whereas hardware and gadgetry are a sure thing with any geek worthy of the name, opera tickets may be a bit risky. Still, you definitely come across some highbrow supergeeks. Somebody, after all, is going to the opera. And it's not me. You might consider offering opera tickets to your programmer.

Symphony tickets are a possibility. Basketball tickets also have a chance. Spike Lee goes to basketball games. Microsoft co-founder Paul Allen owns the Portland Trailblazers, and Bill Gates once attended a game. Football tickets have a chance. They're a longshot but no more so than opera tickets.

Drop Off a Dilbert Cartoon

Bone up a little on your Dilbert and take the time to share a little light anti-corporate humor with your own favorite engineer. Dilbert captures the spirit of company life for many a technoguru.

You may want to post some Dilbert cartoons in front of your cubicle so when the programmer stops by, he'll see the cartoons and laugh.

Preferred by most geeks is the before-Dilbert's-creator-left-the-workplace material. Somehow, someone feeling the pain seems best able to lampoon it.

Give Star Wars Tickets

I know that this is old by now. But wait; read on. Give tickets to one of the new movie theaters showing *Star Wars* in digital video. Digital video definitely "rings the chimes" of programmers, and you can score some useful points by offering the experience. The technology doesn't use film, just lasers. I don't know why that's important, but your geek will know.

Give three tickets. According to an inside source of mine, most geeks are not attached but probably have lots of friends who are. If they take a friend, they have to take the friend and the friend's significant other.

Be Creative

Come up with your own approaches to bribing programmers. If your programmers have a Macintosh, you may want to ask them about the iMac, the PowerMac G3, Mac OS X, and the like. Maybe your ideas will be better than the ones I've suggested. However you decide to get to the objective, always have the intention to pamper and nurture your geek. Life in the technoworld is much easier with that person's cooperation, or a least toleration, than with the tech guru's indifference or even (perish the thought) resistance.

Okay, I admit it. These ploys are pretty transparent. They're likely to backfire, as in "Are you patronizing me?" I don't know, though. Play to a person's weakness, and friendship could bloom. Here's a bonus suggestion. Try talking about *GPS,* or *Global Positioning System.* (GPS sends out satellite signals that you can process in a receiver that, in turn, tells you where you are. Bet you have lots of uses for that.) Try out the subject on your geek, though, and watch the eyes light up.

Part VIII

Appendixes

The 5th Wave   By Rich Tennant

"Hold your horses. It takes time to create a Help file for someone your size."

In this part . . .

Nothing may be worse than being stumped on some insignificant trifle when you are on the path of creating a truly significant Help file. One such trifle can be an unassuming little word that you just aren't familiar with. You find some such specialized RoboHELP words in the glossary. A number of other situations can be disconcerting if you aren't well prepared. Here you can read about our CD-ROM, which offers you nice goodies like trial versions of the software so that you don't have to feel unprepared as you use this book.

Appendix A

Glossary

· ·

I'm not sure whether brevity is a virtue in a glossary, but it's what I offer in this one. Sometimes an unfamiliar term can keep you or me from getting our work done right, and the idea in this glossary is to prevent you from such wasted time. This is a glossary of most-used terms in this book and in RoboHELP Help authoring in general. (For the most part, this isn't a glossary of obscure, specialized technical terms that you'll meet once or maybe never in your life as a RoboHELP author.)

And then, there are times that you just want to look up a term without reading the details that are found in the book's text. Check out the term here.

ActiveEdit: An option in Classic (not in HTML help) that attaches the ActiveEdit button to your Help file when you compile. You click the button to jump straight to the topic that needs editing.

ActiveX Control: Predecessor of the ActiveY control. Not! It's a self-contained program — such as a Calendar, a Chat Program, a Calculator, or a you-name-it — which you can add to a Help page.

ActiveX is the most recent incarnation of Microsoft's OLE (object linking and embedding), and the new name is even less comprehensible than the old one.

Baggage folder: Some dumb thing you don't really want. That's what it sounds like. That's pretty much what the file is, too. Part of Project Manager, the Baggage file has files that RoboHELP couldn't put into its usual folders — .BMP files used in Splash Screens and other specialized, unlikely things. The name sounds like (and almost is) the "garbage folder."

Book: A book is, like, some covers with pages between them that you read. Okay. In RoboHELP, a book is a category you set up in your Table of Contents. Books show up in the .CNT file. A couple things might be confusing. First, books don't happen automatically. You create them. Second, they are actually standard Windows folders but use a special icon. Third, in Windows they usually don't link to topics themselves.

Bookmark: A named location within a topic in RoboHELP HTML. (The Classic equivalent is a mid-topic jump.) You can set up links straight to bookmarks. They're great in big topics so people can jump right to a certain part and not just to the beginning.

Broken Link: Famous 18th century Cherokee chief (not). It's a link that doesn't point to a topic any more (usually because you've deleted the topic it connects with).

CHM file: In Help author parlance, a "Chum file." The compressed HTML Help file you get when you compile an HTML Help project in RoboHELP HTML.

Cnt file: In RoboHELP Classic, the file containing your Table of Contents.

Compile: Smoosh together. In RoboHELP HTML, you use the Microsoft HTML Help compiler when you compile. (You don't have to know you're using it, but you do.) Compiling creates your compressed HTML Help file, using a .CHM extension.

Compress: Squoosh (as opposed to "smoosh.") The compiler automatically compresses (squeezes) your final Help file into a reduced space.

Context-Sensitive Help: Help available within an application (usually within a dialog box).

Dll file: Dynamic Link Library. A DLL file contains programs another program needs so that it can run. Store DLL files in your Windows directory.

Dynamic HTML: HTML that won't stand still for a minute, as in really restless HTML. HTML has been around for awhile. It was static; it just displayed your text, images, and links. Dynamic HTML, a recent breakthrough, allows you to "do things" to the elements of the page (like words, paragraphs, or pictures). You can even control elements using scripts (programs).

External Topic: A topic and all, but not a topic within your current Help project. You can use it in your current project, though.

Form: A form is a box on the screen. It's an area where you can put form elements (buttons and such).

Between you and me, I think the form is more something that the program's interpreter needs than anything you or I care about. (We'd be just as happy to put form elements straight onto a page, not inside a box.)

Form Element: Text Box, Check Box, Radio Button, Drop Down Menu, Push Button — the elements you can put on a form so you can interact with the user.

Your form element will look nice but not actually work until you bribe your programmer to connect the element with a script on the server. (See Chapter 25 to find out how to bribe a programmer.)

Hlp file: A compressed WinHELP Help file.

Hotspot: A clickable area, often on an image. A link to another topic, although a Hotspot may also run a script, display a pop-up window, or do something else.

HTML: Hypertext Markup Language. If we'd known this language would become so widely used, wouldn't we have given it a less pretentious name? HTML is the code that browsers use in interpreting Web pages. How about if we called it "browser code"? Just a thought.

Image: "Image is everything; images are pictures." In RoboHELP, images are files in the .JPG, .JPEG, and .GIF formats.

Index: In fingers, the index is the pointer. The index is the list of keywords for a topic. Click the keyword to go to the topic for it.

Jump: A "link" in WinHELP (RoboHELP Classic).

Keyword: An index entry. The keywords connect with topics in the Help system.

Link: An area in RoboHELP HTML you can click to go instantly to another topic (or to something else, even to a Web page). Links can be either text or images, which makes for lots of good fun (the equivalent in RoboHELP Classic is a jump).

Macro: A special program (coded material) in RoboHELP Classic. Often macros execute when the Help file starts up.

Marquee: Text that scrolls around on the HTML page ad nauseam. Fun at first but annoying after awhile.

Multimedia: Video, animation, and sound you put into your Help files. "Multimedia" sounds really advanced, but you just include the right files into your topics — namely, .AVI and .WAV files (or a number of others).

Page: An icon in your table of contents *(TOC)* representing a topic. You click the page in the TOC to display the topic. If pages can be a little confusing, it is because they aren't identical with topics although they seem the same (they're icons).

Pop-up: "Pop-up" is primarily a term used in RoboHELP Classic. Where a classic jump takes a Help user to another topic, a pop-up displays a small window within the topic (great for definitions).

Programmer: Geek. Technogeek. Geekazoid. Perhaps your most important resource while working in RoboHELP.

Project: A Help project is an electronic file where you store everything else in your help system — books, topics, the Table of Contents, Index, everything.

Project Manager: The perhaps slightly neglected area on the left side of your RoboHELP screen where you see folders you can expand or contract. Helpful for getting organized, but RoboHELP puts much of the material into the folders automatically.

Script: Thinly disguised, supposedly "friendly" name for a program. Scripts may be more modest programs than, say, full-blown Java or C++ programs. They're programs, though.

See Also References: These are references linking a keyword in your index to another topic (besides the main topic that the keyword takes you to).

Smart Indexing: Use the Smart Index Wizard to identify keywords you can add to your Index automatically. You can even do cool things like set up words to "always ignore." You can work with synonyms and antonyms. Smart Indexing is fun.

Style Sheet: A designer bed sheet from Neiman Marcus (yes, I'm kidding). In RoboHELP HTML, a style sheet is equivalent to a template in Microsoft Word. You use the style sheet to set up the formatting in your HTML topics and to keep it uniform. Style sheets work behind the scenes, so they aren't as much fun as Dynamic HTML. But they are a powerful way to keep your topics looking professional.

Table of Contents: Convenient listing of all your topics, often divided into books. People can click on the pages in the TOC to go straight to associated topics.

TOC Composer: Pane on the left side of RoboHELP used to create books in your TOC, which you can drag topics into.

Topic: A topic, in RoboHELP, is the basic unit of information you manipulate to convey information. Wow, that sounds stilted. A topic is, more or less, a document. It's one piece of help. If you're writing about "Birds," "Robins" might be one topic.

TrueCode Editor: A pane in RoboHELP HTML where hardcore techies can work directly with the HTML code for their pages. You can make changes there and see the effect in the WYSIWYG Editor.

URL: A proposed phonetic speller for the name "Earl" — just kidding. Uniform Resource Locator. It's an Internet address in the techie format of http://www.anyplace.com (you can tell from the format who found the Internet first — the tech gurus).

WYSIWYG Editor: The main pane in RoboHELP HTML where you create your topics. WYSIWYG (what you see is what you get) means that you don't have to see a bunch of codes as you write (which was the case as recently as RoboHELP Classic).

Appendix B

About the CD-ROM

*H*ere's some of what you can find on the *RoboHELP 7 For Dummies* CD-ROM:

- ✔ The Real RoboHELP itself — a time-locked, trial version, of course
- ✔ Sample Help files to help you get started
- ✔ PaintShop Pro — shareware for the budding graphic artist in you
- ✔ MindSpring Internet Access — a nice way to connect to the Internet if you're not there already
- ✔ Microsoft Internet Explorer 5.0

Books are nice, and, especially, *RoboHELP 7 For Dummies*. But sometimes when you're reading about a hands-on program like RoboHELP HTML, you may fancy an electronic file to compliment your book. Maybe existing Help files, so you won't have to waste time creating one from scratch; for example, a nice paint tool for working with your images. Or perhaps you're just evaluating RoboHELP and would like to try it out before investing in the product.

The CD-ROM accompanying this book complements what you see in the text with a trial version of RoboHELP, a shareware paint program, Internet access program, and some sample Help files. We're looking for every way we can to help you get off and running as a Help author.

System Requirements

RoboHELP is a program for Windows 95 or later. Make sure your computer meets the minimum system requirements listed below. If your computer doesn't match up to most of these requirements, you may have problems in using the contents of the CD. To properly run the software on the CD, you'll need:

- ✔ A PC with a 486 or faster processor
- ✔ Microsoft Windows 98, 95, or NT 4.0
- ✔ At least 16MB of total RAM (24MB or more recommended)

✔ At least 40MB of hard drive space available to install all the software from this CD (you'll need less if you don't install every program)

✔ A CD-ROM drive — double-speed (2x) or faster

✔ A sound card for PCs

✔ A monitor capable of displaying at least 256 colors or grayscale

✔ A modem with a speed of at least 14,400 bps

If you need more information on the basics, check out *PCs For Dummies,* 6th Edition, by Dan Gookin; *Windows 98 For Dummies, Windows 95 For Dummies,* or *Windows 3.11 For Dummies,* 4th Edition, all by Andy Rathbone (and all published by IDG Books Worldwide, Inc.).

Running the CD in Microsoft Windows

To use the CD in Microsoft Windows, first you have to get the CD running. Once it's running, you can access the materials on the CD and begin working through the examples and programs. The following sections show you how to run and access the files on your CD.

If you are running Windows 95 or 98, follow these steps to open your CD:

1. **Insert the CD into your computer's CD-ROM drive.**

   Give your computer a moment to take a look at the CD.

2. **When the light on your CD-ROM drive goes out, double-click the My Computer icon. (It's probably in the top-left corner of your desktop.)**

   This action opens the My Computer window, which shows you all the drives attached to your computer, the Control Panel, and a couple other handy things.

3. **Double-click the icon for your CD-ROM drive.**

   Another window opens, showing you all the folders and files on the CD.

Follow these step to install the CD programs on your computer:

1. **Double-click the file called** License.txt.

   This file contains the end-user license agreement that you "agree" to by using the CD. When you are done reading the license, close the program (most likely NotePad) displaying the file.

2. **Double-click the file called** Readme.txt.

   This file contains instructions about installing the software from this CD. It might be helpful to leave this text file open while you are using the CD.

3. **Double-click the folder for the software you are interested in.**

   Be sure to read the descriptions of the programs in the "What You'll Find" section of this appendix (much of this information also shows up in the Readme file). These descriptions will give you more precise information about the programs' folder names, and about finding and running the installer program.

4. **Find the file called** `Setup.exe`, **or** `Install.exe`, **or something similar, and double-click the file.**

   The program's installer will walk you through the process of setting up your new software.

To run some of the programs, you may need to keep the CD inside your CD-ROM drive. This is a *good thing*. Otherwise, the installed program would have required you to install a very large chunk of the program to your hard drive space, which would have kept you from installing other software.

What You'll Find

Here's a summary of the software on this CD arranged by category.

Trying Out RoboHELP

Your Help authoring system is a pretty big commitment. You'll be spending hours and hours in it, and, besides, you have to invest in it financially.

Why not "try before you buy"? Here you'll find a 15-day, time-locked version of RoboHELP HTML. It's a trial version, nicely provided by the manufacturer — Blue Sky Software, based in La Jolla, California. You can install it and use it for 15 days from the date you install it.

Here's the Blue Sky Web site:

```
www.blue-sky.com
```

Playing with Sample Files

As you work through the examples in this book or examples of your own, you may not always want to start from scratch (though starting from scratch is fun, too). You may want to try out something specialized, like putting in an expanding Hotspot, and you may not want to create a complete Help file so that you can try it.

On the CD are some sample Help files that I worked with in this book. (Not every file that I mention is here, but these should help you get started.)

These are not finished files. What you see here may not coincide exactly with what you see in any given chapter. I revised and played with these sample files frequently throughout the book.

To use any of the files, copy the contents of a Help folder to your own hard drive. Then use RoboHELP to open the file you want to work with — usually an mpj file in RoboHELP HTML or an hpj file in RoboHELP Classic.

Here is a list of sample files on the CD:

For RoboHELP HTML	For RoboHELP Classic
birds.mpj	birds.hpj
fishing.mpj	flowers.hpj
food.mpj	physiol.hpj
inventrs.mpj	
islands.mpj	
pets.mpj	
weather.mpj	

For good examples of finished files, check out the sample files that come with RoboHELP.

Beautifying Your Graphics

RoboHELP comes with its own graphics tools, but these tools don't pretend to offer the capabilities that come with the full-blown paint or image tools. If you want to work over your images, you can use PaintShop Pro from this CD.

PaintShop Pro is a popular, shareware graphics and photo-editing tool. You can retouch and edit your photos, enhance color, and generally spiff up your images. Its manufacturer is Jasc Software in Eden Prairie, MN.

You can check out its Web site at:

```
www.jasc.com
```

Accessing the Internet

MindSpring Internet Access, from MindSpring. For Windows 3.1, Windows 95/98/NT, and Mac OS. MindSpring Internet Access is a commercial product that gets you signed up to the MindSpring Internet service provider *(ISP)*. If you don't already have Internet access, MindSpring is an excellent ISP that offers Internet access for a low monthly fee. MindSpring also has different Web hosting options depending on the kind of account you have. If you're already on the Internet but would like to learn more about MindSpring and the different service options it offers, you can visit the Web site at:

```
www.mindspring.com.
```

If you already have an ISP, installing MindSpring may replace your current settings. You may no longer be able to access the Internet through your original provider.

If you already have Internet Explorer 4.0 or later installed on your computer, select the Custom Install option when you install MindSpring Internet Access, and deselect Internet Explorer. This will prevent MindSpring from attempting to replace your browser with an earlier version.

Microsoft Internet Explorer Web Browser

For Windows 95, 98, and NT, Microsoft Internet Explorer is one of two major players in the Web browser market. However, just in case you don't have the latest version (at the time of publication), we include a copy of Microsoft Internet Explorer on this CD-ROM. You can always find the latest information about Internet Explorer at the Microsoft support site at:

```
www.microsoft.com/ie
```

If You've Got Problems (Of the CD Kind)

I tried my best to compile programs that work on most computers with the minimum system requirements. Alas, your computer may differ, and some programs may not work properly for some reason.

The two likeliest problems are that you don't have enough memory (RAM) for the programs you want to use, or you have other programs running that are affecting the installation or the running of a program. If you get error messages like `Not enough memory` or `Setup cannot continue`, try one or more of these methods and then try using the software again:

✔ Turn off any anti-virus software that you have on your computer. Installers sometimes mimic virus activity and may make your computer incorrectly believe that it is being infected by a virus.

✔ Close all running programs. The more programs you're running, the less memory is available to other programs. Installers also typically update files and programs. So if you keep other programs running, installation may not work properly.

✔ Have your local computer store add more RAM to your computer. This is, admittedly, a drastic and somewhat expensive step. However, if you have a Windows 95 PC, adding more memory can really help the speed of your computer and allow more programs to run at the same time. This may include closing the CD interface and running a product's installation program from Windows Explorer.

If you still have trouble with installing the items from the CD, please call the IDG Books Worldwide Customer Service phone number: 800-762-2974 (outside the U.S.: 317-596-5430).

Index

browser dependencies. *See* Web
    browser dependencies
bulleted lists, 91–92, 96
buttons
  creating. *See* form elements
  Related Topics, 121–123

• C •

capitalization in indexes, 165, 169
cascading style sheets, 251
CD-ROM
  contents, 355
  graphics tools, 358
  Internet access, 359
  Microsoft Internet Explorer, 359
  MindSpring Web site, 359
  opening, 356–357
  RoboHELP, 357
  sample files, 357–358
  system requirements, 355–356
  troubleshooting, 359–360
centering text
  Classic, 94
  HTML, 86–87
CGI (Common Gateway Interface), 259
CGI scripts, 259. *See also* scripting
    HTML code
check boxes, 263
.CHM files
  compiling, 216
  defined, 352
clipart. *See also* images
  Microsoft library of, 230
Close window, ActiveX control, 257
cnt file, defined, 352
collapsing folders, 194–195
color
  background, 248–250
  creating your own, 86
  horizontal lines, 107
  text backgrounds, 88–90

text (Classic), 94–95
text (HTML), 85–86
COM (Component Object Model),
    254, 263
COM objects, 254
comments tags (<!...->), 265
Common Gateway Interface (CGI), 259
compile, defined, 352
compile settings, changing, 219–220
Compiled File setting, 220
compiling
  .CHM files, 216
  fixing errors, 221–222
  Hotspots (HTML), 119–121
  HTML Help, 215–216
  progress message, displaying, 225
  projects (Classic), 43–46
  projects (HTML), 29–30
  recommended frequency, 339–340
  WinHelp, 220–221
Component Object Model (COM),
    254, 263
compress, defined, 352
Compression option, 225
compression style, selecting, 225
containers, defined, 33
context-sensitive Help
  creating, 297
  defined, 352
Context-Sensitive Help folder, 193
converting
  Classic projects to HTML projects,
    204–206
  Hotspots to Shed image, 126–127
  HTML Help to printed documents,
    304–308, 310
  HTML Help to WinHelp, 207–211
  HTML links to WinHelp, 207
  Microsoft Word documents to
    WinHelp, 209–210
  See Also references to printed docu-
    ments, 310

From PCs
to Personal Finance,
We Make it Fun and Easy!

For more information,
or to order, please
call 800.762.2974.

www.idgbooks.com
www.dummies.com

Dummies Books™
Bestsellers on Every Topic!

TECHNOLOGY TITLES

INTERNET

Title	Author	ISBN	Price
America Online® For Dummies®, 5th Edition	John Kaufeld	0-7645-0502-5	$19.99 US/$26.99 CAN
E-Mail For Dummies®, 2nd Edition	John R. Levine, Carol Baroudi, Margaret Levine Young, & Arnold Reinhold	0-7645-0131-3	$24.99 US/$34.99 CAN
Genealogy Online For Dummies®	Matthew L. Helm & April Leah Helm	0-7645-0377-4	$24.99 US/$35.99 CAN
Internet Directory For Dummies®, 2nd Edition	Brad Hill	0-7645-0436-3	$24.99 US/$35.99 CAN
The Internet For Dummies®, 6th Edition	John R. Levine, Carol Baroudi, & Margaret Levine Young	0-7645-0506-8	$19.99 US/$28.99 CAN
Investing Online For Dummies®, 2nd Edition	Kathleen Sindell, Ph.D.	0-7645-0509-2	$24.99 US/$35.99 CAN
World Wide Web Searching For Dummies®, 2nd Edition	Brad Hill	0-7645-0264-6	$24.99 US/$34.99 CAN

OPERATING SYSTEMS

Title	Author	ISBN	Price
DOS For Dummies®, 3rd Edition	Dan Gookin	0-7645-0361-8	$19.99 US/$28.99 CAN
LINUX® For Dummies®, 2nd Edition	John Hall, Craig Witherspoon, & Coletta Witherspoon	0-7645-0421-5	$24.99 US/$35.99 CAN
Mac® OS 8 For Dummies®	Bob LeVitus	0-7645-0271-9	$19.99 US/$26.99 CAN
Small Business Windows® 98 For Dummies®	Stephen Nelson	0-7645-0425-8	$24.99 US/$35.99 CAN
UNIX® For Dummies®, 4th Edition	John R. Levine & Margaret Levine Young	0-7645-0419-3	$19.99 US/$28.99 CAN
Windows® 95 For Dummies®, 2nd Edition	Andy Rathbone	0-7645-0180-1	$19.99 US/$26.99 CAN
Windows® 98 For Dummies®	Andy Rathbone	0-7645-0261-1	$19.99 US/$28.99 CAN

PC/GENERAL COMPUTING

Title	Author	ISBN	Price
Buying a Computer For Dummies®	Dan Gookin	0-7645-0313-8	$19.99 US/$28.99 CAN
Illustrated Computer Dictionary For Dummies®, 3rd Edition	Dan Gookin & Sandra Hardin Gookin	0-7645-0143-7	$19.99 US/$26.99 CAN
Modems For Dummies®, 3rd Edition	Tina Rathbone	0-7645-0069-4	$19.99 US/$26.99 CAN
Small Business Computing For Dummies®	Brian Underdahl	0-7645-0287-5	$24.99 US/$35.99 CAN
Upgrading & Fixing PCs For Dummies®, 4th Edition	Andy Rathbone	0-7645-0418-5	$19.99 US/$28.99CAN

GENERAL INTEREST TITLES

FOOD & BEVERAGE/ENTERTAINING

Title	Author	ISBN	Price
Entertaining For Dummies®	Suzanne Williamson with Linda Smith	0-7645-5027-6	$19.99 US/$26.99 CAN
Gourmet Cooking For Dummies®	Charlie Trotter	0-7645-5029-2	$19.99 US/$26.99 CAN
Grilling For Dummies®	Marie Rama & John Mariani	0-7645-5076-4	$19.99 US/$26.99 CAN
Italian Cooking For Dummies®	Cesare Casella & Jack Bishop	0-7645-5098-5	$19.99 US/$26.99 CAN
Wine For Dummies®, 2nd Edition	Ed McCarthy & Mary Ewing-Mulligan	0-7645-5114-0	$19.99 US/$26.99 CAN

SPORTS

Title	Author	ISBN	Price
Baseball For Dummies®	Joe Morgan with Richard Lally	0-7645-5085-3	$19.99 US/$26.99 CAN
Fly Fishing For Dummies®	Peter Kaminsky	0-7645-5073-X	$19.99 US/$26.99 CAN
Football For Dummies®	Howie Long with John Czarnecki	0-7645-5054-3	$19.99 US/$26.99 CAN
Hockey For Dummies®	John Davidson with John Steinbreder	0-7645-5045-4	$19.99 US/$26.99 CAN
Tennis For Dummies®	Patrick McEnroe with Peter Bodo	0-7645-5087-X	$19.99 US/$26.99 CAN

HOME & GARDEN

Title	Author	ISBN	Price
Decks & Patios For Dummies®	Robert J. Beckstrom & National Gardening Association	0-7645-5075-6	$16.99 US/$24.99 CAN
Flowering Bulbs For Dummies®	Judy Glattstein & National Gardening Association	0-7645-5103-5	$16.99 US/$24.99 CAN
Home Improvement For Dummies®	Gene & Katie Hamilton & the Editors of HouseNet, Inc.	0-7645-5005-5	$19.99 US/$26.99 CAN
Lawn Care For Dummies®	Lance Walheim & National Gardening Association	0-7645-5077-2	$16.99 US/$24.99 CAN

For more information, or to order, call (800)762-2974

Dummies Books™
Bestsellers on Every Topic!

TECHNOLOGY TITLES

SUITES

Title	Author	ISBN	Price
Microsoft® Office 2000 For Windows® For Dummies®	Wallace Wang & Roger C. Parker	0-7645-0452-5	$19.99 US/$28.99 CAN
Microsoft® Office 2000 For Windows® For Dummies®, Quick Reference	Doug Lowe & Bjoern Hartsfvang	0-7645-0453-3	$12.99 US/$19.99 CAN
Microsoft® Office 4 For Windows® For Dummies®	Roger C. Parker	1-56884-183-3	$19.95 US/$26.95 CAN
Microsoft® Office 97 For Windows® For Dummies®	Wallace Wang & Roger C. Parker	0-7645-0050-3	$19.99 US/$26.99 CAN
Microsoft® Office 97 For Windows® For Dummies®, Quick Reference	Doug Lowe	0-7645-0062-7	$12.99 US/$17.99 CAN
Microsoft® Office 98 For Macs® For Dummies®	Tom Negrino	0-7645-0229-8	$19.99 US/$28.99 CAN

WORD PROCESSING

Title	Author	ISBN	Price
Word 2000 For Windows® For Dummies®, Quick Reference	Peter Weverka	0-7645-0449-5	$12.99 US/$19.99 CAN
Corel® WordPerfect® 8 For Windows® For Dummies®	Margaret Levine Young, David Kay, & Jordan Young	0-7645-0186-0	$19.99 US/$26.99 CAN
Word 2000 For Windows® For Dummies®	Dan Gookin	0-7645-0448-7	$19.99 US/$28.99 CAN
Word For Windows® 95 For Dummies®	Dan Gookin	1-56884-932-X	$19.99 US/$26.99 CAN
Word 97 For Windows® For Dummies®	Dan Gookin	0-7645-0052-X	$19.99 US/$26.99 CAN
WordPerfect® 6.1 For Windows® For Dummies®, Quick Reference, 2nd Edition	Margaret Levine Young & David Kay	1-56884-966-4	$9.99 US/$12.99 CAN
WordPerfect® 7 For Windows® 95 For Dummies®	Margaret Levine Young & David Kay	1-56884-949-4	$19.99 US/$26.99 CAN
Word Pro® for Windows® 95 For Dummies®	Jim Meade	1-56884-232-5	$19.99 US/$26.99 CAN

SPREADSHEET/FINANCE/PROJECT MANAGEMENT

Title	Author	ISBN	Price
Excel For Windows® 95 For Dummies®	Greg Harvey	1-56884-930-3	$19.99 US/$26.99 CAN
Excel 2000 For Windows® For Dummies®	Greg Harvey	0-7645-0446-0	$19.99 US/$28.99 CAN
Excel 2000 For Windows® For Dummies® Quick Reference	John Walkenbach	0-7645-0447-9	$12.99 US/$19.99 CAN
Microsoft® Money 98 For Dummies®	Peter Weverka	0-7645-0295-6	$24.99 US/$34.99 CAN
Microsoft® Money 99 For Dummies®	Peter Weverka	0-7645-0433-9	$19.99 US/$28.99 CAN
Microsoft® Project 98 For Dummies®	Martin Doucette	0-7645-0321-9	$24.99 US/$34.99 CAN
MORE Excel 97 For Windows® For Dummies®	Greg Harvey	0-7645-0138-0	$22.99 US/$32.99 CAN
Quicken® 98 For Windows® For Dummies®	Stephen L. Nelson	0-7645-0243-3	$19.99 US/$26.99 CAN

GENERAL INTEREST TITLES

EDUCATION & TEST PREPARATION

Title	Author	ISBN	Price
The ACT For Dummies®	Suzee Vlk	1-56884-387-9	$14.99 US/$21.99 CAN
College Financial Aid For Dummies®	Dr. Herm Davis & Joyce Lain Kennedy	0-7645-5049-7	$19.99 US/$26.99 CAN
College Planning For Dummies®, 2nd Edition	Pat Ordovensky	0-7645-5048-9	$19.99 US/$26.99 CAN
Everyday Math For Dummies®	Charles Seiter, Ph.D.	1-56884-248-1	$14.99 US/$22.99 CAN
The GMAT® For Dummies®, 3rd Edition	Suzee Vlk	0-7645-5082-9	$16.99 US/$24.99 CAN
The GRE® For Dummies®, 3rd Edition	Suzee Vlk	0-7645-5083-7	$16.99 US/$24.99 CAN
Politics For Dummies®	Ann DeLaney	1-56884-381-X	$19.99 US/$26.99 CAN
The SAT I For Dummies®, 3rd Edition	Suzee Vlk	0-7645-5044-6	$14.99 US/$21.99 CAN

CAREERS

Title	Author	ISBN	Price
Cover Letters For Dummies®	Joyce Lain Kennedy	1-56884-395-X	$12.99 US/$17.99 CAN
Cool Careers For Dummies®	Marty Nemko, Paul Edwards, & Sarah Edwards	0-7645-5095-0	$16.99 US/$24.99 CAN
Job Hunting For Dummies®	Max Messmer	1-56884-388-7	$16.99 US/$24.99 CAN
Job Interviews For Dummies®	Joyce Lain Kennedy	1-56884-859-5	$12.99 US/$17.99 CAN
Resumes For Dummies®, 2nd Edition	Joyce Lain Kennedy	0-7645-5113-2	$12.99 US/$17.99 CAN

For more information, or to order,
call (800)762-2974

DG BOOKS WORLDWIDE

...FOR DUMMIES
BESTSELLING BOOK SERIES

Dummies Books™
Bestsellers on Every Topic!

TECHNOLOGY TITLES

WEB DESIGN & PUBLISHING

Title	Author	ISBN	Price
Creating Web Pages For Dummies®, 4th Edition	Bud Smith & Arthur Bebak	0-7645-0504-1	$24.99 US/$34.99 CAN
FrontPage® 98 For Dummies®	Asha Dornfest	0-7645-0270-0	$24.99 US/$34.99 CAN
HTML 4 For Dummies®	Ed Tittel & Stephen Nelson James	0-7645-0331-6	$29.99 US/$42.99 CAN
Java™ For Dummies®, 2nd Edition	Aaron E. Walsh	0-7645-0140-2	$24.99 US/$34.99 CAN
PageMill™ 2 For Dummies®	Deke McClelland & John San Filippo	0-7645-0028-7	$24.99 US/$34.99 CAN

DESKTOP PUBLISHING GRAPHICS/MULTIMEDIA

Title	Author	ISBN	Price
CorelDRAW™ 8 For Dummies®	Deke McClelland	0-7645-0317-0	$19.99 US/$26.99 CAN
Desktop Publishing and Design For Dummies®	Roger C. Parker	1-56884-234-1	$19.99 US/$26.99 CAN
Digital Photography For Dummies®, 2nd Edition	Julie Adair King	0-7645-0431-2	$19.99 US/$28.99 CAN
Microsoft® Publisher 97 For Dummies®	Barry Sosinsky, Christopher Benz & Jim McCarter	0-7645-0148-8	$19.99 US/$26.99 CAN
Microsoft® Publisher 98 For Dummies®	Jim McCarter	0-7645-0395-2	$19.99 US/$28.99 CAN

MACINTOSH

Title	Author	ISBN	Price
Macs® For Dummies®, 6th Edition	David Pogue	0-7645-0398-7	$19.99 US/$28.99 CAN
Macs® For Teachers™, 3rd Edition	Michelle Robinette	0-7645-0226-3	$24.99 US/$34.99 CAN
The iMac For Dummies	David Pogue	0-7645-0495-9	$19.99 US/$26.99 CAN

GENERAL INTEREST TITLES

BUSINESS & PERSONAL FINANCE

Title	Author	ISBN	Price
Accounting For Dummies®	John A. Tracy, CPA	0-7645-5014-4	$19.99 US/$26.99 CAN
Business Plans For Dummies®	Paul Tiffany, Ph.D. & Steven D. Peterson, Ph.D.	1-56884-868-4	$19.99 US/$26.99 CAN
Consulting For Dummies®	Bob Nelson & Peter Economy	0-7645-5034-9	$19.99 US/$26.99 CAN
Customer Service For Dummies®	Karen Leland & Keith Bailey	1-56884-391-7	$19.99 US/$26.99 CAN
Home Buying For Dummies®	Eric Tyson, MBA & Ray Brown	1-56884-385-2	$16.99 US/$24.99 CAN
House Selling For Dummies®	Eric Tyson, MBA & Ray Brown	0-7645-5038-1	$16.99 US/$24.99 CAN
Investing For Dummies®	Eric Tyson, MBA	1-56884-393-3	$19.99 US/$26.99 CAN
Law For Dummies®	John Ventura	1-56884-860-9	$19.99 US/$26.99 CAN
Managing For Dummies®	Bob Nelson & Peter Economy	1-56884-858-7	$19.99 US/$26.99 CAN
Marketing For Dummies®	Alexander Hiam	1-56884-699-1	$19.99 US/$26.99 CAN
Mutual Funds For Dummies®, 2nd Edition	Eric Tyson, MBA	0-7645-5112-4	$19.99 US/$26.99 CAN
Negotiating For Dummies®	Michael C. Donaldson & Mimi Donaldson	1-56884-867-6	$19.99 US/$26.99 CAN
Personal Finance For Dummies®, 2nd Edition	Eric Tyson, MBA	0-7645-5013-6	$19.99 US/$26.99 CAN
Personal Finance For Dummies® For Canadians	Eric Tyson, MBA & Tony Martin	1-56884-378-X	$18.99 US/$24.99 CAN
Sales Closing For Dummies®	Tom Hopkins	0-7645-5063-2	$14.99 US/$21.99 CAN
Sales Prospecting For Dummies®	Tom Hopkins	0-7645-5066-7	$14.99 US/$21.99 CAN
Selling For Dummies®	Tom Hopkins	1-56884-389-5	$16.99 US/$24.99 CAN
Small Business For Dummies®	Eric Tyson, MBA & Jim Schell	0-7645-5094-2	$19.99 US/$26.99 CAN
Small Business Kit For Dummies®	Richard D. Harroch	0-7645-5093-4	$24.99 US/$34.99 CAN
Successful Presentations For Dummies®	Malcolm Kushner	1-56884-392-5	$16.99 US/$24.99 CAN
Time Management For Dummies®	Jeffrey J. Mayer	1-56884-360-7	$16.99 US/$24.99 CAN

AUTOMOTIVE

Title	Author	ISBN	Price
Auto Repair For Dummies®	Deanna Sclar	0-7645-5089-6	$19.99 US/$26.99 CAN
Buying A Car For Dummies®	Deanna Sclar	0-7645-5091-8	$16.99 US/$24.99 CAN
Car Care For Dummies®: The Glove Compartment Guide	Deanna Sclar	0-7645-5090-X	$9.99 US/$13.99 CAN

IDG BOOKS WORLDWIDE

For more information, or to order,
call (800)762-2974

FOR DUMMIES

BESTSELLING BOOK SERIES

Dummies Books™
Bestsellers on Every Topic!

TECHNOLOGY TITLES

DATABASE

Access 2000 For Windows® For Dummies®	John Kaufeld	0-7645-0444-4	$19.99 US/$28.99 CAN
Access 97 For Windows® For Dummies®	John Kaufeld	0-7645-0048-1	$19.99 US/$26.99 CAN
Approach® 97 For Windows® For Dummies®	Deborah S. Ray & Eric J. Ray	0-7645-0001-5	$19.99 US/$26.99 CAN
Crystal Reports 7 For Dummies®	Douglas J. Wolf	0-7645-0548-3	$24.99 US/$34.99 CAN
Data Warehousing For Dummies®	Alan R. Simon	0-7645-0170-4	$24.99 US/$34.99 CAN
FileMaker® Pro 4 For Dummies®	Tom Maremaa	0-7645-0210-7	$19.99 US/$26.99 CAN
Intranet & Web Databases For Dummies®	Paul Litwin	0-7645-0221-2	$29.99 US/$42.99 CAN

NETWORKING

Building An Intranet For Dummies®	John Fronckowiak	0-7645-0276-X	$29.99 US/$42.99 CAN
cc: Mail™ For Dummies®	Victor R. Garza	0-7645-0055-4	$19.99 US/$26.99 CAN
Client/Server Computing For Dummies®, 2ⁿᵈ Edition	Doug Lowe	0-7645-0066-X	$24.99 US/$34.99 CAN
Lotus Notes® Release 4 For Dummies®	Stephen Londergan & Pat Freeland	1-56884-934-6	$19.99 US/$26.99 CAN
Networking For Dummies®, 4ᵗʰ Edition	Doug Lowe	0-7645-0498-3	$19.99 US/$28.99 CAN
Upgrading & Fixing Networks For Dummies®	Bill Camarda	0-7645-0347-2	$29.99 US/$42.99 CAN
Windows NT® Networking For Dummies®	Ed Tittel, Mary Madden, & Earl Follis	0-7645-0015-5	$24.99 US/$34.99 CAN

GENERAL INTEREST TITLES

THE ARTS

Blues For Dummies®	Lonnie Brooks, Cub Koda, & Wayne Baker Brooks	0-7645-5080-2	$24.99 US/$34.99 CAN
Classical Music For Dummies®	David Pogue & Scott Speck	0-7645-5009-8	$24.99 US/$34.99 CAN
Guitar For Dummies®	Mark Phillips & Jon Chappell of Cherry Lane Music	0-7645-5106-X	$24.99 US/$34.99 CAN
Jazz For Dummies®	Dirk Sutro	0-7645-5081-0	$24.99 US/$34.99 CAN
Opera For Dummies®	David Pogue & Scott Speck	0-7645-5010-1	$24.99 US/$34.99 CAN
Piano For Dummies®	Blake Neely of Cherry Lane Music	0-7645-5105-1	$24.99 US/$34.99 CAN

HEALTH & FITNESS

Beauty Secrets For Dummies®	Stephanie Seymour	0-7645-5078-0	$19.99 US/$26.99 CAN
Fitness For Dummies®	Suzanne Schlosberg & Liz Neporent, M.A.	1-56884-866-8	$19.99 US/$26.99 CAN
Nutrition For Dummies®	Carol Ann Rinzler	0-7645-5032-2	$19.99 US/$26.99 CAN
Sex For Dummies®	Dr. Ruth K. Westheimer	1-56884-384-4	$16.99 US/$24.99 CAN
Weight Training For Dummies®	Liz Neporent, M.A. & Suzanne Schlosberg	0-7645-5036-5	$19.99 US/$26.99 CAN

LIFESTYLE/SELF-HELP

Dating For Dummies®	Dr. Joy Browne	0-7645-5072-1	$19.99 US/$26.99 CAN
Parenting For Dummies®	Sandra H. Gookin	1-56884-383-6	$16.99 US/$24.99 CAN
Success For Dummies®	Zig Ziglar	0-7645-5061-6	$19.99 US/$26.99 CAN
Weddings For Dummies®	Marcy Blum & Laura Fisher Kaiser	0-7645-5055-1	$19.99 US/$26.99 CAN

IDG
BOOKS
WORLDWIDE

For more information, or to order,
call (800)762-2974

FOR DUMMIES

BESTSELLING
BOOK SERIES

IDG Books Worldwide, Inc., End-User License Agreement

READ THIS. You should carefully read these terms and conditions before opening the software packet(s) included with this book ("Book"). This is a license agreement ("Agreement") between you and IDG Books Worldwide, Inc. ("IDGB"). By opening the accompanying software packet(s), you acknowledge that you have read and accept the following terms and conditions. If you do not agree and do not want to be bound by such terms and conditions, promptly return the Book and the unopened software packet(s) to the place you obtained them for a full refund.

1. **License Grant.** IDGB grants to you (either an individual or entity) a nonexclusive license to use one copy of the enclosed software program(s) (collectively, the "Software") solely for your own personal or business purposes on a single computer (whether a standard computer or a workstation component of a multiuser network). The Software is in use on a computer when it is loaded into temporary memory (RAM) or installed into permanent memory (hard disk, CD-ROM, or other storage device). IDGB reserves all rights not expressly granted herein.

2. **Ownership.** IDGB is the owner of all right, title, and interest, including copyright, in and to the compilation of the Software recorded on the disk(s) or CD-ROM ("Software Media"). Copyright to the individual programs recorded on the Software Media is owned by the author or other authorized copyright owner of each program. Ownership of the Software and all proprietary rights relating thereto remain with IDGB and its licensers.

3. **Restrictions on Use and Transfer.**

   (a) You may only (i) make one copy of the Software for backup or archival purposes, or (ii) transfer the Software to a single hard disk, provided that you keep the original for backup or archival purposes. You may not (i) rent or lease the Software, (ii) copy or reproduce the Software through a LAN or other network system or through any computer subscriber system or bulletin-board system, or (iii) modify, adapt, or create derivative works based on the Software.

   (b) You may not reverse engineer, decompile, or disassemble the Software. You may transfer the Software and user documentation on a permanent basis, provided that the transferee agrees to accept the terms and conditions of this Agreement and you retain no copies. If the Software is an update or has been updated, any transfer must include the most recent update and all prior versions.

4. **Restrictions on Use of Individual Programs.** You must follow the individual requirements and restrictions detailed for each individual program in the "About the CD-ROM" appendix of this Book. These limitations are also contained in the individual license agreements recorded on the Software Media. These limitations may include a requirement that after using the program for a specified period of time, the user must pay a registration fee or discontinue use. By opening the Software packet(s), you will be agreeing to abide by the licenses and restrictions for these individual programs that are detailed in the "About the CD-ROM" appendix and on the Software Media. None of the material on this Software Media or listed in this Book may ever be redistributed, in original or modified form, for commercial purposes.

5. **Limited Warranty.**

   (a) IDGB warrants that the Software and Software Media are free from defects in materials and workmanship under normal use for a period of sixty (60) days from the date of purchase of this Book. If IDGB receives notification within the warranty period of defects in materials or workmanship, IDGB will replace the defective Software Media.

   (b) **IDGB AND THE AUTHOR OF THE BOOK DISCLAIM ALL OTHER WARRANTIES, EXPRESS OR IMPLIED, INCLUDING WITHOUT LIMITATION IMPLIED WARRANTIES OF MERCHANTABILITY AND FITNESS FOR A PARTICULAR PURPOSE, WITH RESPECT TO THE SOFTWARE, THE PROGRAMS, THE SOURCE CODE CONTAINED THEREIN, AND/OR THE TECHNIQUES DESCRIBED IN THIS BOOK. IDGB DOES NOT WARRANT THAT THE FUNCTIONS CONTAINED IN THE SOFTWARE WILL MEET YOUR REQUIRE-MENTS OR THAT THE OPERATION OF THE SOFTWARE WILL BE ERROR FREE.**

   (c) This limited warranty gives you specific legal rights, and you may have other rights that vary from jurisdiction to jurisdiction.

6. **Remedies.**

   (a) IDGB's entire liability and your exclusive remedy for defects in materials and workman-ship shall be limited to replacement of the Software Media, which may be returned to IDGB with a copy of your receipt at the following address: Software Media Fulfillment Department, Attn.: *RoboHELP 7 For Dummies*, IDG Books Worldwide, Inc., 7260 Shadeland Station, Ste. 100, Indianapolis, IN 46256, or call 800-762-2974. Please allow three to four weeks for delivery. This Limited Warranty is void if failure of the Software Media has resulted from accident, abuse, or misapplication. Any replacement Software Media will be warranted for the remainder of the original warranty period or thirty (30) days, whichever is longer.

   (b) In no event shall IDGB or the author be liable for any damages whatsoever (including without limitation damages for loss of business profits, business interruption, loss of business information, or any other pecuniary loss) arising from the use of or inability to use the Book or the Software, even if IDGB has been advised of the possibility of such damages.

   (c) Because some jurisdictions do not allow the exclusion or limitation of liability for conse-quential or incidental damages, the above limitation or exclusion may not apply to you.

7. **U.S. Government Restricted Rights.** Use, duplication, or disclosure of the Software by the U.S. Government is subject to restrictions stated in paragraph (c)(1)(ii) of the Rights in Technical Data and Computer Software clause of DFARS 252.227-7013, and in subparagraphs (a) through (d) of the Commercial Computer – Restricted Rights clause at FAR 52.227-19, and in similar clauses in the NASA FAR supplement, when applicable.

8. **General.** This Agreement constitutes the entire understanding of the parties and revokes and supersedes all prior agreements, oral or written, between them and may not be modified or amended except in a writing signed by both parties hereto that specifically refers to this Agreement. This Agreement shall take precedence over any other documents that may be in conflict herewith. If any one or more provisions contained in this Agreement are held by any court or tribunal to be invalid, illegal, or otherwise unenforceable, each and every other pro-vision shall remain in full force and effect.

Installation Instructions

The *RoboHELP 7 For Dummies* CD offers valuable information that you won't want to miss. To install the items from the CD to your hard drive, follow these steps.

1. **Insert the CD into your computer's CD-ROM drive.**

   In a moment, an icon representing the CD you just inserted appears on your computer desktop. Chances are, the icon looks like a CD-ROM.

2. **Double-click the CD icon to show the CD's contents.**

3. **Double-click the Read Me First icon.**

   The Read Me First text file contains information about the CD's programs and any last-minute instructions you may need to correctly install them.

4. **To install most programs, just drag the program's folder from the CD window and drop it on your hard drive icon.**

5. **Other programs come with installer programs — with these, you simply open the program's folder on the CD and then double-click the icon with the words "Install" or "Installer."**

   Sometimes the installers are actually self-extracting archives, which just means that the program files have been bundled up into an archive, and this self-extractor unbundles the files and places them on your hard drive. This kind of program is often called a .sea. Double-click anything with .sea in the title, and it will run just like an installer.

   After you have installed the programs you want, you can eject the CD. Carefully place it back in the plastic jacket of the book for safekeeping.

For more information, see the "About the CD-ROM" appendix.

Discover Dummies Online!

The Dummies Web Site is your fun and friendly online resource for the latest information about ...*For Dummies*® books and your favorite topics. The Web site is the place to communicate with us, exchange ideas with other ...*For Dummies* readers, chat with authors, and have fun!

Ten Fun and Useful Things You Can Do at www.dummies.com

1. Win free ...*For Dummies* books and more!
2. Register your book and be entered in a prize drawing.
3. Meet your favorite authors through the IDG Books Author Chat Series.
4. Exchange helpful information with other ...*For Dummies* readers.
5. Discover other great ...*For Dummies* books you must have!
6. Purchase Dummieswear™ exclusively from our Web site.
7. Buy ...*For Dummies* books online.
8. Talk to us. Make comments, ask questions, get answers!
9. Download free software.
10. Find additional useful resources from authors.

Link directly to these ten fun and useful things at **http://www.dummies.com/10useful**

For other technology titles from IDG Books Worldwide, go to **www.idgbooks.com**

Not on the Web yet? It's easy to get started with *Dummies 101*®: *The Internet For Windows*®*98* or *The Internet For Dummies*®, 6th Edition, at local retailers everywhere.

Find other ...*For Dummies* books on these topics:

Business • Career • Databases • Food & Beverage • Games • Gardening • Graphics • Hardware
Health & Fitness • Internet and the World Wide Web • Networking • Office Suites
Operating Systems • Personal Finance • Pets • Programming • Recreation • Sports
Spreadsheets • Teacher Resources • Test Prep • Word Processing

IDG BOOKS WORLDWIDE BOOK REGISTRATION

We want to hear from you!

Visit **http://my2cents.dummies.com** to register this book and tell us how you liked it!

- ✔ Get entered in our monthly prize giveaway.
- ✔ Give us feedback about this book — tell us what you like best, what you like least, or maybe what you'd like to ask the author and us to change!
- ✔ Let us know any other ...*For Dummies*® topics that interest you.

Your feedback helps us determine what books to publish, tells us what coverage to add as we revise our books, and lets us know whether we're meeting your needs as a ...*For Dummies* reader. You're our most valuable resource, and what you have to say is important to us!

Not on the Web yet? It's easy to get started with *Dummies 101*®: *The Internet For Windows*® *98* or *The Internet For Dummies*®, 6th Edition, at local retailers everywhere.

Or let us know what you think by sending us a letter at the following address:

...*For Dummies* Book Registration
Dummies Press
7260 Shadeland Station, Suite 100
Indianapolis, IN 46256-3945
Fax 317-596-5498

**BESTSELLING
BOOK SERIES
FROM IDG**